MUSIC IN AMERICAN LIFE

Paul Hindemith in the United States

Paul Hindemith
in the United States

LUTHER NOSS

University of Illinois Press

Urbana and Chicago

Library of Congress Cataloging-in-Publication Data

Noss, Luther.
   Paul Hindemith in the United States / Luther Noss.
      p. cm. — (Music in American life)
   Bibliography: p.
   Includes index.
   ISBN 0-252-01563-0 (alk. paper)
   1. Hindemith, Paul, 1895–1963. 2. Composers—Biography.
I. Title. II. Series.
ML410.H685N7 1989
780'.92'4—dc19
[B]   88-10694
                                    CIP
                                    MN

For Osea

Contents

Acknowledgments   xi

PART 1. EARLY Associations, 1920–40

Introduction   1
1. Early Associations with the United States, 1920–37   3
2. The First U.S. Concert Tour, 1937   13
3. The Second U.S. Concert Tour, 1938   31
4. The Third U.S. Concert Tour, 1939   42

PART 2. RESIDENT, 1940–53

Introduction   57
5. Emigration, 1940   59
6. The First Seven Months   63
7. Professor at Yale   83
8. Teacher at Yale   94
9. Performer at Yale   102
10. Creative Work   110
11. Professional Activities   140
12. Recognition, Honors, Citizenship   154
13. Mr. and Mrs. Paul Hindemith of New Haven, Connecticut   159

PART 3. EXPATRIATE, 1953–63

Introduction   169
14. Estrangement, 1953–58   171
15. Reconciliation, 1959–63   182

Notes   199

Bibliography   209

Indexes   211

Acknowledgments

This is a documentary record of Paul Hindemith's long association with the United States, which began in 1920 and continued until his death forty-three years later. That association was a part of his personal and professional life that has received only limited coverage in most of the published biographical accounts, thereby leaving the impression that it was of relatively minor significance.[1] On the contrary, its impact on the course of his creative work was of major consequence. I have written this book in order that the full story of the composer's relations with the United States might be made available and that any misconceptions surrounding them be clarified.

Materials in the Paul Hindemith Collection at Yale University and in the archives of the Paul Hindemith Institute in Frankfurt am Main, West Germany, were the major sources of the material used in preparing this account. The Yale collection, established in 1964, and under my supervision since 1970, is intended primarily as a repository for documents relating directly to the composer's life and work in the United States, and through the cooperation of his former students, colleagues, and friends in this country it has been possible to gather a substantial amount of such material.

The archives of the Frankfurt institute contain the complete Hindemith legacy of music and literary manuscripts, correspondence, journals, diaries, and a great variety of other papers.

The institute, formally opened in 1973, is subsidized by the Paul Hindemith Foundation, a private and nonprofit Swiss corporation that holds title to the entire Hindemith estate by the bequest of Gertrude Hindemith, who died in March 1967. All of the income derived from royalties, performance material rentals and fees, investments, and other sources is allocated by the board of directors to maintain the institute and to underwrite the many special projects carried out under its auspices. Yale University has enjoyed a close association with the foundation and institute from the beginning and its Hindemith Collection has been strengthened significantly by copies from the Frankfurt archives of all of the correspondence and other accounts left by Paul and Gertrude Hindemith that relate to their United States experience. Permission to quote from these documents has been granted, and I have done so frequently and extensively throughout the book so that as much of the story as possible can be told in the Hindemiths' own words.

I am much indebted to the director of the institute, Dr. Dieter Rexroth, and his associate, Dr. Giselher Schubert, for their assistance during my several stays in Frankfurt to do research and for the many courtesies extended to me while there. I had valuable help at Yale from Harold E. Samuel, music librarian, and his assistant, Deborah Miller, and Judith Schiff, chief research archivist in the University Library, in finding pertinent documents deposited in the historical records of the School of Music and the university.

I am grateful to Howard Boatwright, Carl S. Miller, Eckhart Richter, and Keith Wilson for providing me with much useful information about Hindemith's activities at Yale. Each had unusual opportunities to work closely with the composer while he was at the university and thus their accounts have been of particular value.

Thankful acknowledgment of permission to use copyrighted materials in their possession is made to the Paul Hindemith Institute, Yale University, the Library of Congress, Wells College, Aurora, N.Y., and Billboard Publications, New York City.

I owe special thanks to Judith McCulloh, executive editor of the University of Illinois Press, for her initial and continuing interest in this project and for her valuable advice and counsel along the way toward its completion. I am doubly indebted to Osea Noss, who not only devoted countless hours in helping to prepare the manuscript but also added many important details to the story, recalled from her warm friendship with Paul and Gertrude Hindemith throughout their years in New Haven and later.

PART 1
Early Associations, 1920–40

Introduction

Although Paul Hindemith did not become a resident of the United States until 1940, his first direct contacts with this country had been made twenty years previously. Details of these earlier associations are given briefly in chapter 1, fitted into the context of his personal and professional activities in Germany from boyhood until the day he left for New York in 1937 to begin his first U.S. concert tour. The rest of part 1 deals primarily with Hindemith's three extended visits here in 1937, 1938, and 1939, experiences that became compelling factors in shaping his decision to make his home in this country.

Part 1 draws heavily on Hindemith's personal letters and travel journals, particularly those he wrote to his wife Gertrude during the 1937, 1938, and 1939 concert tours. The low fees he received made it impossible for her to accompany him; consequently he took time to write long and meticulously detailed accounts of his experiences, liberally garnished with his frank and often wry observations on the social, cultural, and economic aspects of life in the United States. The letters he exchanged with Willy Strecker, his publisher and close personal friend, and with Ernest Voigt, then president of Associated Music Publishers in New York, also provide valuable information. All of the documents noted above are in the archives of the Paul Hindemith Institute in Frankfurt am Main, and photocopies are in the Paul Hindemith Collection at Yale University.

Data relating to Hindemith's association with Elizabeth Sprague Coolidge and his first public appearance in the United States were obtained from his correspondence with her and with Oliver Strunk, filed in the Music Division of the Library of Congress, Washington, D.C. Additional details concerning Mrs. Coolidge's activities are

1

from *Elizabeth Sprague Coolidge: A Tribute on the 100th Anniversary of Her Birth* by Jay C. Rosenfeld, 1966, an eight-page brochure published privately in Chicago.

Although competent in speaking and reading English by the time of his first U.S. tour, Hindemith by his own admission lacked confidence in writing it and still did all of his correspondence in German. The quotations in English are my own translations, as are those from the letters written by Willy Strecker and Mrs. Hindemith.

Chapter 1

Early Associations with the United States, 1920–37

PAUL HINDEMITH'S first U.S. experience was not a happy one. In February 1920, having completed a new string quartet, he sent it to Pittsfield, Massachusetts, as an entry in an international chamber music composition competition. It was rejected and the score returned, his first (and only) serious rebuff as a composer. Ironically, the sponsor of the competition was Mrs. Elizabeth Sprague Coolidge, who would shortly become one of Hindemith's most ardent champions in the United States, and the composition was his *String Quartet in C Major, Opus 16*, which would be premiered the following year at the Donaueschingen Festival of Contemporary Chamber Music and bring the composer international acclaim.

Mrs. Coolidge, this country's most noted patron of contemporary chamber music in the first half of the twentieth century, had inaugurated her famous summer music festivals at South Mountain near Pittsfield, Massachusetts, in 1918 and immediately announced an international competition to find new works to be performed. Hindemith obviously thought it worthwhile to enter, but he lost. It is not known why the judges decided as they did, but it is quite probable they considered the score too difficult. (The story of how it came to be performed at Donaueschingen is told later in this chapter.)

Hindemith was twenty-five years old in 1920 and unchallenged in his home city of Frankfurt am Main as its most illustrious young professional musician. Born in Hanau on 16 November 1895, young Paul had lived with his family in various suburban towns, and for three years with his paternal grandparents in Nauheim, before moving to Frankfurt with his parents and a younger sister and brother in 1905.

Robert Rudolf Hindemith, father of the family, was the son of a successful merchant who refused to let him pursue a career in music. Robert left home early, was frustrated in his attempts to be a success as a musician, and had to be content with eking out a meager income as a housepainter. Nevertheless, his interest in music remained strong and he insisted his three children begin musical studies at the earliest possible age. He started Paul and sister Toni (two years younger) on the violin and brother Rudolf (four years younger) on the cello, demanding an all-out effort from all three. By the time the family moved to Frankfurt in 1905 he could announce the availability of the "Frankfurt Children's Trio" for engagements, with himself accompanying some of their numbers on the zither. The ensemble was short-lived, but Paul and Rudolf had been launched on their notable careers in music, albeit rather inconspicuously.

Paul's first formal violin study began in 1904 with a local teacher in Mühlheim. Soon after coming to Frankfurt he worked with Anna Hegner, a pupil of Adolf Rebner, professor of violin at the Hoch Conservatory. She was so impressed with the talent and progress of her young student she brought him to Rebner, who agreed to give Paul private lessons in 1907 and obtained a scholarship for him to enter the conservatory in 1908, after he had finished grammar school. This was the end of Hindemith's formal training in general education. He studied at the Hoch Conservatory for sixteen semesters between 1908 and 1917, where his principal teachers were Rebner in violin and Arnold Mendelssohn and Bernhard Sekles in theory and composition. He concentrated on violin during the first seven semesters, adding theoretical studies in 1912. He had worked with Mendelssohn for only a year when the teacher became ill and could not continue. His compositional studies were completed under Sekles over the next three years.

Hindemith compiled a brilliant record at the conservatory, winning every major prize in performance and composition offered by the school. Preparing for a professional career as a violinist had been his primary objective and he made extraordinary progress. By 1915 he was playing second violin in his teacher's professional string quartet, the leading ensemble of its kind in the city, and holding the position of first concertmaster in the Frankfurt Opera Orchestra. His progress in composition was equally remarkable. When he began formal study in 1912 he demonstrated such exceptional ability during the first year that he was urged by the conservatory to continue working in composition as well as in performance. He did so, and by the time his association with the conservatory ended in 1917 he had confirmed his talent for writing with an impressive list of compositions that included a prize-winning *String Quartet in C Major, Opus 2,* a *Concerto for Violoncello and Orchestra, Opus 3,* a *Piano Quintet, Opus 7, Three Pieces for Violoncello and Piano, Opus 8* (published by Breitkopf and Haertel in 1917, the first of his works to be printed), and *Three Songs for Soprano and Large Orchestra, Opus 9.*

Although Hindemith was called into military service in August 1917 and assigned to a regimental band that eventually saw duty near the battle lines on the western front, whenever time and circumstances permitted he continued to write music and during 1918 completed his *String Quartet in F Minor, Opus 10,* a *Sonata in E♭ for Violin and Piano, Opus 11.1,* and *Sonata in D for Violin and Piano, Opus 11.2.*

Hindemith was back in Frankfurt early in 1919 and by 9 March had completed the *Sonata in F for Viola and Piano, Opus 11.4,* which was destined to become one of his most frequently performed works. His music was now given recognition by the newly established Society for Contemporary Music and Drama, whose members organized a public concert of his chamber music that was presented in Frankfurt on 2 June 1919. The program included the *String Quartet in F Minor, Opus 10, Piano Quintet, Opus 7* (the score was destroyed in a bombing raid on Frankfurt during World War II), the *Sonata in D for Violin and Piano, Opus 11.2,* and *Sonata in F for Viola and Piano, Opus 11.4.* Hindemith participated in all four numbers either as a violinist or violist. The concert was a success, and the young composer was lauded by the critics as an exciting new talent with a promising future.

Attending that concert were the brothers Ludwig and Willy Strecker, principal owners and officers of the venerable and world famous music publishing company of B. Schott and Sons in Mainz. They were so impressed they ventured to offer the still not fully tried young composer a lifetime contract for the exclusive publication rights to his music. Confident of his bargaining strength, Hindemith rejected the financial arrangements as initially proposed and demanded better terms. The Schott firm agreed and never had reason to regret its decision.

Encouraged by the success of his professional debut as a composer, Hindemith now devoted all of his free time to writing. By the end of 1919 he had finished *Traumwald, Opus 13,* a set of four songs for soprano and string quartet, *Sonata for Solo Viola, Opus 11.5, Sonata for Violoncello and Piano, Opus 11.3,* the one-act opera *Mörder,*

Hoffnung der Frauen, Opus 12, Three Hymns by Walt Whitman, Opus 14, for baritone voice and piano, and *In einer Nacht, Opus 15,* a suite of fourteen short pieces for piano.[1]

It was now that Hindemith decided to enter his *String Quartet in C Major, Opus 16* in the international composition competition being sponsored by Elizabeth Sprague Coolidge in the United States. He had written the work during January and February 1920 but told no one about either the composition or the competition. Available records provide no clue as to why not, but one might assume he wished to avoid possibly embarrassing publicity in the event the score was rejected, as it was. However, word of its existence finally leaked out early in 1921, and the organizers of the new Festival of Contemporary Chamber Music to be held in Donaueschingen that summer immediately urged him to allow its performance on one of the programs. He demurred, feeling that since he was involved in planning the festival, none of his own music should be presented. But the organizers persisted, and he relented. One of the leading string quartets in Germany, led by Gustav Havemann, was asked to play it, but after seeing the score they decided it would require more rehearsal time than they could afford and declined. Hindemith then offered to play the viola part himself and have his brother Rudolf do the cello, provided two competent violinists could be found. Two members of the Mannheim Opera Orchestra were engaged, Lico Amar as first violinist and Walter Caspar as the second, and thus the ensemble shortly to become famous as the Amar-Hindemith String Quartet came into being.

The *String Quartet in C Major, Opus 16* was presented in Donaueschingen on 1 August 1921, brilliantly performed by the new Amar-Hindemith group, and scored a sensational success, firmly establishing Hindemith's position as foremost among the young German composers. New scores were completed in rapid succession and in a wide diversity of forms, and virtually all were published and performed immediately. Over fifty works were written after *Opus 16* before Hindemith left Frankfurt for Berlin in 1927 to become professor of composition at the Staatliche Hochschule für Musik. Among these were his three one-act operas, two string quartets, six of the seven *Kammermusik* pieces, *Das Marienleben,* the opera *Cardillac,* and the *Concerto for Orchestra,* plus several instrumental sonatas, choral works, and songs. The reaction of the musical public to this music was strong and mixed. Conservatives jeered, appalled by Hindemith's iconclastic assaults on past traditions, and progressives cheered, delighted by his fresh and uninhibited use of new musical ideas and idioms. He became an instant musical celebrity in Germany and word of his remarkable achievements soon spread through Europe and Great Britain.

Hindemith resigned from the Rebner String Quartet in 1921 and the Frankfurt Opera Orchestra in 1923. His primary professional activities as a performer would now be as the violist with the Amar-Hindemith String Quartet and as a concert violist. The quartet concertized throughout Europe for twelve years but Hindemith left the group in 1929, having become too busy with other commitments. On 15 May 1924, he was married to Gertrude Rottenberg, who was the daughter of Ludwig Rottenberg, director of the Frankfurt Opera, the granddaughter of a former mayor of Frankfurt, and a first cousin of the Austrian ambassador to the United States. Educated in French convent schools, trained and knowledgeable in music, gifted as a singer, fluent in French and English, and ardently devoted to her husband and his music, Gertrude was an invaluable aide to Paul Hindemith for the rest of his life.

Hindemith's compositions received comparatively little public attention in the United States during this period except among the few who were particularly interested in contemporary music. Among these was Mrs. Coolidge, who sponsored the U.S. premiere of his *String Quartet in F Minor, Opus 10* at her South Mountain Festival in 1923. Hindemith's name did not appear in the *New York Times* until 1926, when an article on contemporary German composers by Adolf Weissman on 23 August gave Hindemith fairly high marks but not without certain reservations. The *Times* did carry brief accounts of the contemporary music festivals in Donaueschingen beginning in 1922, but Hindemith's name was not cited even though he was by then one of the directors. When the festivals were moved to Baden-Baden in 1927 and held there for the next three summers, the *Times* covered the events more comprehensively and frequent references were made to Hindemith. The paper also carried a long and favorable review of the 1929 world premiere in Berlin of his new comic opera *News of the Day*. Mrs. Coolidge continued to promote interest in his music, sponsoring U.S. premieres in Washington, D.C., of his *Spielmusik, Opus 43.1* in 1928, and *Kammermusik No. 7* (concerto for organ) in 1929.

The breakthrough came in 1930, when Hindemith received two

important commissions from the United States, one from Serge Koussevitzky to write a work for the fiftieth anniversary of the Boston Symphony Orchestra and the other from Mrs. Coolidge to compose a piece for a concert of contemporary music she was sponsoring in her home city of Chicago. Koussevitzky had come to know and admire Hindemith's music while living in Paris from 1920 to 1926, and for a Paris concert he was guest conducting in May 1928 he had engaged the composer to appear as the soloist in his viola concerto, *Kammermusik No. 5*. Correspondence on file in the Library of Congress reveals that there was serious difficulty in agreeing on the fee, with Koussevitzky looking for a bargain and Hindemith refusing to play until he got his price. He did. Two years later Koussevitzky chose Hindemith as one of the few leading contemporary composers who were commissioned to write a piece for his orchestra's anniversary. It was a happy choice, for the composer created one of his most brilliant and widely admired works, the *Concert Music for Strings and Brass, Opus 50*. It was completed in December 1930 and premiered by the Boston Symphony Orchestra under Koussevitzky on 4 April 1931.[2]

Elizabeth Sprague Coolidge cabled the composer in January 1930, inviting him to come to Chicago in October and participate in a concert of contemporary music she was organizing. Hindemith replied by cable that he could not give a definite answer for two months, and when he did it was negative: his heavy concert schedule would preclude his coming over until the fall of 1931. Mrs. Coolidge then tried another approach, hoping it might induce the composer to reconsider. She offered him a commission to write a concerto for piano and chamber orchestra which he would conduct and suggested that the noted Frankfurt pianist Emma Lübbecke-Job be engaged as the soloist. Mrs. Lübbecke and Hindemith had been professional colleagues and close personal friends for many years and the thought of writing a piece for her to premiere in the United States appealed to him. He accepted the commission provisionally in a long letter to Mrs. Coolidge which also included a revealing glimpse of his current attitude about composing. After regretting again that it would be impossible for him to be there and conduct the piece he went on to say:

> I can write a piece for you after this year's Berlin Festival ends in June. However, there are still some problems to be solved. In recent

years I have stopped writing concert music almost entirely and have been composing music mostly for educational and community purposes, for amateurs, children, radio, mechanical instruments, etc. etc. I consider this kind of composing more important than writing for public concert purposes because the latter is mostly a technical exercise for musicians and has little to do with the development of music. Therefore, I must view the piano concerto purely as a business matter. All of the concert music I have written in recent years has been done on commission. The idealism I am happy to apply to endeavors I consider essential to the future development of music I cannot transfer to concert music. On the contrary, I must balance one against the other.

I hope you understand my point of view when I tell you the honorarium you have stipulated for a composition by me is too low. For a commission such as this I must receive no less than 10,000 marks. If you think this figure is too high, I will completely understand your decision immediately. If you agree to this condition, please write and tell me what you would like to have (length, form, type, instrumentation, etc.). The manuscript would become your property, if you wish, and I would agree to your exclusive right to the piece for a half year.[3]

Mrs. Coolidge readily agreed to the fee of 10,000 marks (then $2,385) and suggested that the ensemble be limited to ten or eleven instruments. The composer wrote later in June that he had completed half of the piece and described his instrumentation of ten brass and two harps as "a somewhat unusual combination but I promise good results." It was completed two weeks later and he wrote to Mrs. Coolidge: "I think it turned out to be a useful piece and I hope it will please you a little. You will hear how it sounds before I do. I really enjoyed working on it, and I would be pleased if it is not the worst piece on your program and if the audience will not be too astonished."[4] Mrs. Coolidge asked her longtime friend and associate Hugo Kortschak to conduct the premiere. They had known each other well since Kortschak, as concertmaster of the Chicago Symphony, had founded the Berkshire String Quartet, which became the resident ensemble at the South Mountain Music Festivals beginning in 1918. He was now living in New York, teaching violin at the Manhattan School of Music and also at Yale. Kortschak went to Frankfurt in August to confer with Mrs. Lübbecke and Hindemith about the performance of the piece. (This was the first meeting between the two men, who from 1940 to 1952, when Kortschak retired, were faculty colleagues at Yale.)

The *Concert Music for Piano, Two Harps, and Brass, Opus 49* was premiered in Chicago on 13 October 1930, with Emma Lübbecke-Job as the soloist and Hugo Kortschak conducting. Mrs. Coolidge wrote to Hindemith after the concert, complimenting him on the success of the piece and apologizing for the tepid reviews in the Chicago papers. She explained that the local critics were not very good and should not be taken seriously. The composer must have been pleased by her closing comment: "I count it a wonderful honor to have had a share in the creation of another masterpiece by you, Europe's foremost composer, and hope that you will not doubt my appreciation."[5]

These early contacts with Serge Koussevitzky and Elizabeth Coolidge in the United States proved to be valuable to Hindemith later. Mrs. Coolidge would invite him to be the featured guest artist at her prestigious Washington, D.C., festival of contemporary music in 1937, thereby enabling the composer to come to the United States for the first time. Koussevitzky would invite him as early as 1938 to teach composition at the inaugural session of the Berkshire Music Center in Tanglewood, Massachusetts, in 1940. Both of these appointments were to have a profound effect on the course of Hindemith's future life in the United States.

Paul Hindemith was at the top of his profession in Germany by 1930. His music had gained acceptance by almost all but a residue of diehard reactionaries and he had become a leading figure in the cultural life of Berlin, then one of the world's most exciting centers of progressive contemporary music, art, and drama. He and Gertrude lived comfortably in a handsome apartment with domestic help, enjoying the company and respect of many of the city's leading citizens. It was a happy situation, but it was not to endure.

Newspapers of the burgeoning National Socialist political party had begun to publish articles and letters in the late 1920s highly critical of Hindemith, accusing him of lacking proper respect for German traditions, associating and working with Communist musicians and artists, writing music simply for profit, and other acts deemed felonious by the Nazis. The composer had long since become inured to critical attacks and paid no attention, but the barbs increased in number and intensity as the party grew in strength, and Willy Strecker became concerned. He urged Hindemith to visit the United States and capitalize on the recent successes of his two commissioned works. The composer refused, saying he was much too busy with his composing, concertizing, and teaching to consider doing so.

The situation changed drastically immediately after Adolf Hitler gained complete control in March 1933. Hindemith's detractors now stepped up their vicious attacks to such a ridiculous level that his good friend, the nationally revered conductor Wilhelm Furtwängler, felt obliged to come to his defense in a long open letter published in Germany's leading newspaper, *Deutsche Allgemeine Zeitung,* on 25 November 1934. The Nazi Minister of Culture Paul Goebbels was infuriated and forced Furtwängler to resign his posts as conductor of the Berlin Philharmonic Orchestra and director of the Berlin State Opera, and the director of the Hochschule für Musik ordered Hindemith to take an indefinite leave from the school. All of this received extensive press coverage throughout the world, including the *New York Times,* which ran several stories about Paul Hindemith and his harassment by the Nazis. It was hardly the kind of publicity he would have preferred; nevertheless it did bring his name to the attention of many in this country who had never heard of him before.

The years 1935 and 1936 were a trying time for Hindemith. He left Berlin early in 1935 for a village in the Black Forest, where he spent the next few months in relative seclusion completing the score of his opera *Mathis der Maler.* His teaching at the Hochschule was resumed in June but on a greatly reduced schedule. He continued composing as before, but also devoted much time to working on the first volume of his comprehensive textbook on composition, *Unterweisung im Tonsatz* (known as *The Craft of Musical Composition* in its English translation). He did some concertizing in England and Holland, and accepted an invitation from the Turkish government to outline a plan for the complete reorganization of the country's music education program. He and Gertrude spent six weeks in Ankara in 1935 and again in 1936. Meanwhile he lived constantly under increasing threats against his music by the Nazi regime, which culminated in an official ban on any further public performances of it in Germany, decreed in October 1936. Thus the invitation to come to the United States in April 1937, received in September 1936, could not have been more welcome.

Before he left for the United States in March 1937, Hindemith's situation in Germany worsened: personnel changes were being made in the Cultural Ministry that he felt would lead to additional troubles for him at the Hochschule, and he wrote to Willy Strecker that he was going to resign. Strecker begged him not to, saying that such a move would be construed as an admission of defeat and give great satisfaction to his enemies.[6] Mrs. Hindemith also wrote to Strecker that her husband was "sick and tired of the whole mess and would submit his resignation the day the ship sails."[7] Strecker wrote once again, expressing deep regret over the decision and imploring Hindemith not to leave Germany permanently, for he was confident that conditions would soon return to normal.[8] However, on 22 March 1937 Hindemith wrote to Fritz Stein, director of the Hochschule, submitting his resignation as of 30 September, and he left for the United States on 25 March.

Chapter 2

The First U.S. Concert Tour, 1937

HINDEMITH RECEIVED a cablegram early in September 1936 from Oliver Strunk, then chief of the Music Division of the Library of Congress, inquiring if the composer could come over in April 1937 to appear as the featured guest artist at the Eighth Washington Festival of Contemporary Music. Hindemith cabled back that he was interested but would need further information before he could give a definite answer. Strunk wrote a long letter giving full details about the festival and his hopes of including an all-Hindemith chamber music concert with Hindemith as the soloist in his new viola concerto, *Der Schwanendreher.* Strunk added: "It is understood that your appearance at our festival will be the first you will make in this country and that the performance of *Der Schwanendreher* will be the first American presentation of the work."[1] Hindemith agreed to come.

The officials at B. Schott and Sons were delighted, for they were fully aware of the festival's importance and knew that it would be an ideal stage for Hindemith's professional debut in the United States. This was an international event held under government auspices by an endowment established by Elizabeth Coolidge in 1925, with an invited audience comprised of the musical elite from all parts of the country. Willy Strecker immediately proposed sending a letter to their U.S. agents, Associated Music Publishers [AMP] in New York, reading in part: "Hindemith's appearance in one of the great American concerts is very important and we are convinced that Klemperer, Koussevitzky, and Stokowski will want to have him on one of their concerts as soon as they know he is coming."[2] A draft of the letter was sent to Hindemith, who replied, "I think it would be better if you did not push too hard."

Strecker did alert the AMP officials nevertheless, and asked them to do what they could to find additional engagements for the composer while he was there. This was the first time AMP had been drawn into direct involvement with Hindemith's U.S. affairs and it would not be the last. It was, in fact, the beginning of a long and mutually advantageous association that would continue over the next sixteen years. The AMP office at 25 West 45th Street in New York would serve as Hindemith's operational base for his three U.S. concert tours in 1937, 1938, and 1939; and during his residency from 1940 to 1953 he depended heavily on the officers and secretarial staff to take care of his routine correspondence and most business matters relating to his publications. It was a generally happy relationship until the early 1950s, when serious misunderstandings over contractual agreements arose which required the personal intervention of Willy Strecker to settle.[3]

Ernest Voigt, then president of AMP, agreed immediately to assume the responsibility of overseeing Hindemith's visit and of securing additional engagements for him during the sixteen days he planned to be in the United States after the Washington festival. AMP was a publishing firm and had never been involved with professional concert management, but its officers did the best they could to cope. The three tours they were finally able to put together were hardly models of logistical efficiency, forcing the composer to endure an inordinate amount of inconvenient traveling, but he did not complain.

Hindemith's admonition to Strecker not to be overly zealous in promoting his first visit to the United States belied his real feelings about the undertaking. He well understood that his appearance at the Washington festival was not just another engagement and took it very seriously indeed, particularly in planning the concert of his chamber music. In his first letter to the composer, Oliver Strunk had suggested the following program:

> Third String Quartet, Opus 22 (1921)
> Solo Viola Sonata, Opus 25.1 (1922)
> Die Serenaden, Opus 35 (1925)
> Trio for Heckelphone, Viola, and Piano, Opus 47 (1928)

He had added: "This may not suit you at all and perhaps there are other works you regard as more representative and would prefer to have them performed."[4]

Hindemith replied that he would prefer to have some of his more recent compositions performed and would shortly submit a revised plan. Ten weeks went by before the anxious festival officials received it:

1. Sonata for flute and piano
2. 4 songs of Hölderlin with piano
3. Solo viola sonata
4. Pieces for mixed chorus
5. III sonata for piano

The flute sonata has not yet been performed for I have just written it. A singer is necessary for the Hölderlin songs—either a powerful baritone or tenor. You must let me know soon which it will be in case I have to transpose the songs. These will also be first performances. For No. 3 I will play Opus 25.1. I will make No. 4 out of some older pieces, revising them. Do you have a madrigal chorus available? If not, some other piece will have to be used. The piano sonata is one of three recently published by Schott. You must select a first-class pianist for it, who can also do the flute sonata and the Hölderlin songs.[5]

Hindemith had rejected all but one of Strunk's initial suggestions, replacing them with three works written between December 1935 and December 1936, and one which would not be completed until just before Hindemith left for New York. It is apparent that he was now considering his most recent music as "more representative" of his work than his earlier compositions. One can also assume that this opinion was based, at least in part, on the fact that he had applied the compositional techniques advocated in his new textbook in writing these pieces and wished to take advantage of the opportunity afforded by this conspicuous concert to demonstrate their validity. He did agree to play the 1922 *Solo Viola Sonata, Opus 25.1,* knowing from long experience in performing the work that it was an effective display piece for his virtuosity as a violist. Furthermore, it was one of his early compositions that he listed at the end of the first German edition of *Unterweisung im Tonsatz* as a work that conformed to the theoretical principles defined in the book.

The four songs on Hölderlin texts were written in December 1935 and the *Piano Sonata in B♭ No. 3* in August 1936. The *Sonata for Flute and Piano* was completed early in December 1936, *after* he had accepted the Washington invitation. The "Pieces for mixed chorus" were complete revisions of four of the six *Liedernach alten Texten, Opus 33* (1923) redone in accordance with procedures outlined in Hindemith's new textbook. He did not undertake this project until

15

receiving word that a madrigal chorus would be available. This was not confirmed until early in February 1937, much to his annoyance; nevertheless he decided to proceed as planned and was able to complete the work in time.[6]

Hindemith sailed from Hamburg on 25 March 1937 on the S.S. *Deutschland* and arrived in New York on 2 April. There was time before the ship docked at noon for him to write a note to his wife, confirming his safe arrival and ending with this hint of apprehension: "The so-called Wonder of the World [New York City] will gradually appear on the horizon and soon the mad rush will begin. Keep your fingers crossed for me."[7] He enclosed the manuscript of chapter 6 of the *Unterweisung* that he had completed during the voyage, and left the packet on the ship to be carried back on its return trip.

The composer's first glimpse of Manhattan's renowned skyline prompted the following entry in his travel journal: "One has seen it a thousand times in films and photographs but it is too fantastic to describe. The skyscrapers of Manhattan are absolutely wild, going beyond anything you ever imagined. It looks like a completely berserk castle, with countless sharp and narrow turrets trying to outdo each other. It looks like a fairyland, for it is so improbable that man could have built anything like this. Surprisingly, it is not over-powering, as I expected it to be. On the contrary, it makes a light and even joyful impression."[8]

Hindemith had requested Voigt not to have any reporters or photographers there to meet him when he arrived, and there were none. Voigt had been quite willing to oblige, for, as he wrote to Willy Strecker: "We did not want to steal Mrs. Coolidge's thunder by having him introduced and interviewed here before he appeared in Washington."[9] In fact, there had been very little advance publicity about Hindemith's visit to this country. The Washington officials did not release an announcement until 11 November 1936, published that day in the *New York Times*. It stated briefly that the composer Paul Hindemith had accepted an invitation to appear at the Washington Festival in April 1937 and that his viola concerto *Der Schwanendreher* would have its U.S. premiere. It also noted that this would be "the fifth important work by Mr. Hindemith introduced into the United States by Mrs. Elizabeth Sprague Coolidge." The release ended with this statement: "It is interesting to note that the German Propaganda Ministry has issued instructions to the German press to refrain from mentioning Hindemith, who is accused of 'Kultur-Bolshevism' and 'spiritual non-Aryanism.' "

The previous week, on 8 November 1936, the *Times* had published a brief item by a reporter who was obviously a bit miffed: "News comes to light in various ways. The fact that Paul Hindemith, the German composer, would visit these shores this season, was received indirectly the other day by an announcement that the League of Composers would tender a reception in his honor in April." Hindemith's actual arrival in this country received only a brief factual notice in the paper on 3 April. However, his appearances in Washington and New York would be given full coverage by the *Times* and other leading newspapers.

Hindemith had fully anticipated delays and complications in passing through U.S. Customs and Immigration and was both surprised and pleased not to encounter any. He reported to his wife that a "magical note from the Library of Congress" had been sent to the ship and seemed to have worked the wonder. He stepped ashore in the afternoon, greeted by Ernest Voigt (who waved an orange-colored handkerchief for identification), Merritt Tompkins, president of Broadcast Music Incorporated (AMP's parent company), and two close relatives living in the United States whom he had never seen before. These were his uncle Gustave Hindemith, the brother of his father, and his first cousin Rudolph, the son of Gustave. Voigt described the meeting in a letter to Willy Strecker: "We were joined by his old uncle, the oldest brother of his father, who has been in this country for over 50 years and had never been back or seen any of his family since. The meeting was quite touching, and Hindemith immediately showed that fine, unassuming, and democratic side of his character that has endeared him to everyone over here who has met him."[10]

This is the composer's own account of what happened next on his first day in New York:

> I went up to the group and was welcomed as though I had been there ten times before. We drove to the Hotel Seymour (located near the AMP office and very nice and quiet), where I unpacked a bit and then we all went into the bar for a drink. It is rather strange to learn to know people with whom you are so closely related. The uncle is exactly like what one imagines an immigrant of the 1880's to have been: tall in the saddle, hearty and lively for a man of his 73 years, and he drinks beer like a trooper. He reminds me more of my mother than my father. On the other hand, the cousin is

completely un-Hindemithian. He is a photographer here in New York, a slight and apparently weak man about 45 years old.

After they left, Voigt and I walked over to Broadway. This is also difficult to describe. It is an absolute jungle of electrical displays and I felt like laughing continuously. I finally did when I saw a giant dragon blowing clouds of real steam out of his nostrils every ten seconds. We had dinner in a seafood restaurant, where we ate oysters and broiled lobsters.[11]

Only one week remained before the all-Hindemith chamber music concert was to be given in Washington and the composer devoted most of his time during this period to rehearsals, all held in New York. The festival authorities had engaged outstanding artists, including the flutist Georges Barrere, the tenor Frederick Jaegel, the young Puerto Rican pianist Jesús Maria Sanroma, and the Madrigal Singers from the Dessoff Choir conducted by Paul Boepple. Hindemith was favorably impressed by the work of the flutist, pianist, and madrigal group, but had reservations about the tenor, whom he felt was not as well prepared as he should have been.

However, Hindemith was quite disturbed over the prospects for a successful performance of *Der Schwanendreher.* When he was told that only a single one-hour rehearsal with the orchestra had been scheduled, conducted by Carlos Chavez, he immediately hit the ceiling and threatened to cancel his appearance at the festival if more time were not granted. It was, and proved to be absolutely essential.[12] The orchestra was an ad hoc ensemble of highly competent professionals drawn from radio studios in New York who had never played together before, nor had Chavez ever seen them. Hindemith reported that "the musicians are good but the conductor does not know how to control them," and that the extra rehearsal was "more of an opportunity for Chavez to learn the score than for the players."[13]

There were no rehearsals on Sunday, 4 April, so Hindemith spent the day at his uncle's farm near Port Jervis, New York, going up and back by train with his cousin Rudolph. He was especially pleased to discover that his uncle was a good amateur pianist who had even organized a small orchestra that met regularly to play for its own pleasure. There was a violin available and Hindemith and the old man made music together, delighting the composer as well as the uncle.

Another evening, Hindemith's cousin Rudolph took him out to

dinner, and they went later to the top of the Empire State Building for a view of Manhattan by night. This was Hindemith's rather unusual reaction to the experience:

> I went with Rudolph to see the most important work of man since the Temple of Karnak: New York at night from the top of the Empire State building. It is an incredible sight: the giant city and its harbors and bridges brilliantly illuminated with a million lights—tiny swarms of humanity in the streets surrounded by buildings that seem from this height to be moving—it is all unbelievably beautiful. The planet Venus stands alone and red in the east, almost a fixed part of the display of lights. At first it looks like the tower light of an even higher skyscraper, but then one realizes she goes her own way apart from the other lights and tells us more than the whole scene around her.
>
> That people can accomplish all this for purely commercial purposes is shocking when you realize it was their religious faith that moved the Egyptians to their great achievements. Either God is trying to show today's heathen world what He has done or it is as worthless as it appears when you look at a tree or an animal. So many stones, such great hurry, so much noise—how great it is one can make music and thus possess a stronger counteragent against all the confusion of the old and new worlds than do the philosophers.[14]

When not involved with rehearsals, Hindemith devoted most of his free time to completing the seventh and final chapter of his *Unterweisung im Tonsatz, Part I,* thus finally finishing the project he had begun eighteen months before. It was mailed to Schott on 8 April and in his journal that day he entered the following paragraph to his ongoing account of United States mores intended for Gertrude's enlightenment:

> It is now time to say something about eating and drinking. I am very satisfied. The little restaurant in the hotel is attractive and serves excellent food. It is also inexpensive, with a complete dinner costing between 50 and 80 cents and a wide choice of dishes is available. If you like to start with mussels, and I do, it costs 20 cents more. The oysters and clams are marvelous. You get a sharp tomato sauce with ground horseradish that goes very well with them. The main dishes are somewhere between English and French. For breakfast I begin with porridge and grapefruit, just like an old native. Except for the ubiquitous glass of water the drinks are the same as ours.

The beer (at least at this restaurant) is called "Budweiser" and it is very good.[15]

Hindemith and Voigt slipped quietly into Washington late in the evening on 9 April, having taken the train from New York. The all-Hindemith chamber music concert was scheduled to begin at 11:15 the following morning in the Library of Congress auditorium and the composer was there by 9:30 to make certain everything was in order. This is his account of the day's events:

The concert began on time and Sanroma and Barrere did a first-class performance of the flute sonata. It made a very good impression and the large audience received it warmly. Then came the Hölderlin songs—Jaegel sang them well enough but you could tell he had again been on an overnight train ride. I had the third number on the program [the *Solo Viola Sonata, Opus 25.1*] and was given a long standing ovation when I came out on stage. I played it the way Charles the Great [*sic*] used to do his solo sonatas—casually and impressively. There was heavy applause. The chorus, which followed me, sang magnificently [the *Four Songs on Old Texts*] and Sanroma played the third piano sonata likewise.

There was a gala luncheon after the concert, given by Mrs. Meyer [wife of Eugene Meyer, publisher of the *Washington Post*]. Nadia Boulanger was there and greeted me like a blissful piano teacher congratulating one of her students who had just made his debut—with embraces and kisses in front of the assembled company. I had to sit next to Mrs. Coolidge in the place of honor and we had a long conversation. Like all the others, she said I should move here and that all kinds of arrangements could be made that would be satisfactory to me. She thought the best idea would be for me to be at one of the universities or large conservatories, even if not on a permanent basis. I told her I would think about it.

Mrs. Oliver Strunk rescued me from the polyp-like arms of the rest of the company by taking me for a ride to see the cherry blossoms. . . . Hotel rooms are hard to get here, not because of the music festival but because of the blossoms. There are three or four thousand very beautiful red-flowering trees surrounding a lake, the gift of a former Japanese Ambassador. You see a big artificial swan in the lake with a red houseboat behind him in which the "Queen of the Blossoms" will ride in the evening like an American female Lohengrin.

Then what happened? Another reception, this one in honor of Mrs. Coolidge and all the participating performers. It was in the home of Mrs. Meyer, filled with great paintings, including some fine old Germans and an El Greco. There was no time to look at them, for everyone wanted to shake my hand and ask if this was my first time here. I soon hurried away to get some rest. [Hindemith attended another chamber music concert in the Library of Congress that evening, which he described as very dull.][16]

The account of the luncheon given in his honor is of special interest, for it is the first time he mentions the possibility of moving to the United States. It is significant that he had been in this country only eight days and was already willing to consider coming here. References to this eventuality and speculations about its feasibility appeared with increasing frequency in his letters and journals from then on.

Hindemith's concert had been well received by the capacity audience, but Olin Downes, the respected music editor of the *New York Times*, had reservations. In his long review of the concert, published the following day, he admitted rather grudgingly that the flute sonata and choral pieces had some attractive aspects, but was quite critical of the other works. There were "singular irregularities" in the solo viola sonata, the vocal lines in the Hölderlin songs were "not easy to accept," and the piano sonata "cultivated a folk-art and simplicity we need not take seriously." The composer's decision to offer a program featuring his music written after 1935 did not please Mr. Downes at all: "Was he best represented by his most recent compositions in this form? We did not find the great Hindemith in these works or discover a movement equal in depth or strong modern beauty to certain slow movements of Hindemith's quartets that are known. Mr. Hindemith writes a great deal, and he has often written unequally, but he has a great past, and if he will, future."[17]

The following evening, Hindemith was the soloist in the U.S. premiere of his *Der Schwanendreher*, the final number in a chamber orchestra concert conducted by Carlos Chavez. He wrote in his journal only that the performance had gone better than he dared hope under the circumstances. There was yet another reception after the concert, this one at the home of Secretary of the Treasury Henry Morgenthau. Ernest Voigt was at the concert and had this to say about the concerto performance in a letter written to Willy Strecker a few days later: "It went pretty well. I am qualifying this because that was Hindemith's impression. He did not feel quite 'en rapport' with

Chavez.... The Victor Company had been planning to make a recording of the concerto but this we have had to abandon because Hindemith was not satisfied with the conductor's interpretation."[18] The review by Olin Downes in the *New York Times* the next day simply described the structural details of the concerto and reported that "the composer played with the same assurance, authority, and carelessness of tonal quality he had shown the previous day in playing his solo viola sonata." No mention was made of Chavez's conducting. Downes explained that he would have more to say about the work after its performance by Hindemith with the New York Philharmonic in New York "next Thursday evening."[19]

From various comments in his letters and journal it is evident that Hindemith thoroughly enjoyed his first public appearance in the United States, notwithstanding the problems with the concerto. He had been received with utmost cordiality and respect by the distinguished guests attending the festival, who gave him spontaneous standing ovations, honored him at three gala receptions, and made it known that they would like to have him stay in this country permanently. There is no evidence that Hindemith had ever before seriously considered emigrating to the United States, but the Washington experience suddenly changed his thinking. He could now be assured he would be welcome, and he immediately decided at least to come over again the following year for another concert tour. Meanwhile, he would begin to explore possibilities for more extended stays in the future, including that of emigrating.

Hindemith's next engagement was in Boston, where he flew on Monday, 12 April. With excellent daily express train service between the two cities it is inexplicable that he was booked to go by plane, for commercial flights in 1937 could be and often were harrowing experiences. Hindemith's small and low-flying fifteen-passenger plane was buffeted mercilessly by a severe storm all the way to New York and everyone on board became ill. He changed to a slightly larger plane in New York and the ride to Boston was uneventful, but the composer was still so ill he could enjoy none of it. He was met in Boston by Arthur Fiedler, who was to conduct a performance of *Der Schwanendreher* the following evening with the composer as the soloist. Fiedler was then forty-three years old and in his seventh year as conductor of the Boston Pops Orchestra and several other instrumental groups in the area.[20]

The following morning Fiedler brought Hindemith to a rehearsal of the Boston Symphony Orchestra being conducted by Koussevitzky. The composer noted in his journal: "When Koussevitzky saw me in the balcony, he stopped the rehearsal and introduced me to the members of the orchestra, who all stood up and tapped their instruments. During the rehearsal break, Koussevitzky came to the balcony, embraced me ardently, and said immediately that next year I must perform with him."[21] Koussevitzky meant what he said and Hindemith did perform with the Boston Orchestra the following year. However, Ernest Voigt was highly annoyed with the Boston maestro's attitude and behavior in 1937. In a letter to Willy Strecker he wrote: "When we approached Koussevitzky several months ago he declined to consider engaging Hindemith on the threadbare grounds his roster of soloists for the season was completed. . . . He did not come to the concert, although he had promised to, but sent a long apologetic telegram pleading indisposition. If you knew Koussevitzky you would hardly expect him to lend his august presence to any such unofficial occasion."[22]

The concert on Tuesday evening, 13 April, was given in the Boston Chamber Music Club auditorium before an audience of 250 invited guests. The program included Hindemith's *Wind Quintet, Opus 24.2* and the *Solo Viola Sonata, Opus 25.1* played by the composer, who was also the soloist in *Der Schwanendreher,* conducted by Fiedler. All of the players were members of the Boston Symphony Orchestra. Hindemith noted in his journal that everything went well and that he was pleased.

He returned to New York by train the following day, 14 April, and wrote to Gertrude that evening expressing his overall satisfaction with the way things had been going so far, adding: "I must definitely plan to come to the United States next year. I don't know just how it might be done as yet, perhaps a combination of teaching and concertizing. In spite of all the comical ways music is officially handled over here, it does have its serious and promising aspects. During the final days of my stay here I have appointments with the Directors of the Juilliard School and Curtis Institute. I want to find out which of these ships sails the better."[23] It had not taken Hindemith long to reach a decision about returning to the United States, for this was written only four days after he had told Mrs. Coolidge in Washington that he "would think about it." (A meeting with the Juilliard director did take place and a complete account of this unsatisfactory encounter is given later in this chapter. There is no record of his having met with any Curtis Institute officials.)

Hindemith's New York debut as a concert artist took place on 15 April, when he played *Der Schwanendreher* with the New York Philharmonic Orchestra under Artur Rodzinski in a Carnegie Hall subscription concert. It proved to be something of a fiasco, as the composer noted in his journal:

> The New York orchestra is not as good as the Boston, and the highly touted Rodzinski is not as good as I had expected. . . . The concert was poorly planned, with the thinly-scored concerto coming between Strauss' *Tod und Verklärungand* and Beethoven's *Fifth Symphony.* The piece is therefore under a great disadvantage in an auditorium as large as Carnegie Hall. The harpist played a lot of wrong notes and the trombonist never played his important solo part in the first movement at all. Rodzinski wandered all over the place and he never did get the tempo right in the final movement. I doubt that the audience was able to get much out of the piece.
>
> Nadia Boulanger gave a reception afterwards that was both fashionable and boring. She makes a less convincing impression here than she did in Berlin. I had a feeling she was trying to play musical politics in every way. Stravinsky was there, having also attended the concert sitting conspicuously in the front row. He went around the room telling everyone that the concerto was a "terribly important piece." I disappeared early.[24]

Olin Downes was still unhappy about the concerto and again questioned the merits of Hindemith's most recent music. His review in the *New York Times* read in part: "Hearing the concerto for the second time . . . we liked it less than we did in Washington. It is clear that it contains beautiful motives and striking passages; it is ingenious on the whole but unnecessarily ugly and forced. . . . What then of the earlier Hindemith? Were we wrong in liking him? Or was Hindemith wrong? Did he only write the earlier pieces in a temper, or bad humor? His recent pieces are puzzling. . . . This concerto, expertly written, does not convince this particular pair of ears as music."[25]

The concert was repeated on 16 April and the composer reported that the concerto performance had gone better but was still "not very good." The officials of Schott and AMP had had high hopes that Hindemith's only appearance with a major U.S. orchestra on this tour would be a great success, but these were dashed. The composer was disappointed but not dismayed. He felt that he had played well but that it was impossible to overcome the heavy odds against him of a poorly planned program, an auditorium too large, and the indifferent work of the orchestra and conductor. As a veteran performer he had encountered similar situations before and thought no more about it.

Voigt and his AMP colleagues now decided it was time for Hindemith to have some relief from the heavy pressures he had been under for the past few weeks and on the following night, 17 April, took him to dinner at Duke Ellington's famous Cotton Club and out for a night on the town afterwards. This was an entirely new experience for him:

> AMP invited me and the Oliver Strunks, who came up from Washington, for a night of relaxation at the Cotton Club, a lively Negro cabaret. There is not much besides a lot of scantily clad dark people tap dancing and singing, but it is all done with incredible verve. The orchestra played continuously for about three hours, the wildest I ever heard. Trumpets screamed all the way up to high B♭, trombones and saxophones did elaborate "hot flourishes." The whole thing was really a rhythmic and tonal orgy, done with remarkable virtuosity.
>
> Afterwards we went uptown to a dance hall in Harlem, where two excellent jazz bands alternated in providing continuous music for the extraordinarily lively crowd of black dancers.... For 25 cents you could rent one of the black ladies for a dance, and they danced pert and lively in spite of their evening clothes.
>
> We ended up at the Ubanga Club, where again there was wild and virtuoso music. The floor show featured a black female dancer doing a strip tease. At the last moment all the lights would be turned off. Since they repeated the trick so often in the same way, we went back downtown to a somewhat whiter neighborhood and had a final glass of beer.[26]

Notwithstanding the late night out, Hindemith rose early the next morning and set to work writing a new solo viola sonata. According to his journal, Victor had expressed interest in making some recordings at the end of his stay, and Hindemith did not care to repeat the recording of *Opus 25.1* he had done for Columbia.

That evening he was the guest of honor at a dinner given by the New York League of Composers that preceded a concert of his own music. The program included some of his early piano pieces, songs from *Das Marienleben,* the new flute sonata, and a performance by him of his *Opus 25.1*. He had to attend a reception after the concert that seems to have been something of an ordeal: "I was beset by the mindless chatter of questions of hundreds of violists, composers, autograph hunters, and a lot of wives too old and too fat. It was also frightfully hot in the room. To recover, I dashed out afterwards with the Strunks to the Blue Ribbon restaurant. Later we went to the Cotton Club, where we saw the last performance of the floor show at 2:00 a.m. The music was just as fresh and lively as it was last night."[27] The composer was obviously intrigued by Duke Ellington and his orchestra.[28]

Since efforts to secure an engagement with the Chicago Symphony Orchestra had not been successful, Hindemith had to be content with a relatively obscure appearance at a small private concert sponsored by the Chicago Arts Club. This had been arranged by Hans Lange, the assistant conductor of the symphony and the composer's friend and professional colleague from the early years in Frankfurt. Hindemith, escorted by Merritt Tompkins, arrived in Chicago on Tuesday morning, 20 April, after an overnight train ride from New York, during which he spent most of the time working on the new viola sonata. There was a rehearsal of *Der Schwanendreher* in the afternoon with Lange and a chamber orchestra comprised of players from the symphony, but during the rest of the day and evening and most of the following day Hindemith concentrated on completing the sonata project. The concert was given that evening, 21 April, at the Chicago Arts Club before a small group of invited guests, preceded by a reception and dinner the composer was obliged to attend. The performance was not entirely successful, as he reported in his journal: "My string quartet Opus 22 was played first and beautifully done. Then I performed the new solo viola sonata, which did not make any visible impression. At the end came the ubiquitous *Der Schwanendreher* which, in a room too small and with the brass playing relentlessly, sounded more like a herd of wild sea lions being turned than a swan. Since there had been only one rehearsal the orchestra was hardly confident, and since Lange gave the tiniest possible beats, he almost upset the applecart."[29] He was obviously not satisfied with the new solo viola sonata, and in fact never played it again. (He gave the manuscript to Oliver Strunk, who eventually left it to Princeton University, where it has remained. It was never published but will be included in the complete edition of Hindemith's works that Schott began issuing in 1977.)

The final stop on the tour before returning to New York was in Buffalo, where Hindemith stayed for four days and appeared in two concerts. The visit was arranged by Cameron Baird, a wealthy young industrialist (owner and head of the Buffalo Pipe and Foundry Company) who was also a talented violist, composer, and conductor. Baird knew Hindemith personally from having spent the academic year 1933–34 studying at the Berlin Hochschule für Musik and was delighted to have the opportunity of bringing the composer to Buffalo. Three years later Baird would play a critical role in the negotiations that enabled Hindemith to enter the United States as an immigrant.

The first engagement was with the Buffalo Philharmonic Orchestra on Friday evening, 23 April, as the soloist in *Der Schwanendreher* and conductor of his *Symphony: Mathis der Maler.* The orchestra had not yet attained the level of excellence it would later achieve, and Hindemith reported having to "grind them down hard" in two extra-long rehearsals to prepare the *Mathis* symphony. Apparently it was not enough:

> First, a Haydn Symphony was conducted by Autori.[30] Then came the concerto and finally *Mathis*. The audience all stood when I came on stage. The concerto performance [conducted by Autori] was the best since Boston. The *Mathis* also went well except for the playing of the first flutist. He was so drunk he played everything wrong insofar as he played at all and he kept looking at me with a friendly smile. In the rehearsal one of the brass players had come in too soon before the final chord and I bawled him out. To prevent this from happening in the concert, I gave a light beat on the measure before, whereupon the trumpet did not come in at all and we all sat there with a big hole before the final chord.[31]

The second Buffalo concert, given in a local school auditorium on Sunday evening, 25 April, was planned and prepared entirely by Cameron Baird. It began with *Trauermusik* (1936) and *Die junge Magd, Opus 23.2* (1922), both conducted by Baird. Hindemith then played his *Opus 25.1* solo viola sonata, explaining in his journal somewhat ingenuously, "I did not feel quite ready as yet to do the new one." This was followed by the *Sonata in E for Violin and Piano* (1935) and the program ended with the composer conducting his *Five Pieces for String Orchestra, Opus 44-IV* (1927) and *Ein Jaeger aus Kurpfaltz, Opus 45-III* (1928).

Hindemith took the overnight train to New York later that

evening, escorted to the station by a large delegation of friends and admirers who serenaded him as the train pulled out by singing "Ein Jaeger aus Kurpfaltz." Returning with him to New York was Karl Bauer, an AMP official, who had been in Buffalo all four days at the invitation of Cameron Baird. Hindemith and Bauer, a native of Mannheim, would become close and intimate friends after the composer moved here in 1940. After Ernest Voigt's untimely death in 1943, almost all of Hindemith's dealings with AMP were through Bauer.

Hindemith was back in New York on Monday, 26 April, and in the afternoon had an appointment with the director of the Juilliard School of Music to inquire about the possibility of a limited teaching engagement there in 1938. It was a fruitless effort, as he reported in his journal: "I wanted to put out some feelers, but when I sensed the narrow-mindedness of the Director and saw that he was insecure and suspicious of me I left."[32] Hindemith quite probably did not know that the director, John Erskine, was retiring from his position in two months and would be succeeded by Ernest Hutcheson. Erskine obviously did not wish to become involved with future planning for the institution, preferring to leave this to Hutcheson. Hindemith made no further direct approach to Juilliard or to any other U.S. school, since he never had the need to do so. He bore no grudge against Juilliard and enjoyed very cordial relations with the school in later years.

Hindemith's final public appearance of the 1937 tour was made that evening at the Greenwich House Music School, a private conservatory for young students, where he read a brief speech stressing the value of music study for the young and describing his experiences in writing, preparing, and conducting the *Plöner Musiktag* festival in 1932. Hindemith had written the speech only that morning, and after Voigt had translated it into English, Hindemith had practiced reading it for some of his friends that afternoon at a small and informal reception given for him by the Beethoven Association. It went well that evening, as he wrote in his journal: "Charming little children played some small pieces of mine that were much enjoyed by the audience. I read my speech and apparently mispronounced only two words, so everyone understood me. The school orchestra played my *Five Pieces for String Orchestra*, the final number, nicely and indistinctly. Photographers then got busy, and what next? Another reception, for the last time. I had chills and felt feverish from a cold

I caught on the sleeper ride back from Buffalo and it was difficult for me to keep from running amok around the room."[33]

Hindemith sailed for Hamburg on the S.S. *Europa* at midnight the following day, 27 April. There was a farewell dinner party, hosted by AMP, and he went later to the Metropolitan Opera House to see a performance of Stravinsky's ballets by George Balanchine's American Ballet Company. He was much impressed by Balanchine's choreography, noting in his journal that he would now take seriously Balanchine's requests that he write a ballet for him. Several friends, including the Oliver Strunks, took him to the ship and waved him off.

Hindemith was so thoroughly exhausted from the tour and so plagued by a miserable cold that most of the return voyage had to be given over to rest and recovery. Nevertheless, he took time to write a number of what he termed "duty letters to America." One sent to Ernest Voigt read in part: "I thank you most cordially for all of your efforts on my behalf. I was very happy to find such understanding of my special situation, which is not easy when it involves a composer-conductor-performer combination. I left the States quite satisfied and pleased that I did not disappoint you."[34]

The letter Hindemith wrote to Mrs. Coolidge is of special interest because of his extended comments on the possibility of his moving to the United States. It is quoted here in its entirety.

My dear Mrs. Coolidge,

The great amount of work I have had to do since leaving Washington made it impossible for me to write you until today. The tour I have had was for me interesting and instructive to the highest degree. As far as I can judge, my music did not make a bad impression at the Washington Festival or in the other cities, so I left the country where I was so warmly received with a feeling of artistic satisfaction. That all this was possible is due entirely to you and I thank you most sincerely for the honor of the invitation and for the recognition you let me share. As a small token of my appreciation I am sending you herewith the manuscripts of the choral pieces that were so beautifully performed in Washington, hoping thereby you will remember the composer as favorably as the music.

You were very kind in Washington to urge me to stay a longer time in the U.S. I answered you then somewhat vaguely because I had no idea what the reaction would be to me or my music. Now

29

that I know it is positive I have been thinking a great deal about it and have come to the conclusion that your proposal is right. I would not like to consider a permanent move to America (at least not now), but a teaching position for several months would be possible, and also the happiest solution, since I am no longer so heavily occupied with teaching duties and I want to do more composing. Furthermore, I am also obligated to continue the reorganization work in Turkey which takes several months a year. The School of Music of Northwestern University made such a proposal to me a short time ago, but I did not want to agree before I had your opinion. I do not like to trouble you with these matters but feel obliged to do so after our discussion in Washington. I would also fully understand if you have no interest in any of this and do not reply.

I will close with this and beg you to forgive me for not writing in English. I am fearful of making so many errors that you would not be able to understand me at all. Again with my heartfelt thanks and friendliest greetings, I am

Yours sincerely, Paul Hindemith[35]

Mrs. Coolidge replied promptly, thanking the composer for the manuscripts and saying that they would be deposited in the Library of Congress. She also gave her enthusiastic approval to the idea of his accepting a teaching engagement at Northwestern University, promising to sponsor a performance of his string quartets if he were to come there.[36]

Hindemith also sent a letter to Willy Strecker, which contained these comments on the tour just ended and his plans for returning in 1938: "I am returning from the trip well pleased. It was right to have undertaken it; the time and the situation were the most favorable one could imagine. It was reasonably successful and we can expect much good to come from it. I have enough plans for the next tour and will only wait to see what happens in the next few months. There are possibilities for doing a film and a ballet, plus performing."[37]

Hindemith would return for another tour in 1938, but his thinking that there were "enough plans" proved to be premature.

Chapter 3

The Second U.S. Concert Tour, 1938

P<small>LANNING</small> F<small>OR</small> the 1938 concert tour began propitiously, since important engagements with the Boston and Chicago Symphony orchestras had already been arranged by July 1937. AMP officials were delighted and anticipated no problems in completing a full schedule, but they were wrong. Nothing further could be done until they knew exactly when Hindemith planned to come over and how long he would stay. The composer delayed until October before fixing these dates and by then it was too late to arrange for additional orchestral appearances. AMP could only suggest that Hindemith plan to present small chamber music concerts in colleges. Hindemith was then so preoccupied with major projects (writing the *Symphonic Dances* and the scenario for a ballet based on the life of St. Francis, later called *Nobilissima Visione*), that he readily agreed and told Voigt to arrange anything he could. He added that he would be too busy with European engagements in 1938 to take on any extended assignments in the U.S. involving film, ballet, or teaching, but would be willing to consider these possibilities for a longer tour in 1939.

Finding colleges that could and would sponsor an appearance by Hindemith within the time period he had prescribed was difficult, and AMP was able to make only seven dates. The 1938 tour, which occupied forty-four days between 18 February and 2 April, therefore comprised a total of only eleven appearances, four with orchestra and seven chamber music concerts. This was far below expectations and disappointing to all concerned, including Hindemith. Nevertheless, it proved to be very successful and enabled the composer to make additional personal and professional contacts that would be useful later. It also provided ample free time to discuss and develop plans for the 1939 tour.

Hindemith arrived in New York on 18 February 1938, after an eight-day crossing from Bremerhaven on the S.S. *Deutschland.* Ernest

Voigt was there to meet him and take him to the Hotel Seymour. Passing through U.S. Customs was a bit more complicated this time, for the officials were puzzled by the viola d'amore Hindemith had with him, never having seen one before. His journal entry for the day noted: "I was checked by four officials, one after the other—I doubt whether even the sinners on Judgment Day will be so rigorously examined."

The first concert was not scheduled until 23 February, allowing time for rehearsals with Lydia Hoffmann-Behrendt, the pianist who would be Hindemith's assisting artist in four of the seven chamber music concerts. A prominent concert artist and teacher in Berlin before emigrating to the United States in 1934, Lydia Hoffmann-Behrendt was now living in Buffalo as the wife of a leading architect and city planner and was still active professionally. Hindemith had met her in New York the year before and when he learned that Jesús Maria Sanroma was available for only three of the concerts he engaged her to do the other four.

The first few days of the 1938 tour were in sharp contrast to those of his visit the previous year. In 1937, the composer had been caught up immediately in a flurry of varied and interesting activities, he could look forward to a very important engagement in Washington, and he found New York City fascinating. In 1938, there was nothing for him to do except rehearse a few times with his pianist and practice his solo pieces in the hotel room, and he was not only bored but also annoyed over the small number of engagements that had been arranged. New York City was now depressing, and it rained every day. Comments in his journal for these days reflect his ill humor. The city streets were "ugly and repulsive," the traffic was "chaotic," the skyscrapers now looked "silly," Broadway was a "sad sight," and the city generally was "unbelievably ugly, and it would take a lot of gilt to cover over its flaws." There is a further hint of disillusionment in a letter written to Willy Strecker on 21 February, wherein he refers cryptically to the United States as the "land of limited impossibilities." Such grumbling ceased abruptly after his successful appearance in Boston a few days later and from then on Hindemith was enthusiastic about future possibilities in this country, writing to his wife that they must definitely plan to spend part of every year in the United States.

The first concert, given at Bryn Mawr College near Philadelphia on 23 February, was strictly a professional engagement, unencumbered by social activities of any kind. Hindemith and Lydia Hoffmann-Behrendt came down from New York in the afternoon, played the concert, and left immediately after the performance, which went well according to the composer's journal.

Hindemith may or may not have heeded Olin Downes's critical complaints in 1937 about his more recent music, but it is interesting to note that the chamber music program he selected for his concerts with Lydia Hoffmann-Behrendt in 1938 comprised three early works and only one written in 1936. The same program would also be used in 1939 on his third concert tour of the States. It began with his *Sonata for Viola d'Amore and Piano, Opus 25.2* (1922) and continued with the *Sonata for Solo Viola, Opus 25.1* (1922). The second half included his *First Piano Sonata* (1936), played by Hoffmann-Behrendt, and the *Sonata for Viola and Piano, Opus 11.4* (1919).

Lydia Hoffmann-Behrendt returned to New York, but Hindemith took an overnight sleeper to Boston. The composer was a notorious railroad buff and thoroughly enjoyed riding on trains, but he had reservations about the U.S. variety: "It shook as though it were being driven over a rough pavement. Furthermore, the engineer was one of those typical American kinds, who stop and start so jerkily that it almost tears out your guts. Sleep was impossible."[1]

Koussevitzky kept the promise he had made the year before by having Hindemith as the guest artist in a pair of regular subscription concerts by the Boston Symphony Orchestra on 25 and 26 February. The composer played what he called his "old" viola concerto, *Kammermusik No. 5*, written in 1927, and in honor of his visit Koussevitzky included on the program his *Concert Music for Strings and Brass, Opus 50*, which Hindemith had been commissioned to write for the Boston Symphony in 1930. There was only one rehearsal with the orchestra, held on the morning Hindemith arrived in Boston, 24 February, and described in his journal along with critical comments on his "old" viola concerto.

> The entire orchestra greeted me like a long-lost relative, and they could hardly do enough to show their cordiality. Thus I felt good and listened with the greatest satisfaction to the rehearsal of the piece I wrote for the orchestra's jubilee [*Opus 50*]. Koussevitzky told me repeatedly how much the orchestra liked the piece. One could really sense that in rehearsal for they played with impeccable perfection. They and the conductor understand the spirit and technique of the work so thoroughly that you could not wish for

anything more. I was pleasantly surprised by the piece, for I hardly remembered it. It is serious and very fresh, and not at all ugly.

Next we rehearsed the old viola concerto. I had practiced diligently and was in good form. However, after hearing Opus 50, the concerto with its small instrumentation seemed overloaded and too busy, and the solo part is too difficult. It is also much too difficult for the orchestra, but the people here played it flawlessly. As I wrote to you last year, they are the best orchestra in the world.[2]

The first Boston concert took place on Thursday afternoon, 25 February, and was successful on all counts. This was an arduous day for the composer, for he had to spend the morning in an intensive last-minute rehearsal with Sanroma preparing for a chamber music concert to be given that evening at Harvard University, and they rehearsed again after the afternoon concert. The concert at Harvard was an experience Hindemith never forgot:

> One of the violists in the orchestra promised to drive me out to Cambridge but he was late in coming because a sudden snowstorm had snarled traffic. Thus we arrived late, but it made no difference. Walter Piston[3] was pacing up and down and muttering over and over, "No Hindemith, no piano." There was actually no piano in the auditorium. I had such an urge to laugh that I had to sit down on the steps for a while. It was not determined why there was no piano or who was to blame. I told the confused people they might at least telephone the piano company and find out if one was on the way and said I would begin the concert by playing my solo viola sonata.
>
> I asked for a music stand and there was none to be found. Everyone was laughing by now and I sent one of the students out to see if he could find something and he brought back a bulky lecturn from somewhere. I played my sonata and meanwhile it had been learned there was no way of having a piano delivered. Piston wanted to send everyone home but I said that would never do. After much chasing around I learned there was another auditorium where we might go, even though it was only partially heated. The large crowd tramped through snow and slush to Paine Hall. There were two pianos there and we continued the concert. Sanroma and I both played well.
>
> To console us, we were told that if a piano had been delivered it probably would have been without legs and pedals.[4]

Hindemith had lunch with Koussevitzky the following day and received very encouraging news from the maestro:

He kept saying I must conduct the orchestra the next time I am here, but that could only be two years from now since he cannot have the same guest artist in consecutive years. However, he will play one of my pieces next year. He had great plans for my next trip. He intends to establish in the Berkshires a large and important summer music academy at which I and Stravinsky will teach. It will be in connection with the summer music festival that began there three years ago. They are now building a large new concert hall. At any rate, we will wait and see what happens.[5]

The repeat performance of *Kammermusik No. 5* with the Boston Symphony was given that evening and Hindemith wrote that it was received enthusiastically by the capacity audience.

Hindemith and Sanroma went from Boston to New Haven by train the following day, 27 February, where they were to appear that evening in a chamber music concert in the Great Hall of Jonathan Edwards College, one of the undergraduate residential colleges at Yale University. This engagement had been arranged by Klaus Liepmann, a young German musician who had recently emigrated to the United States and was now holding a nonfaculty appointment at Yale as director of the undergraduate symphony orchestra. Ernest Voigt had asked him only the month before if he could arrange to have Hindemith at Yale on February 27 and Liepmann agreed to try. He was confident the Yale School of Music would be willing to sponsor such a concert and was both surprised and chagrined to learn otherwise. The dean of the school, David Stanley Smith, did not like Hindemith's music and certainly was not interested in promoting it. Liepmann was obliged to proceed on his own and was finally able to complete arrangements for Hindemith's appearance by securing the sponsorship of three of the undergraduate colleges.[6]

Hindemith had known Klaus Liepmann in Berlin and agreed to let the young conductor and string players from the student orchestra open the concert by playing *Five Pieces for String Orchestra* and *Trauermusik,* with Hugo Kortschak as the soloist in the latter work. Hindemith then played his *Opus 25.1* solo viola sonata, Sanroma the *First Piano Sonata,* and the two artists joined in doing the *Sonata for Viola and Piano, Opus 11.4.* There was a reception at the Master's House after the concert and later that evening Hindemith and Sanroma were driven to New York by Liepmann.

The concert at Yale was merely another stop on the tour as far as Hindemith was concerned, who would have had no reason whatever even to imagine that two years later he would return as a member of the faculty and remain for the next thirteen years. His initial impression of the campus, as noted in the journal, is therefore of special interest: "Yale is a large complex of buildings in imported English Tudor style and you get the definite feeling when you step inside any one of them that the people here have no idea of what to do with the money available to them."[7] He learned later and to his occasional annoyance that Yale's financial resources were not as unlimited as its "Tudor" magnificence might have suggested at first glance. (The apparently paradoxical behavior of the Yale School of Music in refusing to cooperate in sponsoring a one-night concert by Hindemith and two years later offering him a faculty appointment was actually not so, but simply the result of a change in the school's administration, fully detailed in chapter 6.)

The following morning in New York, 28 February, Hindemith went to the AMP office and was pleased to learn that Paramount Studios in Hollywood had inquired about the possibility of his doing a film score for them. This development, plus his recent success in Boston and Koussevitzky's promise of future conducting and teaching engagements, prompted the composer to write to his wife: "This is really a strange country, for along with a lot of nonsense there are also incredible possibilities. I think we must plan our annual visits here with these in mind."[8] It is clear he was now simply taking it for granted that he would be coming to the United States each year, with engagements sufficient to allow Gertrude to accompany him.

Hindemith's next engagement was in Chicago as a guest conductor and soloist with the Chicago Symphony Orchestra in a pair of regular subscription concerts on 3 and 4 March. He went out on the Twentieth-Century Limited, boarding the famous train on Tuesday afternoon, 1 March, and arriving in Chicago the following morning. With his avid interest in railroading, which included making and operating his own scale models, he could not resist entering these wry comments on his journal:

> You board it from a red-carpeted platform and gaze with complete astonishment at the Club-Parlor-Reading-Bar-Observation Car, the writing room, and the barber shop, but when you go inside you

have to wonder why the passengers are not also offered a Roman bath, movie theater, swimming pool, bowling alley, shooting gallery, and other vital and spiritual refreshments. The diner was really first class. After dinner I went into one of the parlor cars that had no radio and stretched out in a chair like an original native. There are Negro servants dressed in white-green-gold uniforms. I was too tired to enjoy the radio, typewriter, dictaphone, secretary, or nurse, and so I went to my comfortable bed. Shortly before falling asleep I discovered that the distinguished engineer of this terribly fashionable train was just like all the other jerkers, shakers, and shovers.[9]

Hindemith's 1938 appearance as a guest conductor of the Chicago Symphony Orchestra was the first of some forty similar engagements with major U.S. orchestras he would fulfill over the next twenty-five years. He particularly enjoyed working with the Chicago ensemble, which he conducted twelve times, for its personnel included many German-Americans, several of whom were old friends and colleagues from earlier days. The rapport between the conductor and his players was therefore especially strong. For his concert in Orchestra Hall on 3 March, repeated on 4 March, he chose to conduct the U.S. premiere of his *Symphonic Dances*, a major work completed late in 1937, and *Kammermusik No. 1*, written in 1921. *Der Schwanendreher* was also performed, with the composer as soloist and Hans Lange conducting. Both concerts went very well and Hindemith reported complete satisfaction in his journal, noting also that Hans Lange had done much better in conducting the viola concerto than he had the previous year, when he had "almost upset the applecart."

The world premiere of the impertinent and satirical *Kammermusik No. 1* at Donaueschingen in 1922 had brought storms of protest down on the head of the twenty-seven-year old composer. Its 1938 performance in Chicago seemed to delight the audience, prompting Hindemith to make these comments in his journal:

I don't understand why people got so upset about *Kammermusik No. 1* when it was first performed. It is not made badly at all, and except for a few harmonic and melodic problems due to inexperience there is nothing to make anyone ill. It is not particularly elegant and the heavy use of percussion is simply a concession to the taste of the period. But dear God, look at all the junk being written today in our chemically purified atmosphere, whose technique, invention, musicality, and even meaning are a thousand times worse than this rather inconsequential piece. People who get upset over the use of a siren whistle have far more reason to be irritated today by wind machines and bleating sheep [i.e., Richard Strauss].[10]

Hindemith arrived back in New York on 6 March, having taken a train from Chicago that passed through Pennsylvania. During the journey he recorded some thoughts which clearly reflected his growing interest in the United States:

You ride through the Alleghenies, medium-sized mountains with many rivers and lakes and fairly thick forests, which make a pleasing impression even at this cold time of year. It occurred to me that this is also a native land for people who have their roots here even though they or their forefathers have been here only a few decades. Thus it seems strange to me that so far nothing artistic has grown out of this feeling of being firmly established here. I suddenly thought what great possibilities a native-born American composer must have and I began to identify myself with him. Then I had one inspiration after another and made a rough sketch of two operas, one about the early days in New York and the struggle between the English and Dutch and one about George Washington and the founding of this great country. This is really colossal material and one could make a powerful work out of it.[11]

On 7 March, the day after Hindemith returned to New York, he and Ernest Voigt had a meeting with Metropolitan Opera officials, who had expressed an interest in the possibility of producing *Mathis der Maler.* The world premiere of this great work, completed in 1935, had been scheduled for the 1935–36 season of the Berlin State Opera but it had been canceled by order of the Nazi Cultural Ministry. A first performance was now set by the Zürich Opera in May of 1938. From his journal record of this meeting, it is apparent that Hindemith took advantage of the opportunity to mention his ideas about an "American" opera:

The Metropolitan people were frightfully astonished to have a composer come to them and dissuade them from doing his work— probably the first time ever. *Mathis der Maler* is really not suitable for here, at least not now, any more than *Die Meistersänger* could have been exported when it first appeared because of its distinctly local flavor and theme, to which one must first become accustomed. I advised them to come to Zürich in May to see the premiere, or to send someone, and they said they would like to. They had great misgivings about an opera on American themes, but we will correspond further like old friends until we have agreed on something.[12]

Nothing resulted from this meeting. *Mathis der Maler* has never been performed by the Metropolitan Opera Company, and there is no evidence of further discussion with Hindemith about doing an opera on an American theme.

A chance happening that evening sparked another idea in the composer's mind for a future U.S. project. He was taken by friends to see Walt Disney's latest animated cartoon feature film, *Snow White and the Seven Dwarfs* and he was completely captivated by it, returning alone to the theater the next day and sitting through two consecutive showings. These were his reactions, as noted in the journal: "This is one of the most enjoyable things you could ever see. It is a lively and jovial fairy story, but it also has its serious—and beautiful—moments. Yet it seems a little sad that so much talent, work, energy, and love should be spent on a picture that is made only for entertainment. My mind drifted into thoughts of Rembrandt's "Night Watch," Michelangelo's "Last Judgment". . . . Here is certainly the way to a new art of motion pictures, which one should strive to remove from the realm of pure entertainment."[13] Hindemith went to see the film two more times before returning to Europe and became convinced that Walt Disney was a genius with whom he would like to collaborate in doing a "serious" film. It was not possible for him to do anything about it at the moment except to make plans for seeing Disney in Los Angeles the following year. (The story of that disastrous meeting, which ended forever Hindemith's desire to work with the producer of *Snow White*, is told in chapter 4.)

The concertizing resumed in Detroit on 11 March, where the composer and Hoffmann-Behrendt gave their usual chamber music concert in the Art Museum. On 13 March they performed at the Nichols School in Buffalo. Sanroma came down from Boston to join Hindemith for a concert at Bennington College in Vermont on 15 March, and the final appearance of the 1938 tour was made at Smith College, Northampton, Massachusetts, on 18 March, with Hoffmann-Behrendt again the assisting artist.

Hindemith's first experience as a classroom teacher in an American school came the next morning, when he gave a lecture on

"Inspiration" to the students enrolled in a psychology course at Smith. It was not quite what they expected to hear, according to Hindemith's journal:

> They wanted to hear my thoughts about "inspiration." It must be terribly interesting to learn directly from the composer himself how the good Lord puts on a light here and there in the darkness of his subconscious mind. To the horror of the lady professor, however, I treated the subject entirely from a practical point of view, saying that I did my writing at a desk directly from scratch and rewrote every line three or four different ways until I got it right. I also said you can speak about "disposition" and "inspiration" only in terms that transcend practical and technical matters. This is true not only of my compositions but also the finest examples of Bach, Mozart, and Beethoven. The students left the classroom obviously instructed but also disillusioned.[14]

Hindemith returned directly to New York that afternoon and remained there until sailing for Europe two weeks later. His time was completely free, enabling him to complete his *Nine Songs for an American School Songbook,* which had been commissioned by the Silver Burdett Company in Chicago, and to meet frequently with AMP officials to make plans for the 1939 concert tour. There was also ample opportunity for visiting with friends, who now included several of the leading U.S. musicians active in the city.

The consequences of an evening spent with the choral conductor Hugh Ross merit special mention as further evidence of the high professional and personal respect Hindemith had gained in this country during the course of his two tours. Ross was a member of a committee of distinguished New York musicians headed by Olin Downes that had the responsibility of planning special musical events for the 1939 World's Fair. During his evening with Hindemith he asked the composer for suggestions and was so impressed with what he heard that he reported the ideas to Downes. As a result, Downes invited Hindemith to meet with the committee at its next session on 25 March. He did, and wrote in his journal:

> Today I had a conference with the Music Committee of the 1939 World's Fair in New York. In a recent meeting with Hugh Ross I had suggested the idea of a great international music festival in the amphitheater. Today I expanded on the plan before the full committee, whereupon the chairman, Olin Downes, the critical

overlord of New York (who gave me such bad reviews last year) was full of praise and paid me many compliments (why one thing yesterday and another today?). I doubt if it served any purpose, and the conference ended like most others. It got bogged down in questions of competence, national jealousies, and tactics. The conference was adjourned, with everyone laughing.[15]

Hindemith's doubts were confirmed, for his plan was not followed. Nevertheless, he had to be pleased, and possibly a bit amused, that this illustrious group of musicians had seen fit to ask for his advice.

AMP officials gave the composer a farewell dinner on the evening of 1 April, and Hindemith boarded the S.S. *Hamburg* alone the following night, sailing for Europe at midnight. He entered a brief note in his journal that he thought the tour had gone very well and was "satisfied with the entire experience."

Chapter 4

The Third U.S. Concert Tour, 1939

HINDEMITH WAS in the United States for over eleven weeks in the spring of 1939, a period longer than the first two visits combined. He and AMP officials had decided before he returned to Berlin in April 1938 that it would be advisable to plan for a longer stay in 1939, since there seemed to be enough possibilities for engagements to warrant it. For a variety of reasons most of these never materialized and only fifteen appearances could be arranged, including seven with orchestra and eight chamber music concerts. Nevertheless, the additional time proved to be most advantageous, enabling the composer to investigate more thoroughly than before a number of options for his future activities in this country. Much of it was also needed to accommodate the horrendous amount of traveling Hindemith was obliged to do because of his haphazard itinerary.

The remaining months of 1938 after returning from the United States had been eventful for the composer. He oversaw the 28 May world premiere of his opera *Mathis der Maler* in Zürich, conducted the 2 July world premiere of his *Nobilissima Visione* ballet in London, danced by Leonide Massine and his Monte Carlo Ballet Company, and conducted the 13 September world premiere of his *Nobilissima Visione Suite* in Venice. All three performances drew international attention and were highly acclaimed. Hindemith began writing his *Three Easy Pieces for Violoncello and Piano* and the *Clarinet Quartet* during the return voyage from New York in April, completing both works shortly after arriving in Berlin. By September he had also written the *Sonata for Bassoon and Piano,* the *Sonata for Oboe and Piano,* the *Piano Sonata for Four Hands,* and the first movement of the *Sonata in F for Viola and Piano.*

Their personal situation in Berlin had by then become intolerable for the Hindemiths and they decided to leave Germany permanently, moving to Switzerland in September and settling in the tiny mountain village of Bluche sur Sierre in the canton of Valais. They rented a small chalet overlooking a verdant Alpine valley, surrounded by snowcapped peaks, where they would live until emigrating to the United States in 1940. Hindemith immediately began working on the second volume of his *Unterweisung im Tonsatz,* a practical textbook in two-voice writing entitled *Übungsbuch für den zweistimmigen Satz.* His publishers were most anxious to have the completed manuscript before he sailed for New York in January 1939, but he was unable to oblige. He continued working on it during the voyage over and at odd moments during the first few weeks of the tour, finally completing it in March.

The 1939 tour began on 7 February and continued until 26 April, precisely as originally planned, and proceeded without complications. Hindemith did not keep a daily journal as before but sent frequent letters to Gertrude giving a day-by-day account of his experiences. His concerts are given mostly routine mention as simply having taken place and having gone "well." His nonconcert activities, however, are described in full detail. Most of these concern his diligent efforts to secure future work in the United States and are a rich source of fascinating autobiographical detail. The frank accounts of his encounters with Leonide Massine are particularly valuable, since they are unique: Massine did not describe them in his own published memoirs nor has anyone else.

The composer arrived in Hoboken, New Jersey, on the morning of 7 February 1939 on the Dutch liner S.S. *Volendam,* having sailed from Boulogne on 28 January. Hindemith wrote that reporters and photographers came on board and "soon had me on the stove, but I treated them in the usual fashion." His good friend from AMP, Karl Bauer, and his cousin Rudolph were there to meet him and took him to the Hotel Seymour.

The first engagement was at the Art Museum in Cleveland, Ohio, on 10 February, where Hindemith and Lydia Hoffmann-Behrendt gave a chamber music concert. The program for this and the other five concerts they gave together on the 1939 tour was the same one they had used in 1938 and included Hindemith's *Viola d'Amore and Piano Sonata, Opus 25.2; Viola and Piano Sonata, Opus 11.4; Solo Viola Sonata, Opus 25.1,* and the *First* or *Third Piano Sonata.* Since this program had been well received the previous year, and since keeping the same program would minimize rehearsal problems, they decided not to change it.

Hindemith was back in New York on 12 February, where he would have four free days before leaving for his next engagement in Chicago. The time was used to good advantage, for he was able to complete arrangements for recording four of his works with Victor in April, interview possible English translators of his new theory book *Übungsbuch für den zweistimmigen Satz*, [1] and begin negotiations with George Balanchine over a ballet score.

The brilliant young (then thirty-five years old) Russian-American choreographer George Balanchine had proposed to Hindemith when they met in New York in 1937 that they collaborate on a new ballet. The composer had seen Balanchine's work and was much impressed, but circumstances had prevented his pursuing the idea of collaboration further until now. He had written his *Symphonic Dances* in 1937, hoping that Leonide Massine would be interested in using the work for a ballet, but since Massine had shown no interest, Hindemith went to see Balanchine in New York and offered him the piece. The choreographer was pleased to accept it, provided Hindemith would also write a scenario for it. He agreed to do so as soon as possible and began working on it during the long train ride to San Francisco the following week.

On 17 February Hindemith was the honored guest at a dinner given by the Department of Music of the University of Chicago, after which a program of his music was performed by students. It is interesting to note that he took an upper berth on the ride to Chicago, writing his wife that it was done "to save expenses." This was only one of several occasions during the 1939 tour when he opted for the most economical mode of travel to cut costs. The Hindemiths were experiencing financial difficulties as a result of their move to Switzerland, for most of their funds were being blocked in Germany and they had relatively little income from other sources. This unhappy fact obliged the composer not only to minimize his expenses but also to take advantage of every opportunity to solicit commissions, something he had rarely had to do in the past. The approach to Balanchine was his first such move and there would be more.

Hindemith's next engagement was in San Francisco, where he appeared in a pair of subscription concerts with the San Francisco Symphony Orchestra on 24 and 25 February, conducting his *Concert Music for Strings and Brass, Opus 50,* and playing *Der Schwanendreher* with Pierre Monteux conducting. He had high praise for both the orchestra and Monteux, calling their work "outstanding." The composer arrived in San Francisco on 20 February after a three-day train ride from Chicago that gave him his first glimpse of western country. He was particularly fascinated to see real "cowboys" and was happy to have a one-hour stop in Cheyenne, Wyoming, where he could leave the train and walk around town a bit. He wrote to Gertrude: "This is still genuine cowboy country. Even the non-cowboy citizens wear the appropriate hats, not to speak of the heavy watch chains and cowboy boots. Everywhere in the shops you find a marvelous selection of guns, of shirts in the most unpredictable colors and fabrics of all kinds, of riding boots, spurs, and fascinating saddles. It was a most interesting stop. However, I cannot imagine them playing Mozart in these outfits."[2] Hindemith spent most of his time during the trip to San Francisco carrying out his commitment to Balanchine. "I was diligent on the train ride and made a ballet for Balanchine to dance with the *Symphonic Dances.* It deals with the Childrens Crusade of 1212 A.D. I brought some material about it along with me. It should work well as a ballet."[3] Unfortunately, the ballet would prove to be as ill-fated as the crusade itself.

During his stay in San Francisco, Hindemith had lunch one day with Serge Denham, general manager of the Monte Carlo Ballet Company, who happened to be in the city on business. The two men knew each other from having worked together on the *Nobilissima Visione* ballet the year before, which the company was now performing on a U.S. tour with Leonide Massine in the leading role of St. Francis. The lunch was intended as a social occasion but it proved to be quite otherwise. This is how Hindemith described it and its aftermath:

> When I told him I was writing a ballet for Balanchine he nearly broke into tears. He yawled and yammered and tried every trick to get me to give it up. However, I remained firm, saying I was simply keeping an old promise. I also told him he did not consider me any more important than a few hairs from the head of the ballet company's assistant manager, otherwise they would have been in touch with me before. At this, all hell broke loose.
>
> Denham telephoned Massine in Portland, Oregon, as soon as he could and the dancer became furious. Massine tried to call me several times, but I was always out of my room. He finally got me early the next morning and in his highly agitated boy's voice demanded that if I could not get out of the Balanchine agreement I

should make the work shorter and less important than the one he wanted me to write for him immediately and to have it ready by July. He said I should arrange a contract with Denham at once and that he would meet me in Chicago on my return trip east. He will expect me to have a scenario ready for him by then. I am seeing Denham in Los Angeles tomorrow and will meet with Massine in Chicago.[4]

Hindemith had enjoyed working with Massine in creating the *Nobilissima Visione* ballet late in 1937 and they had become reasonably good friends. (The dancer was one year younger than the composer.) At the ballet's successful world premiere in London, conducted by Hindemith on 2 July 1938, the noted New York impressario Sol Hurok (who was to manage the ballet company's U.S. tour in 1938–39) was present and insisted that the composer come over in October 1938 to conduct the U.S. premiere in New York. Hindemith said he would like to and then heard nothing further. This had irked him considerably and was clearly a factor in his decision to offer the *Symphonic Dances* to Balanchine, whom Massine was now looking upon as a dangerous professional rival. The composer refused to give up his Balanchine commitment but did agree reluctantly to write something for Massine which he would give to him in Chicago. He needed the money.

The composer made an unscheduled stop in Los Angeles before returning East, spending the entire day of 28 February visiting the Fox, Paramount, and Walt Disney film studios in Hollywood with Serge Denham as his escort. Hindemith was to be in Los Angeles for ten days at the end of March and was planning to use some of the stay to investigate possibilities for obtaining a lucrative film contract, convinced that he could make an important contribution to the art. However, he agreed to this preliminary visit on the advice of Denham, who had many friends in the industry and offered to set up the necessary arrangements. Hindemith was not particularly impressed with what he saw at Fox and Paramount, reporting to Gertrude that they were much like the Berlin studios except for being larger. He had looked forward to meeting Walt Disney ever since seeing *Snow White* the year before and was quite disappointed, as he wrote to his wife:

Our last stop was at the Walt Disney Studios. That was quite interesting but there was a bitter aftertaste. Two young fellows took us around and it was interesting to see how Mickey Mouse is produced. However, the place is so tightly regulated that it makes you ill. They have a special school where talented young artists are taught to draw only Mickey Mouse or Donald Duck and are not allowed to try anything on their own. The animators are a bit better off, for they can at least be a little freer to use their own imagination. Naturally, a director oversees all this to make certain nothing original sneaks in. High above all this rules Disney himself. He is a nice fellow about 45 years old and not at all like what you imagine the producer of Mickey Mouse would be. He is obviously a very cocky guy.

I was taken into the holy of holies, where a recording of Stokowski's orchestral transcription of Bach's *Toccata and Fugue in D Minor for Organ* was being played along with the showing of about 100 frames of film. Disney offered a lot of zany opinions about the music, respectfully and unanimously supported by the 12 animators present and seconded by that world wonder Leopold Stokowski, none of which made any sense.

They are making what I wished they would, namely, a serious film. But how!! [The film was *Fantasia*.] It begins with the aforementioned Stokowski recording of the Bach and continues with other masterpieces under his stick waving and suffering from his clumsy rearranging. The program is a mishmash: *Sorcerer's Apprentice, Night on the Bald Mountain, Le sacre du printemps,* and Schubert's *Ave Maria.* I saw the picture sketches for *Le sacre* and they are beautiful but will be absolutely meaningless in the general muddle and totally unsuited to the music.

The people here are too impractical and fussy with details. They could save a lot of work with a better format. I spoke with the great music god Stokowski and had the feeling that in spite of his friendliness he was very insecure and did not particularly like my being there. When I saw what kind of trash he was making and that he was wearing an ultramarine blue silk shirt and a lemon-yellow cravat with his albino-like face I really could not muster up the proper feeling of awe. The last vestige disappeared entirely when I saw one of the arrangers taking apart a fine score like *Night on the Bald Mountain,* deleting and rewriting until not one stone was left on another. When they began doing the same thing with the *Ave Maria* I finally became convinced that the music world could be saved from this evil only by an exterminator. The art should really be saved! Here are all the means at hand for a great film art and you have a scoundrel like that ruining everything. Oh well, perhaps I may still have a chance to do something with it.[5]

Hindemith was clearly disenchanted by what he had seen and heard in Hollywood, but was not yet totally dissuaded. He still believed his visit a month later would prove to be fruitful and that something could be worked out, preferably with Disney.

Hindemith left immediately for Chicago and during the three-day train ride drafted what he called a "comic ballet" scenario for Massine involving maidens at a boarding school and a band of pirates. He met the dancer for an hour in Chicago as planned and reported to his wife: "We had a long discussion in the usual Massine fashion. I gave him the comic ballet script I had written on the train and we talked about all the other plans he had for the future. Unfortunately, I could not agree with any of them."[6]

Between 5 and 10 March, Hindemith and Lydia Hoffmann-Behrendt played chamber music concerts at four colleges: Dartmouth (Hanover, N.H.), Wells (Aurora, N.Y.), Vassar (Poughkeepsie, N.Y.) and Skidmore (Saratoga Springs, N.Y.). It was a tight schedule involving extremely complicated travel arrangements by rail and auto, but everything went smoothly. The composer also gave a lecture on music theory at three of the colleges on the day following the concert.

The engagement at Wells College proved to be of special importance, for it was here that Hindemith and Nicholas Nabokov were brought together for the first time. Nabokov, a young Russian-American composer of considerable repute (and a cousin of the author Vladimir Nabokov), was then chairman of the Music Department at Wells and had long admired Hindemith's music. He now became so impressed with the man himself that he immediately offered to arrange a summer composition course at the college in 1940 for the composer to teach. Hindemith expressed interest and said he would consider it. This was the beginning of Nabokov's involvement with Hindemith's personal problems, which would shortly lead to his playing a key role in facilitating the composer's admission to the United States as an immigrant in February 1940.

Back in New York after the Skidmore College appearance, Hindemith had seven days free of concert engagements but was kept fully occupied with other matters of equal importance. He was able to complete his *Übungsbuch für den zweistimmigen Satz* and sent the manuscript to Schott in Mainz, and as much time as possible was given to work on his new viola-piano sonata, which he hoped to have ready for performance at the final concert in New York on

23 April. Much attention also had to be devoted to the complicated personal problems of Leonide Massine, who was in New York appearing with his ballet company at the Metropolitan Opera House. Hindemith did not wish to jeopardize his chances of obtaining a ballet contract from Massine no matter how much he was beginning to dislike the temperamental and unpredictable dancer.

Meanwhile, he had received the disappointing news from George Balanchine that the projected 1939–40 tour of the American Ballet Company had to be canceled for financial reasons. Consequently, the *Symphonic Dances–Childrens Crusade* ballet plan on which he had devoted so many hours of work on his way to San Francisco was, as he reported to his wife, "down the drain" and there it would remain. This was hardly an auspicious beginning to what he had hoped would be a creatively rewarding association, but he did not despair. At the moment Hindemith was obliged to continue coping with Massine, but when that relationship came to a sour end a year later he again turned to Balanchine. This time there would be no problems, only unqualified success.

Massine rejoiced when he learned of Balanchine's misfortune and immediately arranged a meeting with Hindemith. He told the composer the ballet script about maidens and pirates did not appeal to him and suggested they revive an idea the composer had proposed once before. This was to do a ballet based on paintings by Brueghel and old folk sayings related to the pictures. Hindemith was not exactly pleased to have a second unused ballet scenario on his hands, but quickly agreed to Massine's recommendation, and immediately began to work on it. He was promised a contract to write the music if an acceptable script were prepared and he was more than willing to try.

Hindemith had been finding it increasingly difficult to maintain full respect for Massine in recent weeks because of the dancer's erratic behavior. Much was lost because of an incident on 16 March vividly described by the composer:

> At 5:00 that afternoon I had to go to see Denham to discuss ballet plans for next year. Massine happened to be there, accompanied by an idiotic Russian count and a strange-looking female, waiting excitedly for the arrival of his recent discovery, the phenomenon Salvador Dali. Everyone was tense, and Massine was full of talk about the idea that had prompted him to use the demigod Dali. They want to make a ballet out of the "Bacchanale" scene from the

opera *Tannhäuser*. Massine was not the least disturbed by my objections to it on the grounds you cannot take a piece out of context. In the opera the scene has no ending and goes right on and you should not change the orchestration. Furthermore, the style and handling of the scene are precisely prescribed by Mr. Wagner and both would be seriously abused by Mr. Dali. Massine said Dali admired Wagner greatly and was even thinking of doing a ballet to the "Magic Fire" music from *Parsifal*. He asked me what I thought of this and I got so mad I saw red and roared at him to quit talking such nonsense. That shut him up for a while.

Dali kept us waiting until 6:00 and you can believe I got even madder. Finally the wonderman arrived, a perverted and nasty little guy with slit eyes and a beard. He spoke French and said the stupidist things about music, all of which Massine drank in avidly. When he said he was planning to have Mr. Wagner himself as one of the characters in the ballet I had enough and got out of there as soon as I could. I was so damn mad I walked all the way back to the hotel and it took a long time to recover from all the insolence, arrogance, and stupidity I had witnessed.[7]

Hindemith met with Massine the next morning and vented his spleen over what he had heard and seen the day before: "I told him to quit interfering in artistic matters and just dance, and that I did not wish to work with a ballet company whose artistic director is so insecure and tasteless. He wants me to write for him exclusively, but I said I might do so from time to time at the most. He listened to what I had to say and made me promise to write a ballet for him next year."[8] Later that day Hindemith agreed to a $2,000 contract for the Brueghel ballet that would be formally signed after his return from Los Angeles. It was a decision he would have reason to regret many times over, for it brought nothing but vexation and in the end would never be completed. Needless to say, he never received any money.

The composer was now obliged to make his third coast-to-coast trip by rail in a month. He left New York on 16 March and stopped over for a day in Chicago to consult with Frederick Stock, conductor of the Chicago Symphony Orchestra, about a commission he was being offered to write a piece for the orchestra's jubilee. For reasons unknown the piece was never written. Another stop was made in Denver on 19 March, where Hindemith played a chamber music concert with Lydia Hoffmann-Behrendt.

Hindemith arrived in Los Angeles in the evening of 21 March, where he appeared as a guest artist with the Los Angeles Symphony Orchestra on a pair of subscription concerts on 23 and 24 March. The regular conductor of the orchestra was his longtime good friend from earlier days in Berlin, Otto Klemperer, and the two men enjoyed a happy reunion. The composer played *Der Schwanendreher* with Klemperer and conducted his *Nobilissima Visione Suite* in its U.S. premiere. It was actually a world premiere of sorts, for Hindemith had decided to enlarge the instrumentation by adding more lower brass.

Hindemith's schedule in Los Angeles had been arranged to allow an extra week of free time for exploring the possibilities of work in films. It was not needed, for he very quickly learned all he wanted to know and more from professional colleagues he had known in Berlin who had recently emigrated to the United States and were now involved with film music in Hollywood, among them Ernst Toch. Nevertheless, he remained in the city, thoroughly enjoying the company of his German friends as the guest of honor at a number of pleasant social occasions, and also continued working on his new viola-piano sonata. His hopes of doing any serious work in Hollywood had been dashed, but it is clear from a letter he wrote to Gertrude that there were few if any regrets:

> The net result of my exploration is that it would be impossible to do anything worthwhile here. When I was in Hollywood last month the film music industry seemed more or less comical. This time I have been laughing hard enough to bring tears to my eyes, especially over what I have heard from Ernst Toch. Actually, it is disgraceful. The whole thing is a nightmare of gold-digging madness. Everyone you see or talk with is looking for some of the gold nuggets lying around the place. Whoever gets to the gold trough for a minute—whether through agents, friends, trickery, or accident— eats his fill. It is probable he has waited many years for this to happen. Many achieve power the usual way, through associating with directors or reigning stars, over the bar or in the bed. Almost all are totally without ability.
>
> I was assured that many of the so-called composers around here have given up trying to find out what a 6-chord is because they wouldn't understand it anyway. Small-time orchestral musicians, who crowd around here like maggots under a dead ass, earn $1,000 a week. A bassoonist here keeps two black servants and a cook for

himself alone. Nothing is said about ability or quality, everything depends upon whether it has mass appeal. Others are paid but write nothing, most of them just sit there waiting for the golden signal. The whole thing is much like the spawning of herring—a hundred thousand tiny eggs swimming around in the giant puddle, each waiting for the glorious moment when a producer squirts his life-giving sperm on him. Some of them are then fertilized and the rest can die. What comes out of this is really no more valuable than a herring.

Even Walt Disney, who is far superior to the others in his objectives and the kind of work he does, is impossible. One evening I was with one of my Berlin friends who works for Disney, and was so disillusioned by what he told me that I was actually pleased to get the enclosed letter from Disney, to whom I had written from New York. [The letter is in the Schott archives and was simply a brief note expressing regret that he would be unable to attend Hindemith's concert in Los Angeles, to which the composer had invited him, sending tickets.] I don't see how anyone could work with someone like that who thinks so highly of himself. I think I am pretty well cured of the urge to do anything with the films here. (I once had the completely mad thought I could create something of artistic value.) This idea simply cannot be pursued seriously.[9]

Despite his passion for railroading, Hindemith confessed to Gertrude that his fourth cross-country ride back to New York had been "boring," but he used the time to advantage by working on his new viola-piano sonata. He was back in New York by 4 April and was soon caught up with preparations for his appearances with the Philadelphia Orchestra as a guest conductor. He did two concerts with the orchestra in Philadelphia on 8 and 10 April and one in Carnegie Hall in New York on 11 April, conducting his *Nobilissima Visione Suite*. Critics had high praise for his conducting and for the composition.

The final concert of the tour was given in New York's Town Hall on 23 April, an event arranged by Ernest Voigt and sponsored by AMP as a sort of grand finale. It was an all-Hindemith program of five chamber music works, including one U.S. and three world premieres. Since all but one of the instrumentalists participating were members of the Boston Symphony Orchestra, Hindemith decided to go to Boston on 12 April, staying there over the next eight days, for rehearsals for the New York concert, a recording session with Arthur

Fiedler and the Boston Chamber Music Society Orchestra doing *Der Schwanendreher* for Victor, a performance of his new viola-piano sonata in a hastily arranged informal concert at Harvard University as a dress rehearsal for New York, and meetings with Koussevitzky.

After one of his talks with Koussevitzky, he was happy to report to Gertrude: "He was extremely cordial and told me repeatedly how much he and his orchestra liked my music. They have played the *Symphonic Dances* six times this season in Boston and New York. He said I must definitely plan to teach at his summer academy in the Berkshires next year that will be held in conjunction with the annual summer music festival. He will be in Switzerland this summer and we will discuss the details."[10] It had been long in coming, but Hindemith had a firm offer to work in the United States the following year. He was now assured of returning in 1940 and carrying out his plan of spending part of each year in this country.

Hindemith was back in New York on 20 April and made a recording for Victor the following day, playing his *Trauermusik*. It was an exasperating experience, as he reported to his wife, for the conductor was not up to his assignment and Hindemith was finally obliged to conduct the piece as well as play the solo part.

Hindemith had made only two previous appearances in New York, one being the rather disappointing engagement with the Philharmonic in 1937, when he had played *Der Schwanendreher*, and the other as the guest conductor of the Philadelphia Orchestra in a recent Carnegie Hall concert. AMP officials felt that this was insufficient and therefore arranged the Town Hall concert on 23 April to provide the composer with a better opportunity to display his talents. Hindemith warned them there would be difficulty in selling tickets to such a concert, but they were certain it would be a great success and went ahead. The composer agreed reluctantly to cooperate and chose a program that once again, as at the 1937 Washington Festival, featured works written since 1935.

The concert opened with the *Woodwind Quintet* of 1922, the only "old" work on the program. Hindemith and Sanroma then played the new *Sonata in F for Viola and Piano*, completed only ten days before. The Madrigal Singers, led by Paul Boepple, sang his choral pieces *Five Songs on Old Texts* in their new English version and were followed by Lydia Hoffmann-Behrendt and Sanroma doing his *Sonata for Piano Four Hands*. The final work was his *Clarinet Quartet*, written in 1938. The participation of eight players from the

Boston Symphony Orchestra was made possible only by Koussevitzky's willingness to release them for this occasion, a remarkable gesture of his admiration for the composer. Hindemith could not have hoped for a better group of players and he was highly pleased with their work. The composer had this to say about the concert in a letter to Gertrude:

> The hall was well filled with mostly young people. [Many free tickets had been given to students at the last minute.] "Never-ending applause filled the festival-minded hall" [a quote from a review] when I came on stage. The playing was very good through-out and the concert was a great success. The program was nicely planned, although the audience seemed to get a little tired during the long *Clarinet Quartet* at the end, in spite of its being played exceptionally well.
>
> I have a recording of the entire concert so I don't need to say more about it now. It was broadcast over the radio and a recording was made so it can be sent by short wave to South America. One of the radio critics gave it a rating of "four stars," like cognac. This rarely happens in modern music, but only to Greta Garbo.[11]

Many of Hindemith's old friends from Frankfurt, who had recently left Germany and were now living in New York, attended the concert and came backstage to greet him afterwards: "There was a mass of humanity in the artists' room after the concert remini-scent of a scene from an African safari film, with all the zebras, gnus, and antelopes gathering at the water hole to drink. It was just like Frankfurt 15 years ago. For some reason, I was able to recall all the names and they were pleased to be remembered. . . . I could not get out of there until midnight and then I went out to have a few beers with Nabokov and Bauer."[12] Nabokov had come down from Aurora not only to hear the concert but also to tell Hindemith that plans for the 1940 summer composition course at Wells College were proceeding well and the prospects were pleasing. However, the composer had to tell his friend to defer further action since he now had the Tanglewood offer from Koussevitzky and would have to see how that worked out before making a decision about Wells.

Hindemith was pleased with the way the Town Hall concert had gone, but the anonymous critic for the *New York Times* had reservations. He carped that after the woodwind quintet "the fun was over." He found the viola sonata "sour," the choral pieces "engaging," the four-hand piano sonata "arid," and the clarinet quartet "juiceless." Hindemith's most recent music clearly did not impress him, for he posed this question at the end of the review: "How can a man who has written so much excellent music write so much dull music?"[13]

Hindemith called at the AMP office the morning after the concert and found a disconsolate Ernest Voigt. The concert had been the financial disaster Hindemith had predicted, with ticket sales of only $350 and expenses of $1,400. The composer offered to return the $500 fee he had been paid but Voigt refused to take it. Hindemith was at the Victor studio all afternoon and evening, where he joined Sanroma in making a recording of his *Sonata in F for Viola and Piano* as a violist and the *Sonata for Piano Four Hands* as a pianist. (This is the only recording of Hindemith playing the piano.) Two days later, 26 April, he sailed for Le Havre on the S.S. *President Roosevelt,* with Ernest Voigt and Karl Bauer there to see him off.

Hindemith's third U.S. concert tour had been long and arduous, but as he reported to Gertrude, it had been "more important and successful in every way than the other two combined," and indeed it had. He had two firm offers of summer teaching engagements in 1940 and a signed contract to write a ballet for Massine. He had made four recordings for Victor and completed the *Übungsbuch* and a new sonata for viola and piano. There had also been ample opportunity to satisfy his burning curiosity about the U.S. film industry and the possibility of becoming involved with it: he could now check that off his list once and for all.

Hindemith told Voigt before leaving that he would be available for concert engagements in the United States in April and May 1940, before going to Tanglewood or Wells College for the summer, and requested that planning begin immediately. Hindemith would, in fact, return in 1940, but not on a concert tour. Neither he nor Voigt nor anyone else could know in April 1939 that he would enter this country as an immigrant in February 1940 and remain here for thirteen years.

PART 2
Resident, 1940–53

Introduction

The fact that Paul Hindemith returned to Europe in 1953 after living in the United States for thirteen years has led some foreign writers to suggest that his stay in this country was a period of "exile." It was nothing of the kind. He was happy to be out of Germany and applied for U.S. citizenship almost immediately after his arrival as an immigrant, fully intending to stay here permanently. Being a U.S. citizen was a source of great pride for Paul and Gertrude Hindemith and they never relinquished the right. The composer rejected out of hand many offers of high positions in Germany he received after the war ended, making it clear he preferred living and working in the United States and had no desire to leave. The decision to move to Switzerland in 1953 was made for pragmatic reasons only and not because his affection for the United States had waned.

Accounts of this period are also often misleading in describing Hindemith's teaching activities in the United States by mentioning Yale University as but one of several schools where he taught. Yale was, in fact, the only school where he held a regular faculty position during all thirteen years. Likewise, the Hindemiths never lived anywhere but in New Haven, Connecticut, during this period.

Hindemith did not become as broadly and deeply involved in the national musical scene as he might otherwise have for the simple reason that he was much too busy with his teaching, which he took very seriously. Nevertheless, the record shows that he made some forty-five professional appearances in eighteen different cities while he lived here. His major impact on U.S. musical life was made through his teaching, as will be described in the chapters that follow.

The composer's letters provided much of the information for chapter 5 and almost all of the story told in chapter 6. They were still being written in German and the excerpts cited in English are my own translations. Hindemith began using English in writing to his friends in the United States after settling in New Haven, but continued to correspond in German with Willy Strecker and Karl Bauer.

Reference materials consulted in writing chapters 7 through 12 were chiefly official documents of Yale University, including minutes of the Yale Corporation meetings, the papers of President Charles Seymour and Provost Edgar Furniss, School of Music faculty and student records, catalogs, and pertinent items in the school's historical archives. A daily journal kept by the author was particularly useful in fixing dates and providing information unavailable elsewhere.

Chapter 5

Emigration, 1940

AFTER HIS THIRD U.S. concert tour, Hindemith returned directly to his alpine retreat in Bluche, Switzerland, intending to spend the summer of 1939 relaxing and composing before resuming his concert activities in the fall. The outbreak of World War II in September put an end to any thought of concertizing for the time being, and the Hindemiths resigned themselves to staying on in Bluche indefinitely. They were not entirely dismayed by the prospect, for they had come to enjoy their life as villagers. The composer wrote to friends saying they were raising and canning vegetables, bottling wine, participating in local theatrical productions, and finding it all a most welcome relief from the tensions of Berlin.

Hindemith could now devote as much time as he wished to his writing, and his accomplishments were extraordinary. The important *Concerto for Violin and Orchestra* was done in June and July, a work he intended to use on his fourth U.S. tour in 1940. In September, he completed the *Sonata in C for Violin and Piano*, *Six Chansons* for mixed chorus a cappella, and the *Sonata for Clarinet and Piano*. The *Harp Sonata* was done in October, and the *Sonata for Horn and Piano* and *Sonata for Trumpet and Piano* in November. He also scored four songs from *Das Marienleben* for orchestra and soprano, composed five pieces for male chorus, and three solo songs for voice and piano. His literary activities included preliminary work on the libretto for *Die Harmonie der Welt* and a draft of a scenario for the Brueghel ballet commissioned by Massine.

Although the evidence is only circumstantial, it might be that this tremendous surge of creative activity was the result of renewed confidence in his future gained from Hindemith's three U.S. concert tours, especially the most recent one. His situation at this time was far better than it had been for the past six years, and 1940 promised to be even more so. The tone of Hindemith's frequent letters to Willy

Strecker, mostly dealing with the new pieces he was writing, was invariably optimistic. A passage from one of these is significant in its reference to the instrumental sonatas, which today hold such an important place in the body of his work: "You must be wondering if I intend to 'sonatize' all the winds. I had always thought of making an entire series of these pieces. Firstly, there is nothing decent available for these instruments except the few classic examples. They may not have any commercial value at the moment but will in the long run. Secondly, they serve as a technical exercise for the big job I hope to tackle this spring, namely, the Kepler opera, to be called *Die Harmonie der Welt*, or something like that. Right now I am learning to play the waldhorn and can already do so quite passably."[1] He was absolutely correct in predicting that the sonatas would be commercially profitable "in the long run," for they have been to this day.

Although his interest in the United States had been increasing significantly ever since his first visit in 1937, Hindemith still was not considering seriously any plan to move to "the land of limited impossibilities" permanently. Germany's invasion of Poland on 1 September did not cause any immediate change in that attitude, nor did Hindemith seem to be unduly disturbed by this alarming turn of events. However, some of his friends in the United States did become concerned.

Documents in the Wells College archives, described in an article by Prof. Crawford R. Thoburn published in the school's alumni periodical in 1966, provide details of the sometimes tricky maneuvering that took place in an effort to bring Hindemith safely and surely to this country as an immigrant in February 1940. The composer himself was never directly involved in these shenanigans and there is no evidence that he was even aware of them. They began 7 September, when Ernest Voigt wrote to Nicholas Nabokov at Wells soliciting his help in getting "our friend Paul" to the United States. He feared that Hindemith would now be in serious financial difficulty because his concertizing would be severely curtailed and that everything possible should be done to bring him here. Hindemith would need the guarantee of employment in the United States to obtain an immigrant's visa, and Voigt made the following suggestion:

Do you think you could induce your faculty to make the gesture and offer Hindemith a position at Wells for a fee of $500 per semester plus free housing? This offer, mind you, would not be a genuine one and Hindemith would not think of holding you to it but it would be something he could show to the American Consul. It will be helpful in getting a visa, since teachers are still being admitted into this country. I know that I am conniving and conspiring by suggesting such a thing to you, but desperate straits require desperate measures and that is the situation.[2]

The plotting between Voigt and Nabokov continued over the next few weeks but nothing could be worked out until November, when Wells College agreed to offer $500 for a series of lectures in April, and Cornell University (at Nabokov's instigation) consented to a similar arrangement, thus providing a total amount of $1,000. This would not be sufficient, so Voigt approached Cameron Baird in Buffalo, who agreed to underwrite a $2,500 teaching engagement for Hindemith at the University of Buffalo during the spring term in 1940, beginning in February. Voigt explained the deal to Nabokov: "The professorship offered by Buffalo is in the nature of pretense, so to speak, in order for Hindemith to come over, as Cameron Baird is subsidizing the amount of his salary. He will be asked to give one or two lectures a week, the rest of the time will be his own, the purpose being to discuss and get under way plans for the establishment of a new School of Music at the University in the fall of 1940. Mr. Baird wants Hindemith to be the Director."[3]

Correspondence between the conspirators and Hindemith became highly confused, since communications with Switzerland were already being severely disrupted because of the war. Letters and cables crossed or were never received, and it was not until late in November that the composer finally gained a fairly clear idea of what was being proposed. After a few more cable exchanges, all details had been settled by mid-December and Hindemith accepted. Buffalo, Wells, Cornell, and Boston Symphony officials immediately went into action, sending letters and telegrams to the U.S. Office of Immigration in support of a visa for the composer and it was granted without question. Carrying character references from Wilhelm Furtwängler, the British conductor Sir Adrian Boult, and other music notables, Hindemith sailed from Genoa 6 February 1940 on the Italian liner S.S. *Rex*. It had been agreed that Gertrude should remain in Bluche until Paul could be assured that the situation warranted her coming over to join him.

British military authorities were now stopping all ships passing through Gibraltar to check passenger lists and Hindemith, traveling on a German passport and therefore an "enemy alien," had been quite apprehensive about what might happen. His fears were unfounded, as he wrote to his wife:

> I was ushered into a room full of captains, lists, and ashtrays. A friendly old English Captain invited me to sit down, but I did not trust him completely when I saw on the table in front of him the names of the only four German passengers on the ship. He told me things did not look good in Germany, whereupon I said I really didn't know since I had not been there for two years. Then I presented him with my letters of reference but he did not want to see them and simply said, "Right-o, Mr. Hindemith, goodby and good luck." (I hope the fellow is soon promoted to Admiral.) We then parted with a cordial handshake and the last stone was lifted from my heart. The only contribution I made for this happy experience was a Swiss five-franc note I dropped into the offering box in the Catholic Chapel, because I know that is what you would have done.[4]

Aside from a violent storm during the last two days of the crossing, Hindemith had no more troubles on the voyage. Anticipated problems with U.S. Customs and Immigration officials did not materialize and Hindemith was off the ship by late afternoon on 15 February. Ernest Voigt was at the dock to meet him and take him to the Hotel Seymour; Nicholas Nabokov could not be there but sent a note to the ship extending a warm welcome and expressing his pleasure that the composer was safely in this country. Both men had good reason to rejoice that their efforts to bring Hindemith to the United States as an immigrant, devious or not, had been successful. Hindemith and Voigt had a drink in the hotel to celebrate the occasion and the composer retired early, not having slept for two nights because of the storm.

Less than three years had passed since Hindemith first came to the United States in April 1937. He had told Mrs. Elizabeth Sprague Coolidge then that he was "not yet ready" to move here permanently. Ready or not, he had now at least taken the first step. He was still not fully persuaded he should make his home here, but it would take only two months for him to make up his mind. He would stay, thus opening an entirely new and important chapter in his life.

Chapter 6

The First Seven Months

HINDEMITH'S FIRST seven months as a resident of the United States proved to be an invaluable period of indoctrination for the composer's future career as a university professor in this country. He was exposed to a remarkably broad cross section of musical life in schools of higher learning, working with students at all levels of ability and achievement. He also had an opportunity to observe the varied educational policies and programs in effect at two large and contrasting private universities, a small liberal arts college, and a university school of music. There would be few if any surprises for him when he began teaching at Yale in September.

Most of these experiences were jammed into the first three months, forcing Hindemith to follow a demanding and exhausting schedule of teaching, lecturing, and commuting. Voigt and Nabokov may have thought they had secured sinecures for him that would guarantee the money needed for a visa but this was not the case. Hindemith had to earn every dollar he was paid through hard and honest labor. During a six-week period in March and April, for example, he was teaching and lecturing at four different schools, requiring about 6,000 miles of travel by train and 400 by auto. This was his weekly schedule between 30 March and 15 April:

Fri: Overnight train from Buffalo to New York
Sat: Early train to New Haven, classes at Yale, evening train to New York
Sun: Business conferences in New York
Mon: Early train to New Haven, classes at Yale, evening train to New York, overnight train to Ithaca
Tue: Afternoon lecture at Cornell, auto to Aurora, evening lecture at Wells
Wed: Auto to Ithaca, early morning train to Buffalo, afternoon classes at University of Buffalo
Thu: Classes at University of Buffalo

Fri: Classes at the University of Buffalo, overnight train to New York

The story of Hindemith's activities during these seven months will be told in eight separate sections, since a comprehensive chronological account of the composer's almost incessant comings and goings would only confuse the reader. The following summary will be helpful in understanding how the separate accounts fit into the whole:

—Hindemith lived in Buffalo from 18 February until 12 June, teaching a full schedule of courses at the University of Buffalo until the spring term ended on 24 May.

—Six weekly lectures were given at Cornell University and Wells College during March and April.

—There were three two-day engagements as a teacher and lecturer at Yale University in March and April.

—Hindemith taught at the Berkshire Music Center at Tanglewood from 8 July to 18 August, living in Lenox, Massachusetts, from 22 June to 10 September.

—He took up residence in New Haven on 15 September upon Gertrude's arrival in the United States, and began teaching at Yale on 30 September.

University of Buffalo

Cameron Baird and several of Hindemith's Buffalo friends were at the station to welcome the composer when he arrived in the city late in the afternoon of 18 February. He was taken to the Lenox Hotel, a fine residential hotel that would be his home throughout his stay in Buffalo. Although he described the hotel to Gertrude as being "a storage house for old ladies," he admitted his two-room suite was both attractive and comfortable and that he was well satisfied.

Escorted by Baird, he met the following day with the university chancellor and dean, who received him with utmost respect and cordiality and told him he was completely free to make out whatever teaching program he wished. As a distinguished artist-teacher of international rank, Hindemith could easily have met his obligation to the university by offering to teach only one or two courses at the most. However, knowing nothing of the workings of an American university and probably being overly anxious to accommodate, he agreed to give no less than seven different courses, ranging in content from basic musicianship to advanced composition and requiring thirteen weekly hours of classroom teaching. Moreover, they would have to be crowded into three days, Wednesday through Friday, in order for him to meet his lecturing commitments at Cornell and Wells.

The University of Buffalo was then a private institution (it did not become a part of the State University of New York system until 1965) with a very small music department and only fifteen music majors. Five of the seven courses Hindemith was to teach would be open only to advanced nondegree students who were proficient in music. As a visiting professor at the university, the composer apparently felt obliged also to offer courses available to regular undergraduate students and agreed to give a one-hour class in basic musicianship open to anyone and a two-hour class in elementary harmony for music majors. Both of these were held on the main university campus on Wednesday afternoons, necessitating a five-mile trolley ride from his hotel. These proved to be a crashing bore and his letters to Gertrude were full of complaints about the students.

In contrast, Hindemith enjoyed the other five courses on his schedule, four of which met within walking distance of his hotel. These were small classes of five to ten students that the university had authorized especially for Hindemith and were open only to students who met specific requirements for admission. Most were professional musicians and music teachers from the city and vicinity. Hindemith was especially pleased with his advanced composition class of five highly qualified students, writing Gertrude that it reminded him of "the good old days at the Berlin Hochschule." There were two classes in advanced theory, wherein he used his new theory books in working out problems in harmony and counterpoint.

There was also a special class for seven public-school music teachers who drove down once a week from Niagara Falls to do "graduate" work with the composer. This was Hindemith's first direct encounter with the mysteries of degree credits and he was baffled: "They are interested above all in receiving some kind of 'points' or 'credits' and that is not a joke. No one asks what anyone knows or what he can do, the main thing is whether he has any 'points' or is otherwise 'graduated.' When a student attends any of my lecture cycles, he apparently receives '2 points' because he has submitted himself to this pleasure for two hours each week. Almost all the members of the class are 'graduated' and have a pocketful of 'points,' but their knowledge is not that extensive."[1] The seventh course was actually a two-hour coaching session in ensemble playing, which Hindemith conducted each Wednesday evening at the spacious home of Cameron Baird, who was an active participant as a violist. One of the students was Max Landsberger, who later became a medical doctor and eventually professor of pediatrics at the University of Buffalo. In his reminiscences of the course filed in the Yale Hindemith Collection, Landsberger wrote that the evening would end with a brief period of socializing over a glass of beer before Hindemith was driven back to his hotel by one of the students.

Hindemith began teaching on 22 February and continued without interruption until the term ended in May, never missing a class. This was his first extended teaching engagement in the United States and a success on all counts. Learning in April that he would be leaving to teach at Yale in the fall, his students petitioned the chancellor to do everything possible to retain the composer, but the effort failed. They showed their appreciation, however, by honoring him at a series of farewell parties and dinners at the end of the term.

Hindemith's busy schedule that spring, which took him away from Buffalo three or four days a week, restricted his activities in the city almost entirely to his teaching. His personal associations did not extend beyond his students and a very few friends he had known previously, but these were sufficient under the circumstances. He did not become involved with extramusical affairs at the university and was on the main campus only one afternoon a week to teach his two classes in elementary theory, nor did he make any public appearances in the city as a performer or conductor. It could be said that Hindemith's presence in Buffalo that spring was a well-kept secret. The city itself had not exactly charmed him during his first weeks there primarily because of the harsh winter weather, but when spring finally arrived he found it most attractive and decided to remain there for an additional three weeks rather than return to New York.

Cameron Baird's hopes for establishing a school of music at the University of Buffalo, with Hindemith as the director, faded soon after the composer arrived in the city and told him he was not interested in taking on such a responsibility. He might consider teaching one or two days a week but that would be all. That was the first blow, and the second came when the composer accepted a position at Yale University for 1940–41. Baird abandoned the idea of a new school but tried to obtain a part-time appointment for Hindemith. This failed for lack of funds. He did succeed in establishing a school of music at the University in 1952, but there is nothing in the available records to indicate he ever discussed this project further with Hindemith.

Wells College

Nicholas Nabokov had been greatly disappointed when Hindemith opted to teach at Tanglewood rather than Wells College in the summer of 1940, but was more than willing to arrange for the composer to give a series of six lectures at the college during the spring for an honorarium of $500. No plans for these lectures were made until the two men met at Wells late in February, after which the composer reported to his wife: "I have come up with a very nice plan for my lectures at Wells. They want to have some kind of a new piece for the College chorus to sing at the annual May Festival and I have proposed to compose the piece in class with the girls."[2] One can readily assume that Nabokov had asked Hindemith to write such a work and that the composer rather astutely devised a scheme that would provide the composition as well as material for his "lectures." It proved to be highly successful.

Wells College is an exclusive liberal arts college for women, located in Aurora, New York, that has always maintained a strong program in the fine arts and music. Its musical life was particularly lively at this time with the energetic and outgoing Nabokov on campus, and provided an ideal setting for Hindemith's novel project, called "A Composer at Work."

The first class was held on 19 March, and the composer described what happened: "The first lecture at Wells was really nice. About 70 young ladies were there, plus a large number of the faculty. I had asked one of the English teachers to write a little poem for me and then had the girls compose. After their initial shyness had passed everything went quite well and they sang and dictated melodies that I wrote on the blackboard for general criticism. Although they are not genuine music students, some good things resulted (naturally, under my subtle direction) and the class ended in an all-around happy mood."[3]

Hindemith was there on six Tuesdays between 19 March and 30 April, and the "happy mood" continued throughout. The composition project was completed, a three-voice a cappella setting for women's voices of a poem by George Tyler called *A Song of Music,* to which Hindemith added an optional accompaniment for strings (or piano) before it was premiered at the May Festival under the direction of Nabokov.[4] (The composer was unable to attend.)

Hindemith enjoyed his Wells College experience in spite of the awkward travel arrangements that had to be made. The only practical way of getting to Aurora from Ithaca was by car, a thirty-mile drive north. His Cornell lecture was given on Tuesday afternoon, after which he would be driven to Aurora in time for the evening class at Wells. The following morning he would be taken to Ithaca in time to board an early morning train for the three-hour ride to Buffalo and resume his teaching at the university in the afternoon. His final class at Wells was held on 30 April, but he accepted an invitation to return a week later to be the guest of honor at a gala farewell party hosted by the faculty.

Cornell University

Wells College could offer only $500 and not the $1,000 Nabokov had requested, so he turned for help to his friend and neighbor, Prof. Paul J. Weaver, chairman of the Music Department at Cornell University. Nabokov suggested that Cornell might wish to take advantage of Hindemith's presence in the vicinity and offer $500 for a series of six lectures. Weaver agreed, and worked out a plan with Nabokov for the composer to give a lecture at Cornell in the afternoon and at Wells in the evening of the same day. It would be a heavy schedule for Hindemith, but he was willing.[5]

The engagement at Cornell marked Hindemith's first appearance as a lecturer at a major U.S. university. He was there on six Tuesday afternoons between 12 March and 23 April and was well received by large audiences of over 300 that included students, faculty, and townspeople. The lectures were on topics dealing with music theory and the understanding of music. Unaccustomed to delivering formal lectures, Hindemith reported to Gertrude after the first session that "it felt funny to talk for an hour to a strange group," and after the second that the audience was "large but rather unresponsive." One might wonder what he expected his audience to do except listen attentively, which they obviously did. These initial misgivings soon vanished and he reported happily that many people came up to him after the final lecture to say how much they had enjoyed the series and what a "marvelous and exciting experience" it had been for them.

The composer was honored at several receptions and dinners during his visits to Ithaca, and on one occasion held a special session with members of the mathematics department, at their request, to explain his new theories. Everything had gone well at Cornell and he was pleased. More important, it had been a valuable and timely introduction into what were still for him the unknown ways of U.S. academic life at its highest level, knowledge that would prove most useful as he began teaching at Yale in September.

Yale University

Prof. Richard Donovan, then assistant dean of the Yale School of Music, learned late in 1939 that Paul Hindemith would be coming to the United States in the spring of 1940 and might be available as a guest teacher for a limited period. At the faculty meeting on 10 January 1940 the members instructed Dean David Stanley Smith to request approval from President Charles Seymour to invite Hindemith as a visiting lecturer at a salary of $2,000. Dean Smith, a reputable composer of markedly conservative persuasion who viewed "modern" music with alarm, wrote a letter to the president that included these cautious comments: "Hindemith is widely regarded as the leading German composer. At one time, he was an extreme modernist but lately he has softened his style so that it is accessible to the average listener. . . . I have met the man. He is very friendly, speaks English well, and is modest about his music. I do not think he would proselyte among the students in favor of modernistic [sic] music."[6] President Seymour replied that he liked the idea but was sorry no money was available except $100 from a lecture fund. He suggested approaching the Oberlander Trust, a Philadelphia foundation established to aid political refugees from Europe. The school faculty now lowered its sights and decided to invite Hindemith for six days of teaching and lecturing at a fee of $500. The Oberlander Trust was persuaded to provide the additional $400 needed.

Hindemith received Yale's offer in a letter sent to him in Buffalo on 29 February and immediately accepted. He did so, he wrote to

Gertrude, because he thought "a connection with Yale, the second most famous university in the country, would be very valuable." A mutually acceptable plan was devised for him to be at Yale on three consecutive Saturdays and Mondays between 30 March and 15 April, giving master classes in theory and composition and delivering two public lectures.

Hindemith's first visit on 30 March was sufficient to convince the faculty (including the author, then in his first year as a member) that everything possible must be done to bring him to Yale permanently. It was an electrifying experience for students and teachers alike, and from a letter he wrote to Gertrude the following day, it is clear that Hindemith himself had found it stimulating:

> Yale was a thoroughly enjoyable experience. It began for me at 10:00 in the morning, when I met with ten of Dean Smith's composition students; the Dean and Donovan were also there. The boys and girls played some of their compositions for me and I was supposed to give a critique. It was not a particularly agreeable situation for me and I told them so. If you are critical, you antagonize the teacher; if you equivocate, you displease the students. However, I soon found a solution to the problem after noting the weak point in their instruction. As I have done before, I asked the Dean questions he could not understand and were so far out of his line he could not be upset when I continued at length in this fashion. I made up complete harmonic schemes, changed the format of entire pages, and showed them many new things. Result: general satisfaction, even for the old Dean, who was highly pleased. I was almost as strict as himself. He told me repeatedly the students should now understand I would not let them write as they please!
>
> After lunch with some of the students, I met with a group of about 40 advanced theory students, plus most of the faculty. They wanted to hear about harmony, so I went over my familiar territory at "high speed." It was most interesting. The students asked questions and participated with great enthusiasm. Some of the theory teachers came out with strong arguments against my ideas and I had to struggle hard to refute them. It was one of the most interesting debates on the subject I have ever had. At the end of the two hours there was an air of lively excitement. I had to continue for another hour and a half to discuss problems of teaching theory and again the questions raised by the students and teachers were intelligent and knowledgeable.
>
> I had dinner that evening at Donovan's home along with all the

members of the faculty, after which I again had to talk about theory. They made me explain with hairline precision what I would use in place of traditional harmony and counterpoint and I did so with the help of my new theory books. They seemed to be enthusiastic about all the new ideas and when I left the battlefield at 10:00 to catch a train for New York I had the feeling I had given them something to think about.[7]

He had indeed given the faculty "something to think about," and they stayed on at the Donovans' for another three hours discussing the memorable events of the day. There was unanimous agreement Hindemith should be offered a regular appointment at Yale and Professor Donovan, recently named acting dean of the School of Music for 1940–41, was instructed to take the necessary action. This was done, and when the composer returned for his second two-day visit a week later, 6 April, he was formally invited to join the School of Music faculty beginning in September 1940. He accepted without hesitation and with obvious pleasure, writing to Gertrude the following day: "No time to write more than a note today but I must tell you something very important—our immediate future seems to be assured. Yesterday I was invited to teach at Yale next year, so get ready to come over."[8]

Hindemith had more to say five days later: "I was very happy to be invited to teach at Yale next year. It is the only place in this country where I think I could feel somewhat at home, and the surroundings are nice (not so much the city of New Haven, but Yale certainly is). . . . I am now fully persuaded to stay in this country a long time, for with Yale in the picture, the prospect is totally pleasing."[9]

Professor Donovan had told Hindemith that Yale would offer him a full-time position as visiting professor of the Theory of Music at a salary of $7,500. However, when it was learned that the composer was still planning to teach one or two days a week at the University of Buffalo the following year, the Yale offer was reduced to a part-time position at a salary of $4,000. Hindemith accepted it on these terms, explaining the situation to his wife: "Because of the Buffalo thing, Yale did not want to give me a full-time position. Furthermore, it was too late for anything but a half-time appointment. Thus, I have to be a Visiting Professor at $4,000, teaching five or six hours a week, which is agreeable to me. With Buffalo added at the same salary, we will be able to make out very well."[10] When he learned late in May that there would be no possibility of a part-time position at Buffalo, Hindemith found himself with only the part-time Yale position for 1940–41, certainly not what he had planned on. Nevertheless, he apparently considered it "agreeable" enough, for he made no attempt to have Yale reconsider and increase its offer.

Yale authorities were actually relieved, for it was difficult enough for them to raise even $4,000. Budget appropriations for 1940–41 had long been closed and there was no money for new appointments; consequently officials had to resort to some accounting legerdemain. Half of the amount had to be taken from a fund marked for another purpose, and half from the Howland Memorial Prize Fund, a brilliant but rather devious maneuver. The Howland Prize is Yale's highest honor, awarded only to illustrious world figures in the arts, literature, and government. The honoree receives a large silver medal and a substantial cash award. Since Hindemith was clearly eligible for the prize, it was decided he would be given the medal and the cash bonus of $2,000 would be applied to his salary. To use the money in this fashion was a contrivance of the first order, never done before or since, and to have resorted to this extraordinary device was a clear indication of how eager Yale was to have Hindemith on the faculty. The composer was completely unaware of what was going on. He received the medal from President Seymour during the intermission of a concert by the Boston Symphony Orchestra in Woolsey Hall, Yale University, on 20 November 1940 that featured a performance of his new *Concerto for Violin and Orchestra.*

Rarely, if ever, has Yale moved with such dispatch in making a faculty appointment. Hindemith was named visiting professor of the Theory of Music for 1940–41 by formal action of the Yale Corporation on 27 April, only three weeks after being proposed. His decision to add the six days of teaching in New Haven to his already overcrowded schedule because he had felt "a tie with Yale will be important" had proved to be absolutely right.

Tanglewood

The first session of Serge Koussevitzky's new and soon to be famous summer music academy on the "Tanglewood" estate near Lenox, Massachusetts, was held in 1940. The maestro had invited both Hindemith and Stravinsky to teach composition, but the latter withdrew at the last minute and was replaced by Aaron Copland. Serious discussion of what Hindemith would teach other than advanced composition did not begin until 10 March 1940, when he met with Copland in New York. Hindemith reported the meeting in a letter:

> I could not persuade Copland to let me teach the course in instrumentation and orchestration he is scheduled to give. (How could anyone teach it better than one who has played in an orchestra as long as I have?) Nor could I persuade him to take over the course in form and analysis that I am supposed to teach. (Nobody knows what really happened in the course of music history; furthermore, any ass can tell the difference between a Scarlatti and Brahms sonata.) Such a course makes no sense unless it includes a serious study of rhythm as well as form. However, I will try to work out something.[11]

Hindemith was in New York again the following week to take a bow at a performance of his *Mathis Symphony* by the Boston Symphony under Koussevitzky and attended a meeting of Tanglewood officials the next day. These included the ubiquitous Olin Downes, who seems to have been brought into the planning of every important musical happening in those days. The composer wrote to Gertrude:

> All of the people were there when I arrived. Koussevitzky embraced me and then made a speech to the assembled company, saying the piece his orchestra had the honor and pleasure of playing yesterday was one of the best not only of our time but of all time, and so on and on. I had no idea he thought it was so important! . . . They finally got around to discussing my courses. I told them I did not want to give any stupid old harmony and counterpoint courses in what they call "Form." I then demanded that my composition students should not be allowed to study instrumentation and orchestration with Copland. It was all granted and I will have complete freedom to do as I wish.
> Then we discussed the general course for amateurs who will be enrolled in a separate division of the school and that I am supposed to teach. I said I would conduct it about the same way I am doing with similar classes at Wells and Buffalo [by classroom demonstration of composing]. At this point Olin Downes made a speech, saying that if I were to do that it would be a blessing to this country and also that I had been sent from heaven to cure the ills that have plagued music in this country for the past 50 years. I told him he was asking me to do a lot and he replied he did not know anyone else who could do it better. He said I could not imagine how deeply interested the people of this country are in

learning about music. I reminded him I was already teaching at Buffalo and had some idea of how deeply interested they were![12]

Hindemith arrived in Lenox on 22 June, two weeks before the summer session was to begin, settling in at the home of the Reverend Mr. Driscoll, minister of the local Congregational church, where he had two pleasant and comfortable private rooms. It was also arranged that he would have his meals at a private home nearby, out of the public eye. While waiting for the school to open he took many long walks through the beautiful countryside that he described to Gertrude as being "like northern Switzerland," and added that "for the first time I have begun to feel some genuine affection for this country." He also began writing a cello concerto.

Hindemith's heavy schedule of teaching at Tanglewood began on 8 July and he reported to Gertrude a week later:

The whole thing is like a combination of the Donaueschingen Festival and the Berlin Hochschule and everything going on here seems to be good. I am looked on as a very "famous" teacher and the students are already spreading rumors about all of the startling things I am doing with them. Unfortunately, the advanced composition class is not outstanding, with the exception of a small German immigrant boy. [This was Lukas Foss.] There were some protests in the first class session, partly because of the unusual work I demanded and partly because I flatly refused to look at the scores they had written previously. By proper handling, however, I was able to bring the more stubborn ones around and after yesterday, when I made them work out a strict counterpoint exercise at the blackboard, they are now humble and grateful.

The advanced composition class of seven so-called composers meets four mornings a week in four-hour sessions. I also have two more theory classes, each meeting three times a week. Finally, I give a sort of entertainment course two evenings a week to two separate groups of students who are amateurs (about 100 in each). I am having the students "compose" a mixed chorus and a fugue. It is a lot of fun and everyone seems to be enjoying it.

The boys in my composition class were very upset when I made them sing what they wrote and also study an instrument. My colleague Aaron Copland could not understand this, for his teaching methods are different. He wants to have his students' works performed and always speaks of them as finished composers, while I consider mine to be raw beginners in need of appropriate training. Koussevitzky is completely on my side and heartily agrees with my proposal to forbid any pieces by my students to be performed publicly. This is absolutely necessary if you are going to accomplish anything with students with such a lack of knowledge about theory and composition.[13]

Hindemith's treatment of his composition students as "raw beginners" caused something of a stir, for ostensibly they were among the most promising young talents in the country, selected from many applicants. They had submitted elaborate scores as evidence of their abilities and expected Hindemith would simply proceed from there. His refusal even to look at them was the first shock and his demand that they return to basic counterpoint and start all over again was the second. They apparently recovered, for by the fourth week Hindemith could report to his wife: "The students are now enthusiastic about their work and are complaining that the course lasts only six weeks."[14]

Hindemith may have been somewhat disappointed with his composition class but not with any other aspect of his activities at Tanglewood. His other courses were enormously successful, particularly those he called "entertainment" classes for amateurs in which he demonstrated compositional techniques and had the students "compose." Out of one of these came *The Harp That Once thro' Tara's Halls*, a setting of the old Irish poem for mixed chorus and piano (or harp and strings), which was published by AMP in 1941. Hindemith later provided a German translation under the title *Altes irisches Lied* and the work was published by Schott in 1958 with both German and English texts.

Hindemith was especially pleased that so much of his music was being featured on the public concerts given during the session and that he could participate in some of them. He was invited to conduct the school orchestra in his *Concert Music for Strings and Brass, Opus 50* on 19 July and later wrote to Willy Strecker that "many large European cities would be happy to have an orchestra so good." His *Third Organ Sonata*, completed only six weeks before, had its world premiere on 31 July, played by E. Power Biggs. *Hin und zurück*, a twelve-minute musical skit, was staged by the theater department on 9 August, with the composer sitting happily in the pit playing one of the two piano parts. He was the solo violist in a performance of *Trauermusik* by the school orchestra on 15 August, and his *Mathis Symphony* was given a brilliant reading by Koussevitzky and the Boston Symphony before a huge audience at the final festival concert on 19 August. Many of his woodwind and brass sonatas were done in informal student recitals, and the school chorus worked on the choral parts of *Das Unaufhörliche* as one of its major study projects during the session.

Positive proof of Hindemith's success at Tanglewood came at the end of the session, when Koussevitzky invited him to return in 1941 not merely as a teacher but as the director of the entire school. Hindemith wrote to Gertrude: "I have had long and frank discussions with Koussevitzky about the school. He has offered me no less than the directorship of the whole thing, but I was not interested. When you are finally here, we will again work together in writing new books, scripts, and compositions. That is more important than directing schools, for less important composers can take care of such things. Get over here safe and sound and everything will work out well."[15] (Hindemith did return as a teacher in 1941, repeating the same courses he gave in 1940 and with comparable success. However, he declined to remain on the staff beyond that, for he was then teaching full time at Yale and wished to have his summers free for composing. Furthermore, he no longer needed the money.)

Hindemith decided to stay in Lenox until 10 September, when he left for New York to meet Gertrude on her arrival. The summer session and festival had ended on 19 August and the town was once again quiet and peaceful with "nobody here but the natives, myself, and the dog I know on the next street," he wrote to his wife. It was a welcome respite from the hectic and concentrated activity of the six weeks just passed and he spent the time taking long hikes through the countryside, relaxing, and composing.

Leonide Massine

Hindemith's relations with Leonide Massine had begun to fall apart in the spring of 1939 and were finally broken off completely in April 1940. The composer had been in no hurry to complete the ballet based on Brueghel paintings commissioned by the dancer since no deadline had been set, but learning that Massine and his company would be performing in Buffalo on 14 March, he made a special effort to have the script completed by then. He attended the performance, which featured the famous *Tannhäuser Bacchanale* staged by Salvador Dali. Remembering too well his distasteful encounter with Dali the year before, Hindemith anticipated the worst and was not disappointed. He had the pleasure of writing a long and withering account of the ballet to Gertrude, from which these comments have been extracted:

> It was just plain stupid. The only technique the silly Dali knows is to put together things that do not belong together. . . . Everything was done in a slick-paper magazine style, which has no more to do with art than ads for autos, whiskey, and toothpaste. . . . There was not the slightest trace of anything bacchanalian, and when the famous crutches came out at the end as forty umbrellas they made no more impression than a drop of mustard on a slice of salami. . . . When Massine's wife Tania asked me what I thought about it, I said it was not worth discussing, and that it was a shame so much work had gone into such an asinine production.[16]

Hindemith delivered his completed Brueghel scenario to Massine after the performance and then learned that the dancer wanted him to do the score for a new ballet he had in mind, based on music by Carl Maria von Weber. Massine was in a hurry to get it so the two men began to work on it immediately. Hindemith had doubts:

> We worked at the piano for two hours on a projected Weber ballet. I do not think the idea is any good at all. He thinks of it only as a plain ballroom dance (in Metternich's palace, so he says) with good people milling around with bad people. He has some funny ideas about the music but I will write what I want to write, namely, music based on those charming piano duets by Weber. He wants to start rehearsals next week, but I told him I could not have anything ready until April 20. Besides, I want to know first how much I am going to be paid. I am seeing him in New York this Sunday to discuss it further.[17]

The meeting with Massine in New York on Sunday, 17 March, went on all afternoon and evening, with detailed planning being done on both the Brueghel and Weber ballets. Hindemith reported that everything had gone smoothly and also that he would be paid $1,000 for the Weber score. He planned to "rearrange" the Weber pieces a bit and make a sort of free paraphrase out of them that "could be very nice." Two of the pieces were done in two weeks and delivered to Massine in New York on 31 March. So far everything was going according to plan and Hindemith had no reason to doubt it would continue to do so. Both of the ballets were well under way and he was counting on receiving a sorely needed $3,000 for his work. It was all an illusion.

Massine did not like what Hindemith had done with Weber's music and told him so. The composer was furious:

> The Weber ballet has gone down the drain. I wrote two nice numbers for it, coloring the music lightly and making it a bit sharper. Ever since I gave Massine the music there have been a lot of phone calls between Buffalo and New York. It seems that the music is too complicated for them and that they simply wanted an exact orchestral arrangement of the original Weber. I am not just an orchestrator and furthermore I had already told them what I was going to do.
>
> One really cannot work seriously with Massine. Last Monday night he even proposed that Salvador Dali do the scenic designs for the Brueghel ballet. I howled at him and said I was not going to have anything more to do with him. I will write the Brueghel ballet score this summer so he can have it in the fall and pay me for it. The sheepheads can do what they want with it, but without me.[18]

Hindemith was deeply offended that Massine had expected him simply to do a hack's job of orchestrating the Weber music and never forgave the dancer. His resentment flared up when the two men happened to meet a few days later. The composer was in Boston attending the U.S. premiere of his new violin concerto by the Boston Symphony Orchestra, and Massine, who was performing in Boston, came backstage to congratulate him. Hindemith let him have it, as he reported to Gertrude:

> I have finally broken off with Massine and it was high time. He is an uncultured nonartist and since he is under the thumb of Sol Hurok he is totally useless for higher purposes. His company happened to be appearing in Boston when my violin concerto was played there and he and his satellites came backstage to see me. I was not going to say a word about the Weber fiasco, but when he more or less blamed me for it and said it was a "pity" it did not come off I said it was a "stupidity" but certainly not on my part. When he realized he had lost that round, he still wanted me to set a date when we could work out the scenario and choreography for the Brueghel ballet. I told him he already had the material and could work it out himself. I also said he would get the music this summer and he could do what he wanted with it. I am delighted to be out of this atmosphere of cheap art and evil conniving.[19]

That was the end, for Hindemith never collaborated with Massine again. He wrote Gertrude in August that he had not even looked at the Brueghel scenario since the fracas with Massine in April, but thought he might start working on it later if he still needed the money. He never did write the Brueghel score and was happy to cancel his contract with Massine early in the fall after receiving a commission to do a ballet for George Balanchine, an artist he greatly respected. (This would be *The Four Temperaments*, completed in New Haven on 1 November.) Hindemith received no money whatever for the considerable time and effort expended on the two Massine ballet projects, but the work he had begun on the Weber music would prove fruitful later. It gave him an idea that he carried out with stunning success in 1943 by writing the *Symphonic Metamorphosis of Themes by Carl Maria von Weber*. (Details of this work and of *The Four Temperaments* are given in chapter 10.)

Creative Work

The extraordinary surge of compositional activity that had marked the year 1939 came to an abrupt halt on 25 November with the completion of Hindemith's *Sonata for Trumpet and Piano*, and six months would pass before he could resume writing music on his own terms. Meanwhile, his major creative efforts had to be concentrated on his heavy teaching and lecturing commitments at Buffalo, Wells, Cornell, and Yale. The only composing he did was restricted to class projects and demonstrations. His abortive attempt to satisfy Massine with "paraphrased" orchestral arrangements of Weber's piano duets proved to be a waste of valuable time at the moment.

Hindemith had no completely free time until after his Buffalo classes ended on 24 May, and then he began immediately to compose. His advanced composition class in Buffalo included two prominent and talented young organists, Robert Noehren and Herbert Fromm, with whom he had developed a warm friendship, and they had frequently expressed the hope that he would write another organ sonata. He did so, completing the *Third Organ Sonata* 5 June and reporting later to his wife: "I wrote an organ sonata, intended for your arrival. Robert Noehren played it immediately and was enthusiastic about it. We made a recording of the piece so we could greet you with it when you landed in New York. However, it was all in vain, for you did not come."[20]

The only major composition Hindemith completed during this seven-month period was a *Concerto for Violoncello and Orchestra.* He began to write it in Lenox while waiting for the summer session to open and completed the first two movements before classes began on 8 July. A month later he wrote to Gertrude: "The cello concerto is still not finished. Firstly, I did not have enough time to write, and secondly, I was not satisfied with the third and final movement I had written and so discarded it. At the moment I have no other ideas for it."[21] The concerto was finished on 9 September, one day before he left for New York to meet Gertrude on her arrival from Lisbon.

Hindemith had shown the unfinished manuscript to Serge Koussevitzky in July, who was impressed and immediately asked for first performance rights. The composer readily agreed, writing to Gertrude that the conductor had been so good about playing his music in recent months he was more than willing to let him have this privilege. The celebrated cellist Gregor Piatigorsky happened to be in Tanglewood a few days later, heard about the concerto from Koussevitzky and offered to be the soloist in the premiere. This took place in Boston on 7 February 1941, with Hindemith, now teaching at Yale, in attendance.

Work on two new and important projects was also begun during Hindemith's post-Tanglewood "vacation" in Lenox. One was his *Symphony in E♭,* finally completed in New Haven on 15 December; the other, the third volume of his *Unterweisung im Tonsatz,* an exercise book in three-part writing. This was not completed until 1949, and then only provisionally. (The full story of both projects is detailed in chapter 10.)

Personal Life

Hindemith's letters to Gertrude during his first three weeks as an immigrant in the United States were filled with complaints. He was worried about not having received any offers of future work in this country, the "dumb" students in his elementary theory classes were giving him fits, he was having to borrow money from Ernest Voigt to see him through until his first paycheck from Buffalo was in hand, he was feeling lonely and depressed, and the continually frigid and snowy weather compounded his miseries. Furthermore, he was having serious doubts about staying in the United States, as the following excerpts from two of these letters reveal:

> The last few days have really been wretched for me and I have concluded I could never feel at home living here. . . . I feel the college professors who have been here a long time and those who have arrived recently would try everything to make it difficult for me. I would not mind if I had a good position, but my general disinterest and a certain amount of ill will have not exactly prompted a desire for a longer stay.[22]

> Even if the money situation were to be satisfactory one could only stay here temporarily, that is, if you don't go out of your mind and become an alcoholic, but the liquor here doesn't taste good at all. On my previous trips to the U.S. the situation never seemed to be as fruitless as this, but that was probably because I didn't stay long in one place, nor did I face such an extended obligation.[23]

The pessimistic comments ceased abruptly after 12 March, when his Cornell-Wells-Yale cycle of teaching and lecturing began. His confidence was quickly restored and life and work in the United States did not seem to be so onerous after all. When he was offered a faculty position at Yale for 1940–41 three weeks later all doubts about staying were instantly removed.

With this problem solved there remained only that of getting Gertrude safely to the United States. Hindemith advised her to make plans for emigrating immediately and she was able to book passage on the Italian liner S.S. *Rex*, scheduled to sail from Genoa to New York on 29 May. She sent her luggage to Genoa late in May but remained in Bluche until it was certain the ship would actually leave, for wartime visa restrictions would preclude her readmission to Switzerland if she left the country. Indeed, the *Rex* did not sail, for Mussolini was about to join Hitler in declaring war on the Allies and all Italian liners had been ordered to stay in port.

This was the Hindemiths' first direct encounter with the misfortunes of war and the composer was distraught. When he learned that the U.S. liner S.S. *Washington* was going to Genoa to pick up stranded U.S. citizens, he wrote to Ernest Voigt asking his help to find a place for Gertrude on the ship. Voigt in turn contacted Yale University officials, who sent an urgent message directly to Secretary of State Cordell Hull asking for his intervention. The secretary took the time to send a long telegram to Hindemith expressing his profound regret that he could do nothing, since only U.S. citizens would be allowed passage on the ship. The composer wrote Voigt that he had been very pleased the "Yale people" had been willing to make this special effort in his behalf.

Hindemith had stopped writing letters to his wife after 27 April, since he had been told mail was not getting through to Switzerland, and resorted to infrequent, brief telegrams simply reporting how and where he was. Meanwhile Gertrude had moved from Bluche to a small house in Sierre to await further developments. Learning by mid-July that postal service to Switzerland had improved, Hindemith resumed writing, sending a long letter to Gertrude giving detailed instructions on what she should do immediately. She went into action, traveling to Zürich, Lausanne, and Geneva for consultations with U.S. and Swiss officials, who aided her in securing reservations on a small Greek ship scheduled to sail from Lisbon to New York on 3 September. Going by train from Geneva to Lisbon, which meant crossing France, now occupied by the Germans, was a trying ordeal for Gertrude, but she was there in time. The S.S. *Neahellas*, bulging with tense and worried refugees, sailed from Lisbon on 3 September and arrived in New York about ten days later. Hindemith was at the dock to meet his wife and they came to New Haven on 15 September.

Chapter 7
Professor at Yale

HAVING JUST experienced four months of intensive college teaching in this country, Hindemith took up his duties at the Yale School of Music as though he had always been there. His half-time appointment was to him a mere technicality that he promptly disregarded, and he participated in all areas of the school's activities with unbounded energy and enthusiasm. A letter written to Willy Strecker within a month after he began teaching at Yale reflects the composer's pleasure over his new situation:

> The school is most enjoyable. It is not large but very well equipped; the library is marvelous and there are many talented students. One can do a lot of good work here, and the prospect for fruitful results are as good if not better here than anywhere else. Musical life in the U.S. has advanced tremendously since I first came here in 1937. . . . You sense a striving for essentials, and the eager desire to learn is limitless and almost incredible. There is still a big job to do here, and it seems whatever I can do about it is appreciated. I am going to feel very good working here.[1]

Hindemith's outstanding work as a teacher and scholar very quickly convinced the music faculty to make every effort to secure a permanent appointment for him at Yale. Accordingly, a recommendation that he be reappointed as a full-time professor of the theory of music in 1941–42, with a salary of $6,500, was forwarded to the provost and president in December. Neither needed any special urging, for both were already well aware of the highly favorable impact Hindemith was making on the university. President Seymour asked the composer to come to his office on 25 January 1941, in a letter that read in part: "I need not tell you how appreciative we are of the services you have given at Yale and especially to the School of Music since you came to us. I am anxious to discuss how far the atmosphere of Yale interests you with a view to a permanent position as a Professor at the School of Music. Should such a suggestion be attractive to you all Yale men interested in music would be deeply grateful and we would have the utmost confidence in the future of the School."[2]

Hindemith met with the president, with the Provost Edgar Furniss also present, and was offered a professorship. He then surprised but also delighted the two officials by saying he enjoyed being at Yale but would not stay unless certain changes were made in the educational policies of the School of Music. They were delighted, since their efforts over the past eighteen months to strengthen the various music study programs offered by the university, particularly in the School of Music, had not been entirely successful and they were still open to advice. Here was a rare and fortuitous opportunity to solicit the suggestions of one of the world's leading musicians. Hindemith was asked to describe what he had in mind and the provost requested that he put it all in writing. They assured him changes would be made and he agreed to accept the appointment. The governing body of the university, known at Yale as the Fellows of the Corporation, ratified it on 8 February. The composer was not quite prepared to commit himself to a permanent position at Yale as yet and asked for and was given a term appointment of three years. The president sent him this note: "I am very happy to have the opportunity of writing to express to you my gratification upon your appointment as a Professor in the School of Music. As I told you the other day, the prestige this will give us and your service to the School form cause for profound self-gratification on the part of all Yale men."[3]

Meanwhile, Hindemith had drawn up his plan for changes in the school's teaching program, sending it to the provost on 3 February. No one on the faculty knew about this until a few days later, whereupon there was panic in the ranks. Most feared the worst, namely, that the university administration was conspiring with Hindemith to do a thorough shake-up of the school and that their future at Yale was now suddenly in jeopardy. Their fears were soon allayed somewhat when they learned that the president and provost had not taken a stand either for or against the composer's proposals. To clear the air, Acting Dean Donovan called a special meeting of the faculty on 13 February, at which Hindemith agreed to present his ideas. He did so eloquently and spiritedly, using large charts he had carefully made to facilitate a better understanding of his plan.

The faculty listened attentively but with growing apprehension as it became clear that the adoption of his plan would mean a total reshaping of the school and its teaching staff. He was advocating, in effect, that it be reorganized as a conservatory much like the Berlin Hochschule für Musik, where he had taught for ten years. It was an excellent outline of its kind but there was no way it could be reconciled with the educational policies in force at Yale. There was no discussion after he had completed his presentation (no one knew quite what to say), nor was any action taken.

The faculty had been aware for at least a year before Hindemith joined the staff that changes in the school's policies and programs were needed, but no significant moves could be made pending completion of the administration's formal review and the appointment of a new dean. The composer's proposals for change, formulated entirely on his own, now jolted the music faculty into action. Donovan immediately drew up a counterplan, with the advice and consent of the senior faculty, that was presented at another meeting held one week later, on 20 February. Hindemith was unable to attend. The counterplan differed drastically from the composer's proposal in organizational detail but not so much in its general objectives. It was approved by the faculty.

Hindemith was very upset that his plan had been rejected and immediately demanded a meeting with Donovan. It took place on 24 February, with former Dean David Stanley Smith, Professor Bruce Simonds, and the author also present. The composer and acting dean had it out in a stormy confrontation, with the others serving primarily as witnesses and making occasional attempts at restoring peace. Hindemith finally cooled down, but it was abundantly clear that he was still angry.

It became necessary for the provost to intervene at this point, and he ordered Donovan to appoint an ad hoc faculty committee to work out a viable compromise. Donovan named Hindemith, Simonds (professor of music and chairman of the Department of Music), Hope Leroy Baumgartner (assistant professor of theory), and the author (then university organist and choirmaster and assistant professor of theory). The committee quickly went into action, holding its first meeting on 27 February with the provost attending to make certain deliberations would get under way without further wrangling.

The immediate problem was to convince Hindemith that the faculty was actually in full accord with the general objectives of his plan and that their reservations had been based solely on the fact that they could not be implemented at Yale in the manner he proposed. He cooperated fully, and the committee was able to complete its report by early April. It incorporated most of the major recommendations made by Hindemith and he was content. So, too, were the president and provost, who approved and accepted the report. Thus the protracted discussions over Yale's music study programs that had been going on since October 1939 were finally ended within only two months of President Seymour and Hindemith's meeting on 25 January. By insisting that changes be made, Hindemith had unwittingly saved the school from what might have been disastrous consequences. It had been virtually immobilized for a year and a half, pending a decision by the university administration as to its future, but now it could move ahead once again. By offering Hindemith an appointment when it did, Yale University had, in turn, unwittingly extricated the composer from a serious predicament, since the offer came at precisely the moment when he desperately needed a solution to his vexing personal problem of beginning a new life in the United States.

The committee report submitted early in April had been in the form of "A General Outline for the Reorganization of the School of Music," and there remained the arduous and thankless task of working out the dreary details of specific courses, class schedules, credits, and degree requirements. There were many long sessions over the next two months, all attended faithfully by Hindemith, who was as bored as his colleagues but submitted to the ordeal with good grace. He surely had not expected to be involved in such doings during his first year at Yale; nevertheless it was a valuable learning process for him and henceforth he would feel completely confident that he understood fully the workings of the school. Although his original plan had undergone several modifications, he was no longer unhappy. A letter to Willy Strecker late in May read in part: "The work at the school goes well. I have been made a professor and will stay here the next three years. The school has been completely reformed, essentially according to my plans (lots of work) and will begin in the fall with a program that will not need to be changed."[4]

The composer was not obliged to go through a similar exercise again during his tenure, for the new program went well and no changes of consequence were needed. As a member of several standing committees he made certain that all of the regulations and requirements were strictly enforced. Hindemith set the example by never requesting waivers for his own students; thus any other faculty member who did so found it difficult if not impossible to secure approval.

With his appointment as a full professor Hindemith became a member of the governing body of the school, known as the "permanent officers," who are responsible for passing on all appointments and promotions and have ultimate control over the school's educational policies and programs. The composer took this obligation very seriously and his fellow officers had the highest respect for his opinions and ideas. With his unique qualifications as a great musician with an extraordinary background of professional experience, he was clearly in a position to tell all of his colleagues much they did not know, but would normally do so only if asked or on those relatively few occasions when he felt compelled to speak up. Personal relations between the composer and his fellow faculty members remained cordial throughout his stay. There would occasionally be heated arguments over specific issues in committee meetings but they would end there. To be sure, there were two or three teachers who enjoyed national reputations who were not particularly happy about his presence, for they felt it dimmed their own. Hindemith was aware of this and made every effort to soothe their bruised egos.

Hindemith accepted another three-year appointment as professor in 1944, still preferring not to commit himself to a longer term. However, in 1947 he agreed to take a permanent position as Battell Professor of the Theory of Music. The chair had been vacant since David Stanley Smith retired in 1946, and the permanent officers voted unanimously that it be given to Hindemith. The composer was quite willing to accept a tenured post, for there were now ample reasons to justify his staying in this country indefinitely. He had become a U.S. citizen in 1946 (as had Gertrude), he enjoyed recognition as one of Yale's most distinguished teachers, talented students were coming to him from all parts of the country, he was fully adjusted to living and working here and liked it, and he had time to compose. Many tempting offers of prestigious professional and academic positions in Germany had been made to him immediately after the war ended in 1945, but he rejected them all. He told several of his friends at the time, including the author, that he fully intended to make his home here. Nevertheless, six years after accepting a permanent appointment at Yale he left the United States to live the rest of his life in Switzerland.

His decision to leave evolved gradually, the result of a series of unusual and totally unforeseen circumstances that caused him to reassess his professional priorities. Eligible for a leave of absence, he requested and was granted a leave for the first term of 1948–49 and used it to complete a heavy schedule of conducting engagements in England, Holland, Germany, Austria, Switzerland, and Italy. His visit to Europe happened to come at a time when the U.S. Military Government (OMGUS) in Germany was actively promoting a program of exchange professorships between German and U.S. universities and had been receiving many requests from German institutions to have Hindemith. An OMGUS officer came to Paris in October to meet with Hindemith and urge him to accept one of these offers. The composer said he might give a few lectures in Germany on musical life in the United States provided Yale would extend his leave by two months. The officer accepted the idea and Hindemith wrote to Dean Bruce Simonds requesting the extension and adding: "You know very well how much I dislike irregularities and changes in fixed schedules. . . . Only the fact that I know both the German and American points of view so well makes me consider the proposition. However, if you think the additional two months cannot be afforded I shall be glad to cancel everything and take the boat back on February 2 as originally planned."[5] The Dean replied that an extension would be approved if a satisfactory arrangement for taking care of his classes could be made. It was possible to do so and the extension was approved.

Hindemith's OMGUS-sponsored tour of Germany was a great success. He appeared in six major cities between 23 January and 22 February, delivering ten lectures of which half were on the subject "Music in the United States." He described and commended it in such superlatives that some of his listeners would take issue, refusing to believe what they were hearing. The composer told the author on his return that he had probably overdone it a bit but that it had been intentional, for he wanted the Germans to realize their country was not the only important music center in the world.

Hindemith's return to Germany as a U.S. citizen lecturing his erstwhile compatriots on the glories of musical life in his adopted country made news. Consequently, he was obliged to meet the press in New York on 31 March, the day after his return from Europe. The reporters were particularly eager to have his comment on musical life in Germany today and he was careful in responding to include positive as well as negative statements. The *New York Times* published a long account of the interview and, as might be expected, featured his negative remarks. There was such an angry reaction to this in the German press that Willy Strecker cabled Hindemith to make some kind of statement that would help put out the fire. He did so in the form of a letter that was printed in the periodical *Melos,* a Schott publication. The composer wrote that he had been misquoted (true) and that he still had confidence in the future of music in Germany, once it had fully recovered from the dire effects of National Socialism and the military defeat. That ended the matter.

Returning to New Haven on 1 April, Hindemith was immediately approached by emissaries from Harvard who invited him to be the Charles Eliot Norton Lecturer at their university in 1949–50. The Norton Lectureship is a prestigious appointment awarded only to men and women of world rank in arts or letters and carries with it the privilege of having the lectures published in book form by the Harvard University Press. It was an offer the composer could hardly refuse, yet he was reluctant to ask Yale for another leave of absence so soon after returning from one. He discussed the situation with Dean Simonds, saying that although he would like to accept Harvard's invitation he would understand if Yale felt it could not approve his being away for a year, and he would therefore let the university decide. The university policy on leaves specifically precluded approval of two in consecutive years, but Dean Simonds recommended the rule be waived in this instance. Hindemith was granted a year's leave of absence without pay for the academic year 1949–50. (The story of his work as the Norton Lecturer at Harvard is told in chapter 11.)

The school was now faced with the impossible task of finding a last-minute replacement for Hindemith in 1949–50. None of the several composers and theorists that were approached was available at this late date because of previous commitments.[6] Finally, Charles Seeger, then chief of the music section of the Pan-American Union in Washington, D.C., agreed to come one day a week to conduct a special seminar in music theory for Hindemith's music majors.

Within two months of beginning his work at Harvard in the fall of 1949, Hindemith received a letter from the rector of the University of Zürich, who asked if the composer would be interested in accepting a professorship there. Hindemith had been summarily rejecting all offers tendered by German institutions, since he had vowed never to live in that country again, but this totally unexpected invitation from one of the great Swiss universities now suddenly changed the situation and consequently his thinking. He had spent a great deal of time in Switzerland over the years, liked everything about the country and its people, and felt very much at home there. Furthermore, having a base in Zürich would be highly advantageous in pursuing his career as a conductor. Thus he replied immediately, saying he was interested but stipulating two conditions: he must be free to design his own teaching program and some arrangement would have to be made by which he could retain his ties with Yale.

Zürich quickly agreed to give him full autonomy over his teaching and the composer then worked out a plan that would enable him to maintain his association with Yale. He proposed to Dean Simonds that he would teach at Yale and Zürich in alternate years, hardly a capital idea, but the dean was anxious to keep Hindemith at Yale even if for only every other year and reluctantly accepted. Zürich authorities, caught in the same predicament, could do nothing but agree, and the plan was put into effect in the fall of 1950.

In July 1950 the University of Zürich sent out a press release announcing that Paul Hindemith was leaving Yale University to teach at Zürich without specifying that he would be there only in alternate years. There had been no direct communication between the administrative officials of the two schools about any of these negotiations and the Yale people were irate to learn of the release by reading it in U.S. newspapers. The Yale News Bureau immediately sent out a release giving the correct details, but the damage had been done. The conflicting accounts simply compounded the confusion as to when or if or for how long Hindemith would be teaching at Yale.

He taught at Yale during the entire academic year of 1950–51 and at Zürich in 1951–52, where three of his major students at Yale transferred to continue their studies with him. To compensate for his absence at Yale, the School of Music arranged to have a succession of leading composers and theorists come for one or two days each week to hold master classes and seminars. The composer returned to New Haven in August 1952 and taught a full schedule of courses in 1952–53.

The first term had been in session only a few days when

Hindemith went to see Dean Simonds, who was shocked and dismayed to hear the composer say he had decided to resign from Yale as of the end of June 1953. Hindemith explained that he had found the plan of teaching every other year at Yale and Zürich to be most unsatisfactory, not only for himself but even more so for his students, and it could not be continued. One of the two schools would have to be cut and after weighing the professional advantages of remaining at one or the other he had opted for Zürich over New Haven. All efforts by Dean Simonds to dissuade him were futile.

Hindemith's decision to resign from Yale and move permanently to Switzerland stunned his friends and colleagues, for neither he nor his wife had ever given the slightest hint of such an eventuality. The reaction in the university community troubled Gertrude, as she indicated in a letter to Willy Strecker:

> *Please do not* say anything about our moving back to Europe. People are beginning to ask hard questions as to whether we are leaving America forever, and are deeply disturbed, disappointed, bitter, etc. If you cannot avoid saying anything, simply say diplo- matically that we will always be going back and forth. We don't know where we will live—probably near Zürich in the winter and the rest of the year in a place traversable only by a monsoon. By giving out this or similarly vague information, you will spare us a lot of unpleasantness and me a deluge of inquiries for which I lack the time or the desire to answer.[7]

Gertrude should not have been surprised that she would have to face "hard" questions. Their many friends at the university had never had reason to believe the Hindemiths were not content with their situation in this country and were understandably anxious to know what had gone wrong. Paul and Gertrude assured them nothing had and that they still felt a deep attachment for Yale and the United States and always would. Their moving to Switzerland, they insisted, did not mean they were actually leaving this country, since they would be returning frequently for extended stays.

There were skeptics, however, who were convinced the Hinde- miths had decided to return to Europe because they were unhappy here. Since there was no hard evidence to support their conclusion they resorted to speculations that soon became rumors that eventu- ally took on the guise of facts. Unfortunately, this served to confirm the impression that the Hindemiths had really never enjoyed living in the United States and had eagerly grabbed the first viable opportunity for making a graceful exit. From his conversations with Paul and Gertrude in 1953 and his correspondence with them after they left, the author can attest to the real reason for their decision to leave. Simply stated, Hindemith had decided to close out his teaching activities and devote more time to conducting. Having taught for some twenty-five years he felt he had done his duty, and his marked success as a conductor in recent years had sparked an urge to do more in this field. He had been completely satisfied with every aspect of his work at Yale and considered it an ideal teaching situation, but he wanted to be free of all academic responsibilities no matter how ideal the conditions. Zürich authorities were unaware as yet that they would also be sharing Yale's fate. After completing his final year at Yale in 1952–53 he taught at Zürich during the winter term of 1953–54 and the summer term of 1954 and then resigned, never accepting another teaching engagement.

Hindemith's faculty associations at Yale had not been restricted to the School of Music. He was elected an associate fellow of Jonathan Edwards College in 1941 and a member of "The Club" in 1946, participating actively in both groups. Jonathan Edwards College is one of the residential units of Yale College (there were ten in 1941, twelve after 1962), each housing between three and four hundred undergraduates from the three upper classes, with a master at the head and an attached body of fellows and associate fellows drawn from the faculties of all the major disciplines. At one meeting of the Jonathan Edwards fellows in 1944, Hindemith astounded his colleagues by composing on the spot a solo song for bass voice and piano. Called *Recitativo e Aria Ranatica,* it is a simple setting in traditional idiom of the biological description of a frog as found in the Encyclopaedia Britannica and Charles Dickens's "Ode to an Expiring Frog," and it is inscribed to Hindemith's good friend Carl Lohmann, then secretary of the university and a fellow of the college. Lohmann, a fine amateur singer, performed it in a public concert at Jonathan Edwards a few months later. The song was never published but will appear in the complete edition of Hindemith's works.

Striking evidence of the recognition Hindemith had gained at the university was his election to membership in the Club (it has no other name) in 1946. This organization was founded at Yale in 1838 and comprises an elite self-perpetuating group of some twenty-five members of the faculty and administration, carefully selected on the basis of their eminence as scholars. When he joined in 1946, Hindemith's colleagues included the president, provost, dean of Yale College, dean of the Graduate School, and a Nobel laureate, among others of comparable ranking. Dinner meetings are held twelve times during the academic year, at which one of the members reads a scholarly paper followed by a lively discussion. Records of the Club show that Hindemith spoke three times: in 1946, 1950, and 1953. Members who heard him in 1950 have told the author it was an unforgettable experience. The composer chose as his topic "Close-ups of Musical Performers" and gave hilarious demonstrations of Arabic, Turkish, and Egyptian musicians playing their exotic instruments and singing their songs, as he recalled them from his several extended stays in the Middle East during the 1930s. He prized his membership in the Club and, according to Gertrude, looked back upon it as one of his happiest associations at Yale.

Yale University officials had invited Paul Hindemith to join the faculty because they knew he was a world master of his profession. They soon discovered he was also a scholar and intellectual whose broad knowledge and interests embraced many academic disciplines other than music and he quickly gained recognition as one of the truly great teachers in the university. There was sincere regret throughout the academic community when it was learned he would be leaving Yale in 1953. It was expressed in this note from Provost Furniss in reply to the composer's letter of resignation:

> Your letter of December 12 did not take me exactly by surprise, since both Secretary Lohmann and Dean Simonds had kept me informed on the problems confronting you. Nevertheless, the fact that I was forewarned does not diminish my regret you are withdrawing from our faculty. This regret will, I know, be shared by all the officers of administration and by your many warm friends. I must respect the reasoning which led you to this decision. Please accept my sincere assurance that we are all conscious of Yale's indebtedness to you, and my best wishes for the future.[8]

Chapter 8
Teacher at Yale

THE SCHOOL OF MUSIC'S 1940–41 curriculum had been fixed several months before Hindemith was suddenly and most unexpectedly appointed to the faculty late in April 1940 as a part-time visiting professor of the theory of music. It was too late to make any changes in the existing program; therefore his teaching would have to be done through added special courses. Deciding what these should be proved to be a knotty problem, for there was too little time left to determine precisely what the student situation would be in the fall. It was agreed, with the composer's full concurrence, that their format would have to be one of utmost flexibility, permitting adaptation to whatever the needs might be.

An ingenious plan was devised whereby Hindemith would offer two courses, both called "Advanced Theory of Music" and vaguely described as a "Seminar course for a limited number of especially qualified students." The only distinction between the two was that one was designated as "A" and the other as "B." Prerequisites for admission were defined as the completion of at least two years of previous collegiate training in theory. The A course met for two hours on Saturday mornings and was devoted to a study of the basic principles advanced in Hindemith's *Unterweisung im Tonsatz,* and the B course, meeting for two hours on Monday afternoons, was actually a class in advanced composition for students he felt had some talent for writing music. The scheme worked out well, with about thirty students enrolled in the two semesters, the majority in the theory class.

The complete revision and significant upgrading of the school's educational program and policies, with which Hindemith was deeply involved, enabled him, in his full-time position as a professor, to develop precisely the kind of teaching program he wished to carry out and one that he would follow over the next twelve years. This opportunity came at the time in the composer's professional career when his interest in theoretical problems was at a peak; consequently all of the courses he offered (other than composition) were focused entirely on music theory. He was now convinced that intensive and comprehensive studies in theory were absolutely essential in the training of professional musicians and insisted that a separate major in this field be offered by the school.

The faculty approved and assigned Hindemith the responsibility of outlining the admissions and degree requirements for the major. They were severe, for he was determined there be no doubt in the minds of anyone at the school, faculty or student, that it was a discipline worthy of respect. There were also pragmatic reasons for setting the highest possible standards, since the announcement that Hindemith would be staying on at Yale as a full-time teacher of composition and theory unleashed a flood of applications from talented students all over the country to study with him and he needed a fine screen to determine the best qualified among them.

To be admitted as theory majors applicants had to submit satisfactory evidence of written work done previously in harmony and counterpoint, meet all of the academic and professional qualifications for general admission to the school as a third-year student, and pass with distinction the special qualifying tests in theory. These included a very difficult written examination in harmony and counterpoint,[1] a series of keyboard tests involving reading four-stave scores in four different clefs at sight, transposing four-part scores in two staves, and harmonizing figured and unfigured bass lines. An oral examination in theory was added for good measure, and applicants were also required to demonstrate proficiency in performance.

To earn the bachelor of music degree in theory candidates had to complete successfully a heavy two-year program of studies that included work in music history, performance, and ensemble as well as theory and composition. Final qualification for the degree was dependent upon meeting a set of special requirements in the last term that included demonstrating competence in teaching a class in theory and passing comprehensive examinations in harmony and counterpoint.

Candidates who took their bachelor's degrees with honors could remain for a third year of study leading to a master of music degree in theory. Hindemith had never heard of such a degree before he began teaching at Yale and let it be known he thought it ludicrous to presume that anyone could ever actually *master* the art of music. There was nothing he could do about it except to set the final special degree requirements as high as possible and that he did. Candidates were required to demonstrate not only their ability to write music, by completing special projects in composition assigned two months before the end of the final term, but also their competence as teachers, by conducting classes in harmony and counterpoint under faculty observation and giving a lecture on a theoretical subject.

Admission requirements for the major in composition were even more demanding than those imposed on applicants for the theory major. They reflected Hindemith's conviction that any musician deserving to be called a "composer" must not only possess outstanding creative talent but also be highly skilled in all practical and theoretical aspects of the art. At least four of the applicant's more recent scores had to be submitted in advance and if these offered sufficient evidence of promise he or she would be permitted to take the entrance examinations in New Haven. These were identical with those given to theory applicants but they had to be passed with a superior rating to qualify as composition majors. No matter how impressive their submitted scores may have been, applicants who failed any part of the tests were denied admission as composition majors and obliged to take their degrees in theory. Hindemith admitted only nine applicants directly as composition majors out of the forty-seven who took their degrees under him. He allowed three of his students who had earned the bachelor of music degree in theory to take the master's in composition. Those he assigned to theory had no reason to feel slighted, for they took all of the courses he offered and attended his master class in composition as observers.

Requirements for the bachelor of music degree in composition included the successful completion of a two-year course of studies comparable in content to that prescribed for theory majors except for greater emphasis on composition, a battery of comprehensive tests in theory, and a number of special composition projects assigned at the beginning of the final term.

A third year of study was required for the master's degree in composition, but Hindemith admitted only seven of his students to the program, selecting those he felt had the requisite talent. They carried a full program of studies throughout the year, but Hindemith reserved the right, with the approval of his colleagues, to modify the stated special requirements for the degree. He believed these gifted students would be better served by carrying out projects and assignments in composition adapted to their individual needs and abilities and proceeded accordingly.

Hindemith began teaching a master class in composition in 1941 and continued to do so every year except when on leave. Enrollment was restricted to students he had personally examined and accepted. The other three composition teachers on the faculty gave individual instruction (as stipulated in the catalog), but Hindemith insisted on meeting all of his composition majors as a group.[2] There were two four-hour sessions each week, with the class standing around the piano looking on and listening while the composer, sitting at the keyboard playing over the score of an individual student by his side, analyzed it in minute detail and more often than not made wholesale emendations. His theory majors received their instruction in composition by attending the master class as auditors. Their compositions in progress would be reviewed individually by Hindemith at the end of the "Teaching of Theory" class session. The author knew most of Hindemith's degree students personally and heard many direct accounts of their experiences and reactions. These varied greatly, depending in large part on their ability to withstand the sharp if not withering criticism their scores were likely to provoke. Hindemith considered the craft of musical composition to be a very serious matter and was utterly intolerant of careless or mediocre work. Talented students would be rewarded with occasional compliments and words of encouragement, provided they were diligent, but would be severely reprimanded if they were not. Students failing to fulfill the promise they had shown on admission, for whatever reason, irritated him greatly and were soon made to understand that they had best consider pursuing another musical trade.

When he began teaching the advanced theory seminar in September 1941, the composer was distressed to find that the students were less "advanced" in their knowledge of traditional harmony than he had assumed they would be, since no one had been admitted to the class who had not done at least two years of previous collegiate study in theory. He knew they would resent having to be dragged screaming through a dull review of elementary harmony and consequently devised a wily plan that would provide the essential remedial work but in the guise of an interesting class project. This was to put together a small and concise textbook in traditional harmony. The book was completed by the end of the second term, in May 1942.

Hindemith had initiated the project simply as a useful exercise for his class, but he was so pleased with the result that he was prompted to write this note to Ernest Voigt at AMP:

> I have completed another book: "Lessons for Harmony Students." It was written for the Yale School of Music out of classroom exper-ience, and will probably sell very well, for there is nothing like it in this country and there is a great need for it. Translation will be no problem, for it consists mostly of musical exercises. Do you think it can be published by the end of September? That would be very good for us at the School since we could immediately put it into official use and other institutions would also be interested in it. I will send it to you at the end of the week.[3]

Voigt received the manuscript a week later and assured Hindemith that AMP would have it published by the end of September. However, wartime conditions forced a delay and it was not published until a year later, when it appeared under the title *A Concentrated Course in Traditional Harmony*. It was an immediate success in this coun-try and was soon translated into most of the major foreign lang-uages, including Hebrew and Japanese. Many thousands of copies have been sold over the years and it has become a classic among traditional harmony textbooks published in the twentieth century.

Beginning in September 1943, Hindemith's seminar in advanced theory was replaced by three two-hour year courses that he contin-ued to teach until his resignation in 1953. These were "History of Theory," "Basic Principles of Theory," and "The Teaching of Theory," offering essentially the same studies he had conducted in his seminar. All three courses were required of Hindemith's majors in theory and composition, but they were also open to other qualified students in the school.

"History of Theory" was primarily a lecture course in which Hindemith traced the development of musical theories from the Greeks to the present. Beginning in 1945, he compressed the lectures into the first term and used the second to prepare a concert of early vocal and instrumental music to be performed by the class at the end of the year. The students were required to assist in searching out suitable compositions and in preparing modern performance edi-tions for use in the concert. The Yale Collegium Musicum Concerts, as they were called, attracted national attention not only because of their novelty but also for their excellence. (Further details about these concerts are given in the next chapter.)

Students in Hindemith's "Basic Principles of Theory" course were introduced to the first two volumes of his *Unterweisung im Tonsatz*, now available in an English translation by Arthur Mendel under the title *The Craft of Musical Composition*, and were surprised to learn he had been having second thoughts about some of the ideas he had proposed and was beginning to make certain modifications. Most of the time, however, was devoted to a detailed study of the problems posed in three-part writing, a subject Hindemith intended to cover in the third volume of *The Craft*. He had begun work on it in August 1940 and wrote confidently to his friend Willy Strecker: "I have done all the preparatory work and have decided on the plan. I will work on it in one of my Yale classes and develop it from teaching experience. If all goes well it should be done by the end of the school year."[4] He was being unduly optimistic, for he was never able to complete the book to his satisfaction. (The melancholy story of part 3 of *The Craft* is detailed in chapter 10.)

Hindemith had never taught a class in theory or composition until his appointment to the faculty of the Staatliche Hochschule für Musik in Berlin in 1927, and was unhappily surprised, by his own admission, to find the task much more difficult than he had anticipated. This experience convinced him that practical studies in theory pedagogy should be required of all students planning to do professional work in that field. The "Teaching of Theory" course he gave at Yale placed special emphasis on instruction in basic musicianship skills such as sight singing, dictation (melodic, harmonic, and rhythmic), transposition, and keyboard harmony. Students were required to make up their own exercises to be used on each other and in some of the elementary theory classes in the school. The plan worked out well, prompting Hindemith to prepare a volume of special exercises designed for this purpose that he called *Elementary Training for Musicians*. It was published by AMP in 1946 and was enormously successful from the start. The book continues to be used widely throughout the world and is considered one of the best of its kind ever written.

Another theory textbook that evolved directly from Hindemith's classroom teaching at Yale was completed in June 1948. It was written as a sequel to *Traditional Harmony* and published in German by Schott in 1949 as *Harmonieübungen für Fortgeschrittene.* An English translation by Arthur Mendel was published by AMP in 1953 under the title *Traditional Harmony, Part II: Exercises for Advanced Students.* The title is somewhat misleading, for these are not simply "harmony exercises" but actually problems in composition that are to be solved. They are incomplete small pieces in a variety of vocal and instrumental formats that are to be completed by the student. The text provides a detailed analysis of the problems involved in each of them along with specific suggestions on how they are to be solved, and why. Hindemith tested the exercises on his own students before releasing the book for publication.

The number of advanced students in the school increased greatly after the war ended and included many who had been drawn there by the presence of Hindemith on the faculty. They were disappointed to discover there was no way they could study composition with him unless he agreed to take them as one of his majors in theory or composition. They complained politely to the dean, who asked the composer to consider offering a special course in composition for which they would be eligible. Hindemith readily consented and beginning in 1948 offered a two-hour course called "Exercises in Composition," open to any qualified student in the upper classes. Unfortunately, this came at a time when his teaching was being seriously disrupted by unexpected leaves of absence and he was able to conduct the class for only part of the second term in 1948–49 and the academic years 1950–51 and 1952–53. It was modeled after the "Composer at Work" classes he taught at Wells College and Tanglewood in 1940 and was heavily subscribed.

Undoubtedly Hindemith's most unusual teaching experience at Yale was serving as an instructor of elementary harmony in Yale College during the summers of 1942, 1943, and 1945. Because of the war, Yale College was holding classes the year around and members of the school's faculty were needed to teach the two twelve-week undergraduate theory courses offered in the summer. Hindemith volunteered to relieve the burden on his colleagues by teaching the beginning harmony course for six weeks, an experience he described in a letter to the author (who was away on military leave) as being "rather strenuous" because the boys were musically "dumb" in his opinion. He took keen delight later in telling how one of the young undergraduates in his class came up to him after the last meeting of the term to compliment him on how well he had done and then asked, "Sir, what is your name?"

Approximately 300 individual students took one or more courses with Hindemith during his tenure at the Yale School of Music, and it was a learning experience that most would never forget, as they have attested in many letters and taped interviews filed in the university's Hindemith Collection and its Oral History Project in American Music. A recurring theme is their gratitude for having had the opportunity to work with a master teacher whose unswerving dedication to the highest principles and ideals of his calling had given them a new and deeper understanding of music and of their responsibilities and obligations as professional musicians. Ample proof of his broad impact on their professional lives is found in the impressive record of achievement compiled by these young men and women in their later work as teachers, performers, composers, conductors, early music specialists, and administrators.[5]

Hindemith's presence on the music faculty also had a marked effect on his colleagues. Few if any of them had ever been associated with a teacher of such boundless energy and capacity for work, who would run up the stairs to his classroom on the third floor of Sprague Hall where he would teach as many as sixteen hours a week and who rarely missed a faculty or committee meeting. Compounding their astonishment was the fact that he still found time to write one significant large composition after another.

Paul Hindemith's many accomplishments as a musician have been well documented and duly appreciated, yet most accounts fail to mention a remarkable personal achievement, namely, that he became a distinguished professor at a university of world rank without having had a formal academic education beyond grammar school. Hindemith began early to compensate for this lack through self-study and by the time he joined the Yale faculty in 1940 he was readily and warmly received as a peer by the eminent scholars of the university.

Chapter 9

Performer at Yale

SHORTLY AFTER Hindemith began teaching at the University of Buffalo early in 1940 one of his faculty colleagues invited him to listen to a recently released recording of his 1939 *Sonata for Viola and Piano* made with Sanroma the year before. He had time to hear only a part of it before having to hurry off to his next class, but it was enough to provoke these comments in a letter to his wife: "The only impression I got from the little I heard was that I played better on the *Trauermusik* recording [made at the same time], but I have finally decided to quit playing in public. If it isn't any better than what came out of the phonograph then it isn't worth doing any more."[1]

Displeasure over the sound of a single recording was hardly sufficient reason to prompt such a momentous decision, but it provided an opening for Hindemith to alert his wife that he would not do any more solo viola playing in public, and he never did. He had actually done comparatively little of it in recent years except during his three U.S. concert tours, and it is abundantly clear from his journal that he was finding it an increasingly onerous task. He had enjoyed ten successful conducting engagements with five major U.S. orchestras on these tours and felt these to be far more satisfying artistic experiences. There can be little doubt this was the major reason behind his decision. However, it had no immediate impact on the course of his professional activities since concert life in the United States was being seriously curtailed by the war and there would have been little possibility of his obtaining engagements as a soloist had he wished to continue. Appearances as a guest conductor would have to wait until the war ended.

Hindemith appeared in public concerts at Yale only once as a violist and once as a violinist, both events being part of the 1941–42 Sprague Hall Chamber Music Series. On 13 January 1942 he played viola in a Brahms string sextet performance by an ensemble of faculty and students. On 24 February he performed eight of Heinrich Biber's *Biblical Sonatas* for violin and continuo. Harpsichordist Ralph Kirkpatrick played the continuo, as realized by Hindemith, assisted by Morris Kirshbaum, violoncello, and George Lam, double bass. Hindemith made two appearances as a conductor with the New Haven Symphony Orchestra. He was a guest conductor on 21 April 1941, doing his *Nobilissima Visione Suite,* and conducted the entire concert on 12 January 1948. The program included his *Four Temperaments,* with Lukas Foss as the piano soloist, Weber's *Euryanthe* Overture, and Bruckner's *Symphony No. 3.* The concert went well but the rehearsals did not. Difficulties in securing full attendance drove Hindemith into towering rages and he threatened to walk out of the event unless an extra rehearsal was held on a Sunday morning at 9:00, with every player guaranteeing his presence. One of the principals balked and received a tongue-lashing loud enough to be heard down the street, according to Howard Boatwright, who was the concertmaster.

The composer obviously needed more music-making activity than this and soon after coming to Yale found it by organizing and conducting concerts of early vocal and instrumental music. After a modest beginning in 1943 these soon developed into extraordinary musical events known as the Yale Collegium Musicum Concerts, which attracted attention far beyond Yale and New Haven. Hindemith's interest in historical instruments had been sparked in the early 1920s, when he became intrigued by the viola d'amore, mastered its technique, and performed on it many times in public. His researches into early German folk music during his involvement with "educational" music in the late 1920s, his close association and friendship with Georg Schünemann, professor of musicology and director of the Historical Instrument Collection at the Berlin Hochschule für Musik, and his intensive study of early art music while writing *Unterweisung im Tonsatz* combined to give him both a broad knowledge and profound appreciation of its value. Yale provided him with his first real opportunity to do something significant with this music.

During his first year at the university Hindemith immediately took advantage of the music library's extraordinary resources in early music by preparing, along with musicology Professor Leo Schrade, a selection of over 200 vocal and instrumental scores from the fourteenth through the seventeenth centuries, which he had his

Tanglewood students sing and play during his second summer of teaching there in 1941. This was so successful that tentative plans were made to publish a "Yale Series" of early music in modern performance editions. AMP expressed interest in the project provided Hindemith would oversee it, but he declined for lack of time and the plan was dropped.

Organizing a public concert of early music at Yale posed a problem for Hindemith since he had no adequate performing groups under his official charge. He solved that in the spring of 1943 by persuading three of his faculty colleagues who directed choral groups at the university to collaborate with him in presenting such a concert. The composer planned the entire program and it was given in Sprague Hall on 23 April 1943 as "A Collegium Musicum of the Early 17th Century." Choral works were performed by the School of Music Chorus, directed by the author, and the Bach Cantata Club, conducted by Richard Donovan, and the audience was led in singing three seventeenth-century canons by Marshall Bartholomew, director of the Yale Glee Club. Hindemith was listed on the program simply as one of the thirty instrumentalists participating, playing the bassoon, viola d'amore, and viola da gamba. All of the instrumental and most of the choral music had been transcribed by Hindemith, requiring the writing of some 300 pages of score. This was an enormously time-consuming task for the composer, but he had good reason to feel it had been worth the effort, for the concert was a success and he knew he had made believers out of his colleagues.

Calls to military service had depleted the school's performing ranks so severely by 1944 that Hindemith was obliged to abandon his plan to present another concert of early music in the spring of the year. The situation was sufficiently improved the following year so that he was able to organize a "Concert of French Music from the 13th and 14th Centuries," which was given in Sprague Hall on 14 May 1945. The composer prepared and conducted the entire concert, using a small chorus of twenty-three singers, an instrumental ensemble of ten players, and William Gephart of New York as a guest vocal soloist. Only authentic historical instruments were used, four of them loaned by the Metropolitan Museum of Art in New York. One of these, a vielle, was played by the composer. Hindemith was so pleased with the performance he had the following statement posted on the school's bulletin board:

I want to thank all students who sang and played in our concert of old French music for their faithful and enthusiastic collaboration. The following quotation from one of the numerous letters I received after the concert seems to express the general opinion of those present: "Monday night's concert was a revelation and I wish that many people could have heard it, particularly those who think they understand old music, but who, I am sure, have never dreamed of its having the vitality that you demonstrated in it." If this is true, we can be content that our efforts were not in vain and that we were justified in our attempt to revive this beautiful music.

Paul Hindemith[2]

The 1945 concert marked the first of the series that came to be known as the Yale Collegium Musicum Concerts, but it was not until the following year that these programs assumed the format they would follow throughout the composer's remaining years at Yale.

The school's enrollment doubled in 1945–46, due mostly to the large number of returning veterans applying, many of whom came to study with Hindemith. Now convinced of the potential at Yale for expanding his work in early music and with enough students of his own to do more with the idea, he decided to make the Collegium Musicum concert a part of his class in the "History of Theory." The first term was devoted mostly to a study of the more important theorists and their theories from the earliest period to the present, but in the final weeks plans would be made for a public concert to be given in the spring, described on the program as "a musical illustration for the course in the History of Music Theory." Students were to search out exceptional compositions from specified early periods and edit them for modern performance. They did so, but in the end it was Hindemith himself who did most of the work in preparing the scores for performance. During the second term the weekly two-hour class sessions would be used for intensive studies and rehearsals of the music to be performed at the concert. As the concert date approached, the composer demanded as many extra rehearsals as he deemed necessary to be assured that every number on the program would be given a flawless performance.

The first of his five major Collegium Musicum programs, "A Concert of 14th- and 15th-Century Music, Given by Students of Advanced Theory," was presented in Sprague Hall on 20 May 1946

105

and was a landmark event, as described in the following press release:

> Mr. Hindemith has arranged for the use of a number of late medieval instruments in an effort to organize an orchestra nearly identical with that shown in Hans Memling's painting "Christ Surrounded by Angels" (Flemish, 1480), which depicts ten angels playing the following instruments: psaltery, tromba marina, lute, natural trumpet, cornetto, trombone, organetto, small harp, the vielle. In addition, a rebec, small drum and cymbals, and another trombone will be included. This is the first time that such an authentic orchestra of the 15th century has ever been presented in this country for actual performance. . . . The instruments to be used have been furnished by courtesy of the Metropolitan Museum of Art in New York and the Yale University Collection.[3]

The concert attracted a capacity audience that included many prominent musicians from New York, Boston, and elsewhere in the area. The audience was so enchanted by what they had heard that everyone stood and cheered at the end.

Hindemith's only reason for presenting these concerts was his conviction that this music was too good simply to be the subject of countless doctoral dissertations in musicology and not to be heard. He also knew that an ordinary routine performance could be deadly dull and defeat the purpose; thus he arranged the program as a fast-moving musical revue, with a variety of fascinating sights and sounds that left no opportunity for the audience to become bored. This is what they heard in 1946:

> An extended Dunstable motet for mixed chorus
> Three 15th-century instrumental pieces, one played by rebec, organetto, vielle, and lute, and two by rebec, bass recorder, vielle, trombone, and lute
> A Dufay *Mass* for mixed chorus
> An anonymous isorhythmic motet for mixed chorus
> Two pieces by Binchois and Grenon, sung by women's chorus
> Four chansons for solo soprano with instruments:
>> by Binchois, with rebec, vielle, and lute,
>> by Binchois, with krummhorn, vielle, and lute,
>> by Hayne, with harp, rebec, vielle, organetto, trombone,
>> by von Wolkenstein, with psaltery, cornetto, vielle, trumpet, drums, and cymbals
> Three pieces for men's chorus

Two canons by von Wolkenstein, sung by the audience and
chorus
Three instrumental dance pieces, played by the 15th-century
"angelic" orchestra of harp, psaltery, rebec, vielle, lute, cornetto,
krummhorn, bass recorder, trumpet, trombone, organetto,
drums, cymbals

Hindemith took a completely pragmatic approach in adapting
this early music for modern performance. His primary objective
was to make it interesting for the listener, and if this meant cutting
a few historical corners so be it. No notes of the original score
were ever changed, but vocal parts might be shifted or reinforced
by instruments to achieve a better balance of sonorities, and
the instrumental scoring was done in whatever way he felt the
most attractive sound would result. The texts were always sung
in the original language, which in 1946 meant Latin, French,
German, and Italian. The composer knew the languages well and
made certain the singers would articulate them perfectly through
long and intensive drills. He also knew how to play all of the
historical instruments being used and insisted the instrumentalists
do likewise by giving each of them special lessons if needed.
Hindemith overlooked nothing in preparing his first major demonstration of the viability of early music, and the tumultuous
ovation when it was done gave proof that he had succeeded
brilliantly.

Participating in the 1946 concert was a chorus of forty-seven
singers, all but three being members of Hindemith's history of
theory class,[4] and seventeen instrumentalists, also from his class,
playing fourteen different instruments. Hindemith did all of the
conducting and played the vielle in the instrumental ensembles that
needed no director. The superb soprano soloist was Helen (Mrs.
Howard L.) Boatwright, who would be featured again in the 1947
and 1953 concerts.

Hindemith had a chronological plan in mind for these concerts,
and in 1947 the program was devoted to "Music of the 15th Century."
The demand for tickets was so heavy the concert had to be given on
two evenings, 22 and 23 March 1947. The capacity audiences in
Sprague Hall heard impeccable performances by a variety of vocal
and instrumental ensembles presenting a fascinating program of
engaging works by Obrecht, Okeghem, Agricola, and lesser-known
composers of the period. Participants included sixty-five singers,

ten instrumentalists, and Helen Boatwright as the guest soloist. Hindemith conducted and also played the tenor viola da gamba in the instrumental ensemble.

The next concert featured "Music of the Early 16th Century" and was presented in Sprague Hall on the evenings of 20 and 21 May 1948. It followed the same format as before and delighted capacity audiences. The guest artist was tenor John Garris of the Metropolitan Opera Company. The chorus had now grown to seventy-four, and seventeen players were used in the instrumental ensembles. A special effort was made to assemble a group approximating a court orchestra of the sixteenth century as depicted in a painting hung in the Yale Art Gallery. Hindemith opted not to join the instrumental ensemble in this concert. Among the more important composers represented were de la Rue, Senfl, Isaac, Josquin, and Stoltzer. The concert was repeated in New York on 27 May, where it was presented in the Metropolitan Museum of Art and highly praised by the press.

Hindemith's absences on leave precluded his organizing concerts of early music in 1949 and 1950, but the series was resumed in 1951, when on 21 May he conducted a program of "Music of the 16th Century" in Sprague Hall and a public rehearsal the preceding evening. A chorus of eighty-nine singers and fourteen instrumentalists performed works by Byrd, de Monte, Palestrina, A. Gabrieli, Handl, Gesualdo, di Lasso, and Le Jeune. The composer played the viola da braccio in the orchestra and led the audience in singing an exuberant canon he had written for the occasion as an encore at the end of the concert. The program was repeated in New York on 4 June in the Cloisters.

The last of Hindemith's notable Collegium concerts was presented in Sprague Hall on 14 May 1953, with a public rehearsal on the thirteenth.[5] (There had been no concert in 1952, since he was teaching at the University of Zürich.) For his valedictory appearance he selected a program of representative works from the fourteenth through the early eighteenth centuries, performed by a chorus of sixty singers, an instrumental ensemble of twenty-two players, and soprano Helen Boatwright as the guest artist. It began with an *Organum* by Perotin and ended with J. S. Bach's great motet *Singet dem Herrn* and included other works by Dufay, G. Gabrieli, Weelkes, Monteverdi, and Gesualdo. The printed program contained this testimonial to Hindemith: "The singular character of the Collegium—the uniform enthusiasm of the members, the essentially nonprofessional outlook, and finally, the quality of the guidance provided through the years by its director, Mr. Hindemith, have made it an institution paralleled in only a very few places in this age." There was a repeat performance on 21 May at the Metropolitan Museum of Art in New York, an event that moved Jay Harrison, critic for the *New York Herald-Tribune,* to write:

> The appearance of Paul Hindemith conducting the Yale Collegium Musicum provided a radiant crown for the music season just ended. He gave the most enjoyable "old music" program to have greeted this town in many a year. It was, moreover, impeccably performed. Soloists, chorus, instrumentalists—all who touched music made music. Not a phrase was mislaid, not a color blurred. It was eloquent, elegant, passionate rendering. It was serious, devout. And it served to remind us of an ideal in performance that is easily forgot in this day of last-minute preparation and resulting mediocrity. The entire program was performed with fervor, power, and directness. And it was conducted by a man to whom these elements are second nature. Indeed, his program of the evening has left us with the season's brightest treasure.[6]

Hindemith never assumed the active role of a crusader for the revival of early music performances. He was quite content to let his Collegium concerts speak for themselves, and they spoke eloquently. There were very few, if indeed any, practical studies in the performance of early music offered by institutions in this country before he began his remarkable series at Yale, and today there are many. There is little doubt that his pathfinding efforts at the university had much to do with focusing attention not only on the pleasures provided by such music but also on the importance of including work in this field as a part of the making of a complete professional musician.[7]

Chapter 10
Creative Work

HINDEMITH'S PRODIGIOUS creative activities continued unabated during his residency in the United States. He wrote six orchestral pieces, three concertos, eleven chamber works, from duo sonatas to a septet, approximately thirty-five songs for solo voice and piano, an oratorio, three smaller works for chorus and orchestra, two ballets, a symphony for band, a large work for solo piano, and extensive revisions of an earlier opera and song cycle. He wrote three theory textbooks that were published, a fourth that was published post-humously, an important book, and an extended essay, both published to high critical acclaim. This impressive record is all the more remarkable for having been accomplished while Hindemith was heavily involved as a full-time university professor and teacher. This chapter covers the period from September 1940 through June 1953, and describes circumstances relating to the completion of these projects in considerable detail, since much of this information is lacking from the biographical accounts published previously.

Shortly after taking up residence in New Haven, Hindemith received a commission from George Balanchine to write a ballet score and by November 1 had completed *Theme and Four Variations: The Four Temperaments,* for solo piano and string orchestra. Having severed relations with Massine in April, he was now free to write for Balanchine and did so with pleasure, for he greatly admired the choreographer's work. Several writers have made the reasonable suggestion that Hindemith may have borrowed some of the musical ideas he had in mind for the Brueghel ballet he was to have done for Massine in writing *The Four Temperaments,* but from letters he sent to Ernest Voigt at AMP it would appear not. This note was sent in early October:

> I am going to start writing the Balanchine ballet tomorrow. I am thinking of doing it this way: a small instrumental introduction

serving as a theme, not to be danced. Then four different variations (danced) based on the theme, each one corresponding to one of the temperaments—one melancholy, one sanguine, one phlegmatic, and one choleric. The whole work will offer about a half hour of music and an opportunity for all kinds of dancing. Has Balanchine thrown his 250 "bucks" on the table? Not that I need the money at the moment, but his credibility is a bit nebulous, to say the least. He can have the first piece next week.[1]

The final installment of the score was sent to Voigt on November 4, together with the composer's wry comment that the piece was "really worthy of a better project." He received Balanchine's payment of $250 (through AMP) in December, much to his surprise, but heard nothing directly from the choreographer for over five months, much to his annoyance. He learned from Voigt in April 1941 that Balanchine was planning to use the ballet on a forthcoming South American tour, prompting this reply: "If the camels of the caravan carrying my *Four Temperaments* into the deserts of our six Pan-American republics I will not be any more surprised than I have been for a long time over Balanchine's blitzkrieg operations [*sic*]. Nevertheless, I would like very much to know what he thinks of the piece. It would be good if you could get the sheik to let me know. Inschalla!"[2] Hindemith sent this progress report to Willy Strecker five weeks later: "The little ballet I wrote for Balanchine last fall will be performed in New York next month as a sort of dress rehearsal for the company's South American tour. It is said to be very good and I am supposed to conduct it, but as always when you are dealing with ballet projects you never know until five minutes before the show."[3] The composer's skepticism was well founded, for there was neither a New York performance in 1941 nor a South American tour. In fact, the world premiere of the ballet was delayed for five years, chiefly because of the war, and did not occur until 20 November 1946, when it was staged by Balanchine in New York. Hindemith's engaging music and Balanchine's brilliant choreography combined to make the work an instant success and it has remained a staple in the ballet repertory. It also proved to be highly successful as a concert piece, and continues to be one of his most frequently performed orchestral works. It was first done as such in Boston on 3 September 1944, with Lukas Foss as the piano soloist. Hindemith was obviously pleased with the work himself, for he conducted it on seventeen of his concerts.[4]

Two movements of his *Symphony in E♭*, begun at Tanglewood in August 1940, had been completed by October, when Hindemith received the Balanchine commission. He set aside the symphony to write the ballet score, resumed work on it in November, and completed it early in December. The idea of writing a symphonic work scored for the traditional romantic orchestra, something he had deliberately avoided doing before, seems to have been prompted by his having heard (and thoroughly enjoyed) the brilliant sounds of the Boston Symphony Orchestra almost daily at Tanglewood. He undoubtedly hoped Koussevitzky would be interested in performing it and the conductor was, telling the composer he would have his orchestra give the first performance in the spring of 1941.

Everything was going well as late as December, when Hindemith wrote to Voigt that the symphony was nearing completion and that "Koussevitzky is more than enthusiastic about it." The score was sent to Voigt on 11 December, with a note requesting that a photocopy be sent immediately to the conductor, for it had been scheduled for performance and "Koussevitzky needs time to study this large work thoroughly." Two months later plans had collapsed, as the composer reported to Voigt: "Koussevitzky cannot do the symphony this spring but will play it several times next year. That's fine with me, because I can now give it to Chicago. I am sending it to them right away."[5]

Available records provide no further information about the Chicago plan, but it is clear that this fell through as well. Irked by Koussevitzky's decision to postpone the premiere until the following season, the impatient composer happily accepted an offer from Dimitri Mitropoulos to have his Minneapolis Symphony give the first performance on 21 November. Hindemith was in Minneapolis for the final rehearsals and the concert, reporting to Voigt on his return:

> Minneapolis was a great success. Mitropoulos was outstanding as was his orchestra. He conducted it without the score and with great drive, carrying everyone along with him. He will conduct the piece in New York on Christmas Day! That will be a bigger jolt to my Boston friend [Koussevitzky] than the Minneapolis premiere, about which he wrote me a nasty letter. Furthermore, the situation is clear: he released the piece in February after he saw he could not program it during the past season. If he still had any interest, he had plenty of time to say so. As you know, he did not make a peep. Nevertheless, the piece must be quite good, if he is so annoyed.[6]

Koussevitzky had to be unhappy over having his mighty Boston ensemble upstaged by a provincial orchestra from Minnesota, of all places, and Hindemith obviously enjoyed this opportunity to remind the conductor not to be quite so casual in his further dealings with him. No lasting harm was done, for Koussevitzky did perform the *Symphony in E♭* in Boston on 23 January 1942 and several times thereafter.

Christmas 1940 would be their first as U.S. residents and to mark the occasion Hindemith's gift to Gertrude was a song for soprano and piano that he wrote using the Latin text of a portion of the Nativity story in the Gospel of St. Luke, *Exiit edictum*. He added another for good measure after Christmas by writing *Cum natus esset,* from the Nativity story in the Gospel of St. Matthew. Gertrude received a similar gift in 1943, when he wrote *Ascendente Jesu in naviculum* (Matthew 8: 23–27) for her, and in 1944, with *Pastores loquebantur* (Luke 2: 15–20) and *Nuptiae factae sunt* (John 2: 1–11). (Hindemith apparently considered these songs to be more or less a private family matter and made no effort to have them publicly performed or published. The noted German soprano Irmgard Seefried happened to learn of their existence in 1951 and obtained the composer's permission to sing three of them in a Vienna concert on 2 April that year. They were so well received that Schott published them immediately and urged Hindemith to add more songs to the series. He eventually found time to do eight more between 1958 and 1960 and all were published by Schott under the title *Thirteen Motets.*)

There was no time for Hindemith even to think about writing any new music during the first seven months of 1941. His heavy and critical involvement in the planning of the complete reorganization of the School of Music demanded endless hours of his attention. He also arranged and copied over 200 pages of early vocal score for use in his Tanglewood classes that summer. There were many conferences at AMP in New York concerning the English translations of the first two volumes of *Unterweisung im Tonsatz,* projects that were far behind schedule. Nevertheless, Hindemith was able to continue some of his creative activity in spite of these distractions. Work was done on the third volume of the *Unterweisung,* and his pocket date book for 1941 reveals tharesumed work on the revision of *Das Marienleben* in March and May.

It was not until he had completed his teaching obligations at

Tanglewood that summer (described in chapter 11) that Hindemith finally had time to compose. He and Gertrude remained in their attractive rented country house near Lenox until his Yale classes began in late September. He immediately began to compose and soon wrote to Ernest Voigt: "I have written a sonata for English horn and piano and if you find any interest in it we could sell photocopies of it. I have written it on transparent paper and a copy would come to $1.40. If we sell it for $3.00 we would both become rich and you could go on your planned vacation in your own yacht!"[7]

The Hindemiths were back in New Haven by 22 September and two weeks later he had completed a sonata for trombone and piano. Voigt had not replied to Hindemith's letter about the English horn sonata, but he sent it to AMP anyway, along with the trombone sonata. There was still no word from Voigt and the composer was irked, sending this note late in October: "I have not heard from you in a long time. If the trains to New Haven have to depend on carrying your news, the New York, New Haven, and Hartford Railway would have to cease service and the Post Office would also have to shut down and the rails would be rusted. At least I would like to know whether the two sonatas I sent to you two weeks ago ever got there, and if so, what you plan to do with them."[8] The confusion was eventually cleared up and the two sonatas were published by AMP in 1942, in the facsimile format recommended by Hindemith. This was an ideal solution to the publishing problems faced by the composer at that time. The Schott firm in Mainz could no longer print his things because of the war, and AMP had no publishing facilities since it was primarily a distributor. Hindemith's remarkably legible manuscripts were about as good as engravings, and duplicating them through photolithography was entirely satisfactory. Most of his compositions issued by AMP during the war were done in this manner.

On 7 November 1941, Hindemith completed a set of variations for violoncello and piano on an old English children's song *A Frog He Went A–Courtin'*. The composer wrote to Voigt asking if he would be interested in publishing the piece, but apparently he was not, and the work did not appear in print until it was issued by Schott in 1952. There is some evidence this brief virtuoso piece was written in response to a suggestion from Hindemith's friend Gregor Piatigorsky, who had once complained to the composer about the lack of effective contemporary "encore" pieces in the cello repertory, urging him to write such a work to satisfy the needs of concert cellists everywhere.

During some short break in his 1941 schedule, Hindemith dashed off four very short duets for bassoon and cello as "house music" he and Gertrude could play for diversion. Mrs. Hindemith, a good musician and a trained singer with some professional experience, had begun to play the cello in recent years, an effort sustained by her husband's encouragement and occasional small pieces written to accommodate her abilities. He could play all of the standard orchestral wind instruments and was especially proficient as a bassoonist. The four duets were written accordingly, but it would seem he did not take them seriously. He gave the manuscript almost immediately to his musicologist friend Karl Geiringer, who eventually loaned it to Schott for publication. The duets were issued in 1969 under the rather vague title *Stücke*.

Hindemith's heavy schedule left no time for composing in 1942 until the school year ended in June. (He did contrive to find a few hours on 13 and 14 May to write *A Little Sonata for Violoncello and Piano* as a gift to Gertrude for their eighteenth wedding anniversary on 15 May. The piece was never published, but it will be included in the sixty-four volume complete edition of Hindemith's works that Schott began issuing serially in 1976 under the sponsorship of the Hindemith Foundation.) However, as soon as the second term ended, Hindemith began composing and continued throughout the summer, writing an incredible amount of music. He wrote to Voigt early in September:

> As more grist for your mill I am sending you a brand new sonata for two pianos. It is a respectable and fairly large piece and it is certain to be well received. I have written the score so that it can be photographed immediately, as is, like you did with the English horn and trombone sonatas. . . . Are you interested in some new publications? I have about two dozen songs in German, French, English, and Latin out of which you can make a selection. Furthermore, there is a volume of easy, pleasing, and merry three-voice fugues for piano. So, choose what you want, as long as songs and fugues are not rationed and fixed with ceiling prices [a reference to wartime measures then in effect].[9]

The *Sonata for Two Pianos* was commissioned by the professional two-piano team of Celius Dougherty and Vincenz Ruzicka and completed on 28 August. It was published immediately in the facsimile format suggested by Hindemith and premiered by Dougherty and Ruzicka in Town Hall, New York, on 20 November 1942.

Voigt had known there might be a two-piano sonata coming and was prepared to publish it, but the new songs and "merry fugues" came as a surprise and he moved slowly in deciding what to do with them. Ever since 1920 Hindemith had enjoyed the happy situation of having almost everything he sent to Schott in Mainz published immediately and he was perhaps under the impression it would be the same with AMP. Unfortunately for the composer, the New York company was not in a position to do the same, but they did the best they could under difficult circumstances.

Hindemith sent a total of twenty-six new songs, twenty-two having been written by late summer, three more in December, and another in January 1943. Ten were settings of German texts, nine of English, five of French, and two of Latin. Why he decided to write so many songs at this particular time remains an unanswered question. They were not commissioned, nor had AMP suggested the idea. In fact, the company waited three years before publishing any of them and then released only eight. (The remaining eighteen will appear in the complete edition.)

The eight 1942 songs published by AMP in 1945 were all on English texts. One, *La belle dame sans merci* (John Keats) was published separately as *No. 1* of *Two Ballades. No. 2* did not appear until 1980, thirty-five years later, when Schott published *Bal des pendus,* written in 1944 on a text by Jean Arthur Rimbaud. The other seven were published in a series called *Nine English Songs* that included one done in 1943 and another in 1944. The 1942 pieces selected were *Echo* (Thomas Moore), *Envoy* (Francis Thompson), *The Moon* (Percy B. Shelley), *On a Fly Drinking out of His Cup* (William Oldys), *On Hearing "The Last Rose of Summer"* (Charles Wolfe), *The Wildflower's Song* (William Blake), and *The Whistlin' Thief* (Samuel Lover). Completing the series of nine were *Sing on, There in the Swamp* (Walt Whitman), done in 1943, and *To Music, to Becalm His Fever* (Robert Herrick), written in 1944. The songs have done well over the years and were reissued by Schott in 1978 in a new one-volume edition.

Hindemith had begun writing the three-voice piano fugues immediately after completing the two-piano sonata and had done six when he first mentioned the project to Voigt in his September letter. The AMP chief apparently expressed interest, for the composer went full speed ahead and within six weeks had completed one of his masterpieces, the astonishing *Ludus tonalis.* His sketches for the work show clearly that he intended initially to write only twelve fugues, representing each of the notes of the ascending chromatic scale, as in J. S. Bach's *Well-Tempered Clavichord.* However, he very shortly changed and enlarged the format significantly by putting the twelve fugues in a sequence of keys following the pattern of his "Series 1" in the first volume of *Unterweisung* and separating each of them by a brief but complete piece called an "Interlude" that served as a subtle modulation into the new key. The entire work was framed by a "Prelude" and "Postlude," the latter being a retrograde inversion of the former. He completed the twelve fugues on 17 September, six "Interludes" by 21 September, the "Prelude" and "Postlude" by 4 October, and the remaining five "Interludes" by 12 October. He then wrote to Voigt: "It will be a volume of about 90 pages and the final copy will be ready in about two weeks. I am thinking of calling it "Ludus tonalis" because of its didactic (not to say sophisticated) quality. Our Latin experts here at Yale think the title is very apt. I cannot find anything better in German or English to describe as clearly what it is and at the same time hinting at the *Well-Tempered Clavichord* and *Art of Fugue* (the form, that is, not the quality)."[10]

Hindemith was very proud of *Ludus* and wanted to have it published without delay, preferably in an engraved edition. When he heard from AMP that engraving would mean an indefinite delay whereas a facsimile edition could be issued much sooner, he sent these testy comments to Voigt:

> I greeted your decision about *Ludus tonalis* with a dry and laughing eye. Naturally, it would be better if it could be engraved—we agreed to that at our last meeting. On the other hand, I think it is precisely today—when every sniveling juvenile has a symphony in his head, when every orchestral conductor performs the most impossible crap because it is either American or Russian and otherwise has no interest in anything but orchestral music, when music is rated only by how it works on the sex glands—it is precisely today that something must appear which shows what music and composition really are. [Here he berates AMP at length about previous delays in publishing his work.] If you think that in spite of all difficulties there is a possibility of publishing *Ludus,* you can do so with confidence. It makes no difference to me if I have to do the

work of copying the score, for it has to be copied anyway. . . . You should make your decision on the basis of your responsibility to music history.[11]

The composer's grumbling brought results, for *Ludus tonalis* was published by AMP in 1943 in a handsome engraved edition, precisely as Hindemith wished. The first edition was quickly sold out and a second had to be rushed into print.

Ludus tonalis was first performed at an all-Hindemith concert given at the University of Chicago on 15 February 1944, played by Willard MacGregor, a gifted young American pianist who had been a pupil of Arthur Schnabel in Berlin. The program also included the *Sonata for Flute and Piano,* played by Ernst Liegl, principal flutist of the Chicago Symphony, and MacGregor, and the four-hand piano sonata, played by MacGregor and the composer. Hindemith had given a lecture at the university the day before on "The Status of Music and Musicians in Ancient and Modern Times."

Preparation of materials for the Yale Collegium Musicum concert on 23 April and a three-week confinement while recovering from a severe attack of influenza and the gout, plus many other disruptions during the spring of 1943, seriously impeded Hindemith's compositional work, but he somehow contrived to complete a new string quartet by 15 May. He had not written one since the fourth quartet some twenty years before, apparently having lost interest in composing another. Now, however, he had been urged by the Budapest String Quartet, then rated as one of the best in the world, to write one for them and he was pleased to oblige. Hindemith called it *String Quartet in E♭* but it is generally known as the *Fifth String Quartet.* It was premiered by the Budapest ensemble in Washington, D.C., on 7 November 1943 and published by AMP in a facsimile edition.

The year before, on 12 December, when Hindemith was in Philadelphia at the invitation of Eugene Ormandy to attend a performance of his *Mathis der Maler* symphony by the Philadelphia Orchestra, the maestro used the opportunity to ask the composer to write a piece that his orchestra could premiere, and Hindemith promised to let him know if and when he had a work to offer. While vacationing in New Hampshire the following July he completed the sketch for a brief (six minutes) work for full chamber orchestra, doing the final score after returning to New Haven in August. This was his *Cupid and Psyche (Farnesina): Overture to a Ballet,* and he decided to offer it to Ormandy for first performance. It was far from being the kind of attention-getting new work the conductor had hoped to receive from Hindemith, but he accepted it. It was premiered by the Philadelphia Orchestra on 23 October 1943 with Ormandy conducting and Hindemith on hand to take a bow.

This is Hindemith's description of the work, as printed in the program for the first performance:

> The Overture is part of a ballet that follows in its action the Apuleius story of Cupid and Psyche as it is depicted in the paintings at the Villa Farnesina in Rome. The music of the entire ballet has the same character as the overture, it is serene and light and tries to be the musical equivalent of the lovely gaiety the Farnesina paintings display. I planned the piece some years ago but the music is not yet finished. I think that is more or less all I can tell you. I don't know what else can be said about the piece "in absentia" without going into technical details.

The composer had his tongue well in cheek while writing these notes, for there never was such a ballet score nor would there ever be. The "overture" received tepid reviews in Philadelphia and Virgil Thomson gave it faint praise when it was played by Ormandy and his orchestra in New York on 25 January 1944. He commented in his *Herald-Tribune* review that it was "jolly, easy to listen to, but difficult to understand in detail." He could not tell what themes represented either Cupid or Psyche, and wondered if this was probably "another of Hindemith's elaborate musical jokes, the sort of thing he surely does best." Perhaps it was.

Ormandy was apparently not impressed by the work, for he never performed it again. However, he retained his high regard for Hindemith's music, frequently performing the major orchestral works and making magnificent recordings of them with the Philadelphia Orchestra in later years.

Hindemith's enormously successful orchestral piece *Symphonic Metamorphosis of Themes by Carl Maria von Weber* was also written in the summer of 1943. The third and fourth movements were done in the first two weeks of June, before the Hindemiths left on their New Hampshire vacation, and the first and second movements were written after they returned to New Haven in August. The genesis of this masterpiece actually dates back to March 1940, when

Hindemith and Leonide Massine had their monumental falling out over how some of von Weber's four-hand piano pieces should be arranged for a ballet score. Massine had summarily rejected what Hindemith was trying to do and the composer had been furious. He had given much thought to the project and was sufficiently satisfied by the possibilities to put the sketches aside for later use in some other form. He kept the idea very much in mind, writing to Ernest Voigt on 9 October 1942, "I am thinking of composing a *Weber Suite* for symphony orchestra and also for band." The opportunity for carrying out his plan would come the following summer.

The full score was published in a facsimile edition by AMP in 1945, but the world premiere took place in New York on 20 January 1944, played by the New York Philharmonic under Artur Rodzinski and with the composer in attendance to acknowledge the hearty applause of an audience that had thoroughly enjoyed what critic Olin Downes of the *New York Times* called "diverting and delight-ful music—one of the most entertaining scores Hindemith has ever given us."[12]

Olin Downes was particularly intrigued by how the Weber themes were used, and had these amusing comments to make: "As for what Mr. Hindemith has done with the Weber themes he must take the full responsibility. He has remarked that because these are by no means the best of Weber themes, he has felt the freer to treat them as he pleases! Nothing like frankness between friends, and the wonderful Carl Maria is safely in his grave! We confess we have no knowledge of the themes used for 'homage to Weber' in the peculiar manner of Hindemith."[13]

There was no reason whatever for Hindemith to refuse to iden-tify the Weber themes he used, but he decided to have a little fun by telling the critics and scholars to go find out for themselves. When the piece is played today the audience is duly informed through program notes that the first movement is on a theme from Weber's *Piano Duet, Opus 60.4,* the second from his *Overture to Turandot,* the third from *Piano Duet, Opus 3.2,* and the fourth from *Piano Duets, Opus 60.2* and *Opus 60.7.*[14]

Five additional projects completed in 1943 remain to be noted. During a July vacation in New Hampshire Hindemith revised and enlarged his *Frau Musica,* first written in 1928, providing it with an English text. He had been persuaded to do so by AMP, who felt the piece would thereby attract more performances in this country, and they were right. The revision was published by AMP in 1945.

I.

Im Hintergrunde der mit Schleiern behängten
Bühne sieht man wie eine Art Traumbild,
jedoch mit lebhaften Farben gemalt, die
Stadt Jerusalem. Sie ist von waffentragenden
Sarazenen bewacht. Vorlagen für dieses Bild
~~vorstellungen~~ möge man sich den
illuminierten Darstellungen fränkischer früher
Buchillustration suchen. Die Häuser stehen
grau, mauerbewehrt und in perspektivisch
in einem grauen Wallringe, der sich auf
einer starkgrünen Wiese mit großen bunten
~~Blumen~~ Blumen und primitiven Bäumen
erhebt. Der tiefblaue Himmel trägt in
gotischen Buchstaben die Aufschrift „Hiero-
solyma". Die bewachenden Bewaffneten
sehen größer aus als die gemalte Stadt,
auch sie sind in Kleidung und
Haltung den genannten Vorlagen weit-
gehend angenähert.

First page of the scenario for *The Children's Crusade,* a ballet written for George Balanchine in 1939 to be performed to the music of *Symphonic Dances.* In the right margin under the heading "Measure and rehearsal number" Hindemith gave precise directions for fitting the music to the story. The ballet was never produced. Holograph in the Paul Hindemith Collection, Yale University.

House at 134 West Elm Street, New Haven, rented furnished by the Hindemiths from September 1940 to October 1945. No changes have been made except for the addition of a garage. Photo taken in 1987 by Michael Marsden of the Bureau of Public Information, Yale University.

House at 137 Alden Avenue, New Haven, purchased by the Hindemiths in 1945 and their home until leaving for Switzerland in 1953. The house was painted white during the Hindemiths' occupancy, but no other changes have been made. Photo taken in 1987 by Michael Marsden of the Bureau of Public Information, Yale University.

Paul and Gertrude Hindemith in the garden of their home on Alden Avenue, New Haven, c. 1950. Paul Hindemith Collection, Yale University.

Title page of the scenario for *The Parable of the Blind,* a ballet based on paintings by Pieter Brueghel and pertinent old sayings. Holograph in the Paul Hindemith Collection, Yale University.

Beginning of the first scene of the "Brueghel" ballet scenario, based on the painting *Conflict between Carnival and Lent* and the old saying, "Whoever is annoyed by things that give pleasure to others will not rest until the world goes under." Holograph in the Paul Hindemith Collection, Yale University.

First page of the unpublished song for solo bass and piano, *Recitativo e Aria Ranatica* ("The Frog"), written in 1944. Holograph in the Paul Hindemith Collection, Yale University.

Hindemith and Robert Shaw with AMP officials, New York, November 1945. Negotiations for writing the *Lilacs Requiem* had just been completed. Standing: Karl Bauer, Hugo Winter, Kurt Stone, Arthur Mendel, Hindemith. Seated: Robert Shaw, Gretel Urban. Paul Hindemith Collection, Yale University.

Cover page of the *Billboard* magazine, featuring a publicity photo of Benny Goodman and Hindemith looking over the manuscript of the clarinet concerto the composer had just written for the noted band leader. Photo by "Popsie, New York." Reproduced by courtesy of Billboard Publications, New York.

Hindemith in his Sprague Hall classroom at Yale. Photo taken in 1949 by Ben Quashen, one of his students. Paul Hindemith Collection, Yale University.

Hindemith hosting a garden party at his home for his degree students at Yale in May 1949. From left to right: Howard Boatwright, Michael Brotman, Harold Blumenfeld, George Hunter, John Cowell, Carl Miller, Hindemith (in front), Robert Hickok (behind), Anthony Barbieri, Alvin King, Leonard Berkowitz, Leonard Sarason, David Kraehenbuehl, Francis Widdis, Peter Ré. Paul Hindemith Collection, Yale University.

Full-length murals painted on paper by Hindemith and hung on the walls of their Alden Avenue home for the farewell party they gave on 3 May 1953. Photos by Charles T. Alburtus of the Yale News Bureau. Paul Hindemith Collection, Yale University.

Hindemith rehearsing Yale School of Music students for the special concert he conducted at the university on 19 February 1960. Photo by Charles T. Alburtus of the Yale News Bureau. Paul Hindemith Collection, Yale University.

Hindemith with the author and Mrs. Noss at the St. Maurice Abbey near Blonay, Switzerland, July 1960. Photo taken by Gertrude Hindemith. From the author's private collection.

After Hindemith completed his six-week teaching obligation in Yale College during August and early September, he and Gertrude spent a week in the Berkshires at South Egremont, Massachusetts, where he wrote his *Sonata for Althorn and Piano.* He did this on his own, probably wishing to fill out his series of instrumental duo-sonatas. AMP was not interested in publishing it, but it was released by Schott in 1956.

In November and December the composer prepared a modern performance edition of Monteverdi's *L'Orfeo,* based as closely as possible on the original score, including the use of authentic early instruments or their modern reproductions. A myth has persisted over the years that the opera was staged at Yale in 1944, but it was not. Wartime conditions precluded any such possibility and Hindemith was well aware of that. After sending the score to several prominent musicians in New York he knew to be interested in opera production, but who also found it impossible to do anything about it at the time, he put the score away and waited for a more propitious time. It came in 1954, when Schott agreed to publish vocal and instrumental parts for a 5 June performance in Vienna, conducted by Hindemith. He conducted it in Frankfurt in May 1960, and in Rome and Perugia in October 1963, shortly before his death. Monteverdi scholars are agreed that Hindemith's is the most successful of the many attempts to arrange a viable modern performance edition of *L'Orfeo.*

Two solo songs complete the list of Hindemith's 1943 compositions, both noted previously: Walt Whitman's *Sing on, There in the Swamp* (one of the *Nine English Songs*) and *Ascendente Jesu in naviculum* (one of the *Thirteen Motets*), written in November and December respectively.

During all of 1944 and the first seven months of 1945, Hindemith wrote only one ballet score of modest proportions, four solo songs (mentioned above), and three short movements of a relatively small string quartet that would be completed in December 1945. This was an unusually small number of new works to be completed over a nineteen-month period by the normally prolific composer, and there had to be a reason. He was not unduly burdened by his work at the school or by other outside commitments and would have had ample time to do more composing, yet chose not to. The fact that he resumed composing in earnest immediately after the war ended in August 1945 provides strong evidence that his reduced creative activity was the direct result of personal concerns brought on by the conflict. German cities were being bombed relentlessly by the Allies during 1944 and the Hindemiths could only agonize over the fate of their families (including their mothers) and friends, since there was no communication possible.[15] It was a constant worry, and the composer would have found it extremely difficult to free his mind of these concerns long enough for any sustained period of writing.

The single significant work Hindemith completed was the ballet *Herodiäde*, commissioned by the Elizabeth Sprague Coolidge Foundation for the distinguished dancer Martha Graham. It was subtitled "An Orchestral Recitation of a Poem by Stéphane Mallarmé" and scored for small chamber orchestra. The work was written in New Haven during the first two weeks in June 1944 and premiered in Washington, D.C., on 30 November 1944 with Miss Graham in the title role. It was not published until 1955 and then only in a piano reduction. The orchestral score and parts are available on rental only.

The orchestra recites the poem, a colloquy between Herodiäde and her nurse, by means of a single melodic line ranging from the lowest to the highest registers of the orchestra and fitted exactly to every syllable of the French text. In later performances of the ballet, narrators were sometimes used to declaim the text, a practice that riled Hindemith considerably. When he learned of a 1955 New York production where this was done, he sent a sharp note to AMP: "The piece is *not* made for declamation since the declamation is given to the orchestral instruments and any additional speaking is a superfluous doubling. (I always thought any ass would know that.) AMP should rent the material only if the text is not to be spoken. Naturally, the text can be sold."[16] *Herodiäde* poses perplexing choreographical problems and thus is not often done as a ballet, but the orchestral score is frequently performed as a concert piece.

Their August 1945 vacation in Maine was a particularly happy one for the Hindemiths. Their major worries about family and friends in Germany were finally over and they could fully relax for the first time in many months. Hindemith began immediately to write a piano concerto that had been commissioned by his colleague and friend Jesús Maria Sanroma, and completed the first movement in Maine and the other two in New Haven by 29 November. The three-movement *Concerto for Piano and Orchestra* was premiered 27 February 1947, when it was played by Sanroma in Cleveland with the Cleveland Symphony under George Szell. The composer made a two-piano arrangement of the concerto during the summer of 1946, the only version of the work to be printed. (The score and parts are available on rental.)

Hindemith began writing his *Sixth String Quartet* in December 1944, wrote two more movements during the spring of 1945, and added a fourth and final movement in December 1945. This is a brief work of only fifteen minutes' duration, uniquely constructed with a purposely simplified cello part in the first three movements. These were especially written for a string quartet that was comprised of two gifted young violinists studying at the school, Blanche Raisin and Jean F. Harris, Hindemith as violist, and Gertrude as cellist, whose limited skills on the instrument had to be accommodated. The two violinists were graduated in June and Hindemith did nothing more with the piece. Late in the fall of 1945 he apparently decided that the first three movements were of sufficient musical interest to warrant publication and added a fourth. It was completed on 30 December and this time he did not restrict the cello part. Schott did not publish it until 1948, but it enjoyed a prestigious premiere in Washington, D.C., on 21 March 1946, when it was performed by the Budapest String Quartet. Cellists playing this quartet must surely wonder why their part is patently so much less demanding than those of the other three players, but they can be assured the listener is not in the least aware of it.

The question is sometimes raised as to whether the music Hindemith wrote while living in the United States was in any way affected by his new environment. He answered this himself in a letter written to Willy Strecker early in 1947. His close friend had urged him to return to Germany, convinced his surroundings would thereby be more compatible for writing such a "German" work as the Kepler opera he had in mind to do. The composer rejected the argument, saying: "The Rhine is not any more important than the Mississippi, Connecticut Valley, or the Gobi Desert—it depends on what you know, not where you are."[17] He probably would not have written some of the things he did had they not been commissioned by U.S. institutions and individuals, yet their form and substance were in no way affected by the fact that he was living here, with one notable exception. This was his setting of Walt Whitman's *When Lilacs Last in the Dooryard Bloom'd* as an oratorio for baritone and mezzo-soprano soli, chorus, and full symphony orchestra, subtitled "A Requiem for Those We Love."

The *Lilacs Requiem* (its commonly used short title) is a distinctly "American" work in its concept and construction. Hindemith had been deeply saddened by the death of President Franklin D. Roosevelt in April 1945 and by the terrible casualties suffered by both sides in World War II. He greatly admired Walt Whitman's poetry and felt that this tribute to the memory of President Abraham Lincoln and the Civil War dead, with its eloquent plea for peace, brotherhood, and the reuniting of former enemies in a spirit of humanity and democracy, was an ideal text for the musical expression of his own reflections. Furthermore, he was immensely proud of having recently (11 January 1946) been sworn in as a U.S. citizen and wanted to manifest his gratitude in some tangible way.

The young and highly talented choral conductor Robert Shaw commissioned Hindemith to write a work for his Collegiate Chorale in December 1945 and the composer used this opportunity to create the oratorio. Writing began on 17 January 1946, was completed on 20 April, and the work was presented in New York's City Center on 14 May by the Collegiate Chorale with Shaw conducting and baritone George Burson and mezzo-soprano Mona Paulee as the soloists.[18] Many regard this profoundly moving work as one of the finest compositions of its kind yet written in this country for use on occasions of national mourning or similar commemorations. (After her husband's death in 1963, Gertrude Hindemith gave the complete original full score of the *Lilacs Requiem* to Yale University, enclosing this note: "It really belongs to New Haven and to our life on Alden Avenue with its fence of lilacs. . . . So, herewith I send the music back to the source from whence it came. May it radiate around old Yale through the spirit and love of the author.")[19]

In June of 1946, Hindemith and Gertrude drove their yellow Pontiac convertible to Mexico City, where Hindemith had accepted an engagement to conduct the National Symphony Orchestra of Mexico in a pair of concerts featuring his own compositions. Remaining in the country until September, he did no composing, but took time to make a two-piano arrangement of the piano concerto he had completed in 1945.

Before leaving for Mexico, Hindemith had accepted a commission from the Dallas Symphony Orchestra to write a large orchestral piece, agreeing to have it ready for a first performance on 1 February 1947. He planned to begin writing it as soon as he returned to New

Haven but his inordinately heavy teaching schedule made that impossible. The wave of returning veterans had crested and he found himself having to supervise the degree studies of twenty majors and to cope with some 100 students in his three advanced theory courses. Work on the Dallas score finally began in the middle of November and it was completed on 30 December. Time was now running out and he was obliged to enlist the help of some of his students in copying parts over the Christmas vacation.

This was the *Symphonia Serena,* whose relaxed and pleasing sounds totally belie the rather frantic circumstances surrounding its creation. The score and parts reached Dallas with only three weeks to spare, but the first performance took place on the scheduled date, conducted by Antal Dorati, and was a critical success. Hindemith dropped his plan to attend when he became annoyed by the preconcert publicity emanating from Dallas. In his opinion, undue attention was being paid to the conductor and orchestra at the expense of the composition and composer and he resented "being relegated to a secondary role."[20]

Along with the many offers of important positions Hindemith received from Germany after the war ended, all of which he happily refused, there also came many invitations to guest conduct leading orchestras in other European countries, all of which interested him very much indeed, and a concert tour was arranged for the summer of 1947. Since several important engagements had to be scheduled in April and May, he was given permission to arrange his teaching so he could leave before the second term ended. However, before embarking for Genoa on 2 April he still had another commissioned work to write.

A Symposium on Music Criticism was being sponsored by Harvard University during the first three days in May and Hindemith was asked to write a work to be performed by Robert Shaw's Collegiate Chorale at a special concert on the second day. He selected a medieval Latin poem describing the Last Judgment, *Apparebit repentina dies,* and set it for mixed chorus and ten brass instruments. Work on it was begun as soon as the *Symphonia Serena* was on its belated way to Dallas, and the piece was ready by 21 February. This powerful and difficult composition was given a brilliant first performance in Harvard's Memorial Church on 2 May 1947 by the Collegiate Chorale and ten Boston Symphony players, with Robert Shaw conducting.

The European visit in the summer of 1947 was the Hindemiths' first since emigrating to the U.S. in 1940 and they were there for over five months, returning to New Haven in late September. The composer met a heavy schedule of conducting engagements in Italy, Austria, Switzerland, Holland, Belgium, and England, but time was also reserved for a six-week Swiss holiday in July and August, during which he wrote most of the *Concerto for Clarinet and Orchestra*. The work was completed on 20 September, four days after returning home.

The concerto was commissioned by Benny Goodman, who had actually approached Hindemith through an intermediary in January 1941 about writing one. The composer agreed and the "King of Swing" was delighted, but further negotiations ended abruptly after Germany invaded Russia in the summer of 1941. The intermediary was Eric Simon, a Viennese clarinetist and conductor who had fled to the United States recently and was then coaching Goodman on the playing of classical clarinet music. Simon gave his correspondence with the composer to the Hindemith Institute in 1970 and included this note: "The true story is that after Germany invaded Russia in the summer of 1941, Benny did not want to have anything to do with anything German, in spite of Hindemith's complete integrity."

Goodman revived the project in 1947 and negotiations for a commission were finally completed. Hindemith sent this progress report to Hugo Strecker, Willy Strecker's son and manager of Schott's London office, in December: "Benny Goodman is studying his part for the clarinet concerto and is only waiting to let loose. I originally wanted to do the first performance with him here in New Haven, where I am conducting the New Haven Symphony Orchestra on January 12 [1948], but that did not work out."[21] Much to Hindemith's annoyance, Goodman waited three years to "let loose," not performing the concerto until early in December 1950, in Philadelphia with the Philadelphia Orchestra under Eugene Ormandy. It was not done on one of the regular subscription concerts but on a so-called "Student Concert," further irking the composer. Under the terms of the commission, Goodman had exclusive performance rights to the concerto for three years and just made it under the wire. The primary reason for the delay was that his renowned dance orchestra was so heavily booked all over the world there simply was no time for him to learn the work, much less perform it. A story was circulated that Goodman did not really like the piece and waited as long as possible before playing it; however Professor Keith Wilson of Yale, who coached Goodman a bit for the premiere, reported that Benny thought highly of the work and enjoyed playing it.

Hindemith was prevented by illness from attending the premiere, but Gertrude stopped off in Philadelphia on her way to New Haven from Washington, D.C., long enough to hear the final dress rehearsal of the concerto. She described her experience to Willy Strecker in a letter written a few days later:

> Benny Goodman played marvelously and with flawless technique, but his tone is almost too smooth. The musicians applauded vigorously and it is said he was very successful at the concert that evening. Unfortunately, he seemed to be rather academic, and I was astonished to detect a certain dryness in his playing. It might be that he did not feel 100% at ease with such a difficult work, but undoubtedly will after repeat performances.
>
> Unfortunately and incomprehensibly it was done at a "Student Concert" and not well advertised. I do not know who made this clever arrangement for a world premiere. Eugene Ormandy seemed very enthusiastic and asked for more world premieres and first performances, but he has not scheduled the piece for any of his regular concerts in Philadelphia or New York. We are shaking our heads in disbelief. Naturally, I am very enthusiastic about the concerto.[22]

Two years later, Ormandy again asked Hindemith for a new work he could premiere and received this curt note from Gertrude: "My husband was rather disappointed with the treatment you gave the clarinet concerto which, in his opinion, is worth more than just a "First American" performance at an afternoon youth concert."[23] Ormandy had his secretary send Gertrude this equally curt reply: "Ormandy would like you to know that Benny Goodman was engaged for a very important *evening* concert for students, where other important works are always being played, and that it was Mr. Goodman who offered the premiere for this concert, realizing the importance of the event. May I have your reply to this letter as soon as possible so I can forward it to Mr. Ormandy."[24] Gertrude's reply, if indeed she ever wrote one, is lost. (The holograph score of the concerto is now at Yale University.)

Relations between the Hindemiths and Benny Goodman remained very cordial over the years. In 1959, for example, Goodman was appearing in Vienna with his orchestra and happened to note that Hindemith was also in the city to conduct a concert. Gertrude reported, "Benny phoned us all of a sudden" and the three enjoyed a pleasant dinner evening in one of Vienna's historic restaurants.

Hindemith's classes in the fall of 1947 were again filled to capacity and demanded his full attention. He had been commissioned by Gregor Piatigorsky to write a cello-piano sonata but could not begin work on it until late in January 1948. Piatigorsky had hoped to play the sonata on a New York recital in March, but the composer decided to redo the final movement at the last minute and the premiere had to be postponed. The highly regarded 1948 *Sonata for Violoncello and Piano* was premiered by Piatigorsky at Tanglewood in the summer of 1948 and published by Schott the same year.

Late that spring, Hindemith rescored seven pieces from *Livre de dancerie* by Claude Gervaise and Estienne du Tertre, published by Pierre d'Attaignant between 1547 and 1557, enlarging the instrumentation from an ensemble of three violas and two celli to full chamber orchestra. He conducted them later in some of his European and South American concerts and they were so well received that Schott published them in 1958 as a *Suite of French Dances*.

The year 1948 was also marked by the long-delayed publication of Hindemith's completely revised version of *Das Marienleben*, the lengthy (sixty minutes) song cycle on texts by Rainer Maria Rilke he had written twenty-five years earlier. He had begun the revision in 1936, intending to have it published along with his *Unterweisung im Tonsatz* as a demonstration of how the theoretical principles outlined in the book might be applied. This plan was abandoned when it became apparent the revision would require too much time. He worked on it intermittently over the next few years and in September 1941 reported to Willy Strecker that the revision had been completed. He proposed to AMP that a facsimile edition be printed, insisting that the song texts should be in English as well as German. When no satisfactory translator had been found by November 1942 and with the war worsening, publication was postponed indefinitely. Meanwhile, further revisions were made. Shortly after V-E Day in the spring of 1945, Hindemith recommended to AMP that a facsimile edition be issued, printed on rag paper and elegantly bound, to be sold at a high price to "collectors." Heavy work at the school in the fall precluded his making a copy of the score and he withdrew his suggestion, agreeing to a regular engraved edition. However, no engravers were available and publication was again delayed.

Developments in the protracted saga of *Das Marienleben II* now took an astonishing turn. The composer wrote a very long letter to Willy Strecker from Mexico City in July 1946 wherein he poured out a stream of bitter complaints about his erstwhile fellow countrymen in Germany, who had been sending him "hundreds of letters" since the war ended. He was highly resentful of their total lack of remorse for Germany's actions, their self-righteous attitudes, their harsh demands for financial aid and help in getting to the United States, their insinuations that he was obligated to return and restore musical order in the country, and much more of the same. Consequently, he had decided that *Das Marienleben II* should not be published in Germany until it had been released in the United States, as a mark of his disdain.

Publication plans remained stalled in the United States and Hindemith eventually got over his pique. He authorized Schott in June 1948 to proceed with the publication. In July, he wrote the extended foreword, giving a detailed explanation of why and how he had revised the work and sent it off to Mainz. *Das Marienleben II* was published about three months later in an engraved and exclusively German edition, with no English translation of either the song texts or the foreword. The world premiere followed shortly in Hannover, Germany, where on 3 November 1948 it was performed by Annaliese Kupper and Carl Seemann. The first U.S. performance was given by Jennie Tourel and Erich Itor Kahn at a New Friends of Music concert in New York's Town Hall on 23 January 1949.

Hindemith returned to Europe for the second time while on sabbatical leave during the first term of 1948–49, staying an additional two months at the request of the U.S. Military Government of Germany. He and Gertrude sailed from New York early in August and did not return until late in March 1949. Conducting engagements in England, Germany, and Italy kept him fully occupied until mid-November, when they took a brief holiday in Taormina, Sicily. While there he wrote the first four movements of his five-movement *Septet for Wind Instruments,* the first composing he had been able to do since completing the Piatigorsky cello sonata in March. It was completed in Rome on 7 December and first performed in Milan on 30 December, played by members of the Teatro Nuovo Orchestra.

Lecture engagements in Germany under the aegis of the U.S. Military Government claimed most of Hindemith's time during January and February, but the first three weeks in March were free and the Hindemiths used them for a vacation in Switzerland before sailing from Cherbourg for New York on 25 March 1949. Again the composer took advantage of the break to do some writing and completed a *Concerto for Horn and Orchestra*. He had recently conducted the Mozart horn concerto with Dennis Brain as the soloist and had been so impressed by the extraordinary artistry of the young Englishman that he decided to write this work for him. To make certain he would conduct the first performance with Brain as the soloist Hindemith wrote to Strecker: "I think the horn concerto should be reserved for me during the next year. This means I will not have to give up any of my trump cards and, furthermore, 99% of all the conductors seem to have lost so much of their good sense that it is best if someone shows them first how it should be performed."[25]

The concerto was premiered in Baden-Baden on 8 June 1950, played by the Southwest [Germany] Radio Orchestra with Dennis Brain as the soloist and Hindemith conducting. It was a great success and the composer was delighted, presenting Brain with a copy of the printed score, inscribed "To the unsurpassed original performer of this piece from a grateful composer." The original manuscript of the score is now at Yale University.

In the spring of 1948 Professor Otto Luening, composer and member of the music faculty at Columbia University, offered Hindemith a commission to write an orchestral work to be premiered at the school's Fifth Annual Festival of Contemporary American Music in May 1949.[26] It is noteworthy that Hindemith was now being recognized publicly as an American composer and he was more than pleased to accept. The two men, who had known each other for several years, enjoyed a lively discussion about the state of contemporary music and agreed there was a need for orchestral scores "of greater transparency and less bombast." The composer kept this in mind in carrying out the Columbia commission. The work he would eventually write was the thirteen-minute *Concerto for Woodwinds, Harp, and Orchestra,* scored for solo flute, oboe, clarinet, bassoon, and harp, and a chamber orchestra of two horns, two trumpets, trombone, and strings. Having been advised by Luening that his piece would be played by the CBS Symphony, a superb ensemble comprised of the finest instrumentalists in New York, he took advantage of the opportunity to write a virtuoso work displaying their abilities.[27]

Hindemith did not write a note of the concerto until he returned home from his European visit almost a year later, and only six weeks before the work was scheduled for performance. Meanwhile, Columbia officials had received no word from him and were understandably anxious. He stopped to see Luening in New York the day after landing there and assured him the piece would be ready in time. It was completed on April 29, leaving only sixteen days for the orchestra to rehearse the work. This fact did not concern Hindemith, for he was confident the CBS players could cope, and they did.

The concerto was premiered at the final concert of the festival, given in Columbia University's McMillin Academic Theater on the afternoon of 15 May 1949 and conducted by Thor Johnson, then director of the Cincinnati Symphony. Hindemith had been given the option of having his piece played on any day of the festival and chose 15 May, the twenty-fifth anniversary of his marriage to Gertrude. Obviously intending from the beginning to commemorate the day in the music, Hindemith did so by the remarkable feat of quoting the entire melodic line, including repeats, of the *Wedding March* from Mendelssohn's incidental music to *A Midsummer Night's Dream* from beginning to end in the final movement. It is played throughout by the solo clarinet while the other instruments go their own way totally oblivious of the clarinet's loud and relentless blowing of nothing but the tune of the wedding march. The audience was momentarily stunned, since there was no explanation in the program, but then sat back and thoroughly enjoyed the ingenious and hilarious musical joke. It was not until after the concert that the composer divulged his reason for having done this. He had also contrived to keep it a secret from Gertrude, who was both touched and highly amused. The Hindemiths celebrated their anniversary alone that evening by having a merry time at a German restaurant in Manhattan's Yorkville district.

In the spring of 1948, Hindemith was also asked by the Connecticut Academy of Arts and Sciences to write an unspecified work to be performed at the celebration of its 150th anniversary in the fall of 1949. A member of the academy, Hindemith agreed, saying he might write a string quartet and arrange to have the Budapest String Quartet play it. He sailed for Europe and gave no further thought to the project until returning to New Haven in April 1949. His plan for doing a string quartet had been dropped somewhere along the way and he now considered writing a sonata for bass clarinet and piano, provided his faculty colleague Keith Wilson would agree to perform it. Wilson, a distinguished professional clarinetist, demurred, saying he was not proficient enough on the instrument for such an assignment. The composer then asked Wilson if trumpeter Robert Montesi and bassoonist William Skelton, advanced students at the School of Music whose outstanding performance abilities were known to Hindemith, would be returning in the fall. Learning they would be, he decided to write a two-movement *Concerto for Trumpet, Bassoon, and String Orchestra.* Most of it was written on the last two days of September and it was played at the academy's anniversary celebration on 4 November 1949. The soloists were Montesi and Skelton, the string orchestra was comprised of School of Music students, and Keith Wilson conducted. The event took place in the Yale Art Gallery auditorium before an audience of about 300 invited guests, including representatives from thirty learned societies here and abroad.[28]

(Three years later a brief scherzo written in New Haven was added as a third movement, and in 1954 the three-movement version was issued by Schott in a reduction for trumpet, bassoon, and piano. Although this has made it convenient as a teaching piece for trumpet and bassoon, its widespread use has led, unfortunately, to frequent performances by only the two soloists with piano. These are totally unsatisfactory in conveying the real musical value of the work, for the piano cannot possibly reproduce the subtleties of the string scoring.)

Professor Marshall Bartholomew, then director of the Yale Glee Club, had been urging Hindemith to write a male chorus for his group ever since the composer came to Yale in 1940, but without success. The club was to make a concert tour of Europe in the summer of 1949 and Bartholomew tried once again, for he was anxious to have a work by Hindemith on the program. The idea of having a work of his sung in Europe by one of the more famous U.S. choral groups apparently appealed to Hindemith as further evidence of how close his ties with this country had become, and he agreed to write a piece. Bartholomew recorded the following in his personal diary:

April 29, 1949. Paul Hindemith telephoned me and asked me to come to his home and pick up a ballad for men's voices he had written for the Yale Glee Club. He had made a sketch during the train ride from New York to New Haven [the ride takes ninety minutes] and written the score at home and presented it to me ready for performance and publication—all done within 24 hours. He had chosen the text from a book of poems he had purchased in a bookstore near the Grand Central Railroad Station in New York. It was entitled *The Demon of the Gibbet,* written by Fitz-James O'Brien.[29]

The Demon of the Gibbet, a short piece of only three minutes' duration, was published by Schott-London in 1950 and later by Schott-Mainz under the title *Galgentritt,* with a German translation by Hindemith. Though the glee club did sing it on tour in 1949, the work has not found an enduring place in the male chorus repertory largely because of some ungrateful vocal scoring in the lower voices.

There are several entries in the composer's 1949 pocket diary during June and early July indicating that he was devoting much of his time to the third volume of *The Craft.* He recorded on 14 July that "chapter 20 of *Part III* is finished," which meant the entire volume was then complete. However *Exercises in Three-Part Writing,* begun so confidently in August 1940 and continued as a major classroom project during his earlier years at Yale, eventually began to raise more questions than answers and Hindemith was never entirely satisfied with it. He deferred its publication in 1949, planning to reorganize the entire series, but he never found time to finish the project before his death. Mrs. Hindemith released the 1949 manuscript of *Part III* for publication and it was issued in 1971 by the Atlantis-Verlag of Zürich.

The Hindemiths left in their own car on 20 July for Colorado Springs, Colorado, where the composer spent the first week in August as a visiting lecturer and conductor at Colorado College. Following this, they enjoyed a two-week holiday in Taos, New Mexico, where on 17 and 18 August Hindemith wrote a *Sonata for Double Bass and Piano.* No positive answers are available to the question as to why he created this particular piece now, when he was still obligated to do a work for the Connecticut Academy, prepare six important public lectures to be delivered at Harvard, and compose an orchestral piece for the Louisville Symphony Orchestra. There is a hint in a letter written to his friend Willy Strecker in October assuring him he would send "the sonata" as soon as he had it checked by a professional bassist in New York. This would suggest that Schott had asked him to write the sonata. The company rushed it into print early in 1950 and it was premiered in Vienna on 20 April that year.

"It was terribly hard work from start to finish, but everything turned out all right," wrote Hindemith to Willy Strecker late in 1949. He was referring to the preparation of the six Charles Eliot Norton Lectures he had delivered at Harvard University during October and November. It had been a far more formidable task than he had anticipated, demanding an inordinate amount of his time and energy, but he could be pleased with their enthusiastic reception by capacity audiences. He called the series "Stability and Inflation in Musical Values," delivered as six weekly evening lectures under the titles "Boethian and Augustinian Trends in Music," "Scientia bene modulandi," "Building Materials and Tools," "Performers and Listeners," "Problems of Education," and "Conquest and Subjugation of Style." They were extensively revised and expanded in writing his *A Composer's World: Horizons and Limitations,* published by the Harvard University Press in 1952 as *The Charles Eliot Norton Lectures, 1949–50.* (This title is not factually accurate, for the book contains eleven chapters, none of which corresponds precisely to any of the six lectures, although all of their substance is incorporated.)

Writing the book proved to be more difficult than writing the lectures. Hindemith told the author one day as he began working on it that it was necessary for him to rewrite everything in German to make absolutely certain he was saying precisely what he wanted to say and then translate it into English. Other commitments precluded his doing any sustained work on it until the fall of 1950, when he refused all outside engagements and concentrated on the book. It went slowly at first because he was concerned about his English, as Gertrude reported to Willy Strecker in November:

> The book is now going much better since the Harvard University Press editor was here the other day. Arthur Mendel had been so critical of Paul's English he even suggested that Paul should write it in German and that he (Mendel) would translate it into English. The Harvard man came, read some of it, and was most enthusiastic about Paul's "personal style" and the special "flavor." He will make only a few small changes but wants to leave most of it as it is because he finds the natural style so convincing. I, too, find that Paul's style is very punchy and sharp, but naturally I cannot be certain since it is a foreign language. In any case, we were inclined to accept Mendel's judgment, since he knows English perfectly. We were all the more pleased when the Harvard editor expressed

himself so enthusiastically. Since then the book has been moving ahead full steam.[30]

Gertrude sent a progress report to Strecker six weeks later: "The Harvard book is going well. We [Gertrude was doing the typing] have been writing it out in the desired format with noteworthy speed. I will be glad when you have a chance to read it, for I am sure you will be astonished. Every page is full of marvelous ideas and very well expressed. Seven chapters have already been sent to the editor, with only four more to go."[31] Work on the book had to be interrupted frequently during the spring of 1951 because of other obligations and it was not until 15 July that Hindemith could record in his pocket diary, "Harvard book finally finished." It was published the following year.

In 1956, Hindemith's lawyer, Oscar Cox, suggested the possibility of having the Harvard book published by another company in a paperback edition, as had been done with Stravinsky's Charles Eliot Norton Lectures. This prompted Hindemith to reply:

I have not heard from the Harvard Press people recently, but as the book still sells rather regularly—annual royalties being rather stable at $100—they might still want to keep it for themselves. I remember they had printed 5,000 copies, which except for a few hundred seem to have been sold. To cover this year's sales they probably made a reprint, and this, too, may be an obstacle to the transfer of the book. In general, I would think there is not much demand for a book of this kind that a paperback edition would be necessary. With Stravinsky, the case is different. He is more agreeable anyway, and if he offends people it is only the composers and other musicians, while grouchy old Hindemith cannot keep his mouth shut and offends almost everyone on earth.[32]

(A paperback edition was published by Doubleday Anchor Books, New York, in 1961 and a reprint edition was issued in 1969 by Peter Smith Publications, Gloucester, Massachusetts. Hindemith translated the book into German in 1959, making further revisions and additions. This was published the same year by Atlantis-Verlag of Zürich under the title *Komponist in seiner Welt: Weiten und Grenzen.*)

In the summer of 1949 Hindemith accepted a commission from the Louisville Symphony Orchestra for a composition to be premiered on 1 March 1950. It was not until 10 December, after the six Harvard lectures, that serious work on the piece could begin. The four-movement *Sinfonietta in E* was completed on 19 January 1950, all of it written in New Haven. The first performance was in Louisville, Kentucky, on 1 March 1950, with the composer conducting.

Hindemith's obligations as the Norton lecturer at Harvard were over by 2 April 1950 and two weeks later the Hindemiths sailed for Europe, where they would stay until returning to New Haven late in September. There were many concert engagements but they also reserved time for an August holiday in their favorite Swiss canton of Valais. While there Hindemith wrote an address he had been invited to give at the Bach Festival in Hamburg on 12 September. This was his *Johann Sebastian Bach: ein verpflichtendes Erbe.* The Schott firm had a limited edition published by the Eggebrecht-Presse of Mainz for distribution to its friends and patrons at Christmas in 1950, and a regular trade edition was issued by Insel-Verlag in 1953. Hindemith made an English translation that was published by the Yale University Press in 1952 under the title *Johann Sebastian Bach: Heritage and Obligation.*

Hindemith resumed his full teaching schedule at Yale in the fall of 1950 and was obliged to devote all of his free time to preparing *A Composer's World* for publication by Harvard. It was not until mid-January 1951 that he was able to get back to writing music again, one year after completing the Louisville Symphony commission. A representative of the U.S. Army Band in Washington, D.C., called on Hindemith at his New Haven home late in 1950 and invited him to be a guest conductor at one of their concerts scheduled for February. He agreed to come but suggested that if his appearance could be arranged for a later date, "I just might write a little something." It could be and he did. The new date was 5 April and the "little something" was no less than the monumental *Symphony in B♭ for Concert Band,* which he completed by 19 March. Hindemith conducted the first performance, played by the U.S. Army Band in the Departmental Auditorium, Washington, D.C. The composer gave the original manuscript of the score to the U.S. Army Band archives, inscribed "To Captain Hugh B. Curry [director of the band] after a very pleasant time with the Band and with many thanks."[33]

Hindemith had served in a German Army band during World War I and echoes of that experience are frequently heard in his music in the form of marches, march rhythms, and march parodies. He wrote a major work for band in 1926, his *Concert Music for Wind*

Orchestra, Opus 41, but that was scored for the standard middle-European military band instrumentation. Writing for a U.S. concert band was a different matter and he consulted his Yale colleague Keith Wilson, then director of the Yale University Band, for advice on the scoring. The resulting *Symphony in B♭ for Concert Band* gained instant recognition as a masterpiece of its genre and is regarded today as one of the few truly great works in concert band literature.

The Hindemiths lived in Zürich from August 1951 until returning to New Haven in September 1952. The composer taught classes in music theory at the University of Zürich, had many conducting engagements throughout Europe, and took time to complete two major compositional projects, preparing the *Symphony: Die Harmonie der Welt* and revising his 1926 opera *Cardillac.* The symphony was done on a commission from Paul Sacher, founder and conductor of the Basel Chamber Orchestra, for a concert commemorating the twenty-fifth anniversary of the ensemble. The composer used the opportunity to provide a sampler of the music he was beginning to write for his opera *Die Harmonie der Welt* in the form of a three-movement work that he described in the program notes as being "concert arrangements of pieces from the opera." It was premiered by the Basel Chamber Orchestra in Basel on 25 January 1952 with Paul Sacher conducting. The first U.S. performance was given by the Minneapolis Symphony Orchestra in Minneapolis on 13 March 1953, conducted by the composer.

Hindemith attended a performance of his 1926 opera *Cardillac* in Venice while on leave from Yale in 1948 and was disturbed. He had not seen the opera for many years and he now found the moral implications of the story indefensible and decided it must be completely revised. Work on the revision began immediately, for the Zürich opera had agreed to produce it in 1949. However, the offer was shortly withdrawn because of internal problems at the theater and the project was set aside. A firm offer by Zürich to stage the new *Cardillac* in June 1952 sent the composer back to work and he devoted most of his free time in the fall of 1951 and spring of 1952 to rewriting much of the libretto and making significant changes in the dramatic action. The result was, in fact, virtually a new opera. The first performance was given in Zürich on 20 June 1952, and critics and scholars have not agreed to this day on the relative merits of the two versions. Hindemith initially refused to permit further performances of *Cardillac I,* but later relented, suggesting the possibility that he had come to look on it as less flawed than he once thought.

Hindemith wrote only two compositions during his final year at Yale: an eight-minute *Sonata for Four Horns,* and *Canticle to Hope,* which would eventually become *Part 3* of *Ite, angeli veloces.* The horn quartet was completed on 29 October 1952 and the composer described the work in a letter to Willy Strecker:

> You will soon be receiving a *Sonata for Four Horns.* Naturally, such a piece has no commercial value at all and you don't have to pay me anything for it. I simply want to have it published because it is a nice piece. A contract can be drawn up later, but only for royalties, with no advance payment. Please do not offer any special first performance rights, for anyone can perform it if he is interested. I wrote it for the Salzburg Horn Ensemble, who serenaded me early one morning in the railroad station while I was still in the sleeping car.[34]

Schott published the work immediately and it was premiered in Vienna in June 1953 by members of the Vienna Symphony.

Hindemith was asked in 1952 by the United Nations Educational, Social, and Cultural Organization (UNESCO) to write a choral and orchestral work to be performed at a world conference in Brussels in July 1953. The theme of the meeting was to be "The Role of Music in the Development of Youths and Adults" and the composer agreed without hesitation. He requested UNESCO to have a leading European poet provide a text that would permit audience participation, and the venerable and renowned French author Paul Claudel was approached. Claudel was initially reluctant, not being wholly in sympathy with the objectives of the United Nations, but he finally agreed and on 6 March 1953 sent Hindemith a poetic paraphrase of the eighteenth chapter of Isaiah that he called *Canticle to Hope.* The composer was disturbed to learn from Claudel that this was only the last of three parts of the complete text, for time was running out. He expressed his concern to the poet, who replied that the three parts were not related and could be treated independently. Hindemith could then proceed immediately to set the *Canticle to Hope* to music, and the piano-vocal score was ready by early May. Preparations for leaving New Haven permanently in June prevented further work on the music until they were on the ship sailing from New

York to Le Havre between 3 and 9 June. The full score was finally completed by 19 June, only three weeks before it was to be performed.

The *Canticle to Hope* was written for mezzo-soprano solo, mixed chorus, orchestra, band, and audience. It was premiered in the Brussels Palace of Fine Arts on 9 July 1953, with Hindemith conducting the huge ensemble comprised of instrumentalists from the "Orchestre international des jeunesse musicales" and a massed chorus made up of groups from several countries attending the conference. The first and second parts were written in 1955 and the complete triptych, now called *Ite, angeli veloces,* was premiered in Wupperthal, Germany, under Hindemith's direction on 9 June 1955. *Canticle to Hope* was the last composition Hindemith wrote as a resident of the United States. However, several of the important compositions he wrote after moving to Switzerland had direct ties with this country and will be described later.

Chapter 11

Professional Activities

HINDEMITH TOOK his responsibilities at the Yale School of Music very seriously and did not accept any outside engagements that would interfere unduly with his work at the university, refusing many more invitations than he took. Most came from educational institutions asking him to give lectures, a fact that disturbed Gertrude, for she feared her husband was coming to be looked upon more as a "professor" than as a professional musician. However, Hindemith was not concerned, for he welcomed the opportunity in those years to promote his new theoretical ideas. There were relatively few conducting engagements and he would have been happy to accept more had they been offered. They were not, primarily because his ability as a conductor was not generally known in this country, and since he did not wish to engage the services of a concert agency, he could only sit back and wait. The lack of conducting engagements in the United States became a vexing problem for him after moving to Switzerland in 1953.[1]

There were few outside engagements during the war years, for obvious reasons, but their number increased substantially after the war ended in 1945. During his first year at Yale, 1940–41, Hindemith had only two: one at Wellesley College, where he conducted the College Orchestra in a performance of his *Five Pieces for String Orchestra* on 4 December 1940; the other in Boston, where he was the honored guest at the first performances of his new *Concerto for Violoncello and Orchestra* by Gregor Piatigorsky and the Boston Symphony under Koussevitzky on 7 and 8 February 1941. Hindemith was very pleased with the success of the concerto but highly outraged over the poor work AMP had done in preparing the performance materials, and he let Ernest Voigt have a piece of his mind:

> The cello concerto was a very great success. You will see in the Boston papers that it was thoroughly praised without exception.

Less pleasant (not to say impossible) is the matter of the performance materials. Koussevitzky could not use the smeared photocopy of the score, and it was really impossible to read the horrible mess by lamplight from a distance and in a hurry. So I had to give him my manuscript. We simply *must* have better copies for performance and I urgently advise you to see that this is done.

The situation was even worse with the copyist and proofreader. I refuse to have anything more to do with them. In the string parts, for example, there were on the average between 50 and 100 corrections that had been made by the proofreader and I found 15 to 20 more that he had missed. This is really scandalous and totally impossible. Not to mention the copyist, who should be thrashed with a wet rag for such sloppy writing. The situation is simply terrible and I cannot understand how anything like this is possible. It beats me how you could have worked so long with such rubbish. You have got to find a solution for the future.[2]

AMP evidently did "find a solution," for similar complaints do not appear in Hindemith's letters after this.

Hindemith's next invitation was to conduct his *Nobilissima Visione Suite* at a subscription concert of the New Haven Symphony Orchestra on 23 April 1941. Such invitations would be summarily refused in later years, for he resented being asked to conduct only his own music as an implication that he was incapable of interpreting the music of other composers.

That summer, the Hindemiths rented an attractive country house about ten miles from Lenox, Massachusetts, where they lived while the composer taught his classes at Tanglewood. (Gertrude drove him back and forth in the Packard they had recently purchased.) Hindemith greatly enjoyed teaching a new course he had designed, which he described in a letter to Willy Strecker:

I was very busy with a historical course in which about 150 people sang and played their way through music from the 12th through the 16th centuries. It had never been tried this way and was very successful, providing a highly valuable experience for all participants. There was a concert every Saturday for six weeks in which every group performed what they had learned during the week. The total program comprised about 200 pieces, most of them never before sung or played except at the time they were written. Everyone had a score and you can imagine the advance preparation that meant for me. We worked at it from March on and the total cost was only $60. How about hiring me to do the same for Schott?[3]

The success of this practical course in early music performance during the summer of 1941 was a significant factor in Hindemith's decision to inaugurate a similar program with his students at Yale, which evolved into the remarkable Collegium Musicum concerts described above. Koussevitzky implored Hindemith to remain on the Tanglewood faculty, but the composer refused. He told the author in the fall of 1941 that he had found the teaching conditions intolerable that summer. He was continually forced to move his classes from one room to another without advance notice, much to his and his students' inconvenience, and swore he would never put up with that kind of treatment again. As a matter of fact, he was no longer interested in the assignment, for he did not need the extra money and preferred to keep his summers free.

Hindemith's first public appearance "west of the Hudson" as a U.S. resident came in November 1941, when he attended the premiere of his *Symphony in E♭* in Minneapolis by the Minneapolis Symphony Orchestra under its brilliant conductor Dimitri Mitropoulos. The first performance of a new symphony by a world-famous composer who would be there in person was a cultural event the musical public and press of this progressive city did not take casually. The local newspapers covered it extensively prior to the concert on 21 November, and their music editors wrote long reviews lauding both the new symphony and its performance, accompanied by large newsphotos of the composer and conductor acknowledging an ovation. (Hindemith remembered this visit with special pleasure and was delighted when he was asked to return in 1953 to conduct an entire concert by the orchestra.)[4]

On his way back to New Haven Hindemith stopped over in Chicago to deliver a lecture at the University of Chicago on 4 December, speaking on the subject "Difficulties in Understanding Modern Music." This had been arranged so that he could also discuss with university officials an offer of a teaching position they had made to him. Hindemith told the author on his return home that although the Chicago salary would be much greater than what he was receiving at Yale he had not accepted the bid, feeling that the professional advantages he enjoyed living and working in New Haven were too important for him to give up. The University of Chicago offer was only one of many he received from U.S. schools during his first years as a resident, all of which he turned down. He was determined to remain in New Haven and teach at Yale and was not interested in any offer to go elsewhere, no matter how tempting it might be. Attempts to lure him away eventually ceased when it became clear there was no way it could be done.

The only other outside professional engagement Hindemith accepted during the academic year 1941–42 was at the Hartt School of Music in Hartford, Connecticut, where he directed three stage performances of his twelve-minute musical skit *Hin und zurück* (1927) on 12, 13, and 14 May 1942.

(Hindemith was quite willing to attend certain performances of his music—such as premieres or other especially significant occasions—but he disliked intensely being trotted out on stage after a routine performance of one of his well-known compositions simply to pamper the conductor's ego. However, he agreed to accept Eugene Ormandy's invitation to do just that and attended a Philadelphia Orchestra concert on 12 November 1942 that included his *Symphony: Mathis der Maler,* for he had high regard for the conductor and his orchestra and there was also the possibility of working out an agreement for a commission. The consequences of this visit were described in the previous chapter.)

Striking evidence of the widespread interest Hindemith's theoretical writings were attracting within the higher musical circles in this country was the invitation he received from the New York chapter of the American Musicological Society to give a lecture on "Music Theories" at their meeting on 24 May 1943. Furthermore, he was asked to write an article on the same subject for the leading musical journal in the United States, the *Musical Quarterly,* which published the article in its issue of June 1944.

Hindemith made only three outside public appearances during the 1943–44 school year, but all were of special importance since they were associated with world premieres of compositions he had recently completed. Details of these engagements were given in the previous chapter, thus only a brief summary is needed here. He was in Philadelphia on 29 October 1943 for the premiere of *Cupid and Psyche* by the Philadelphia Orchestra under Eugene Ormandy, in New York on 20 January 1944 for the premiere of *Symphonic Metamorphosis of Themes by Carl Maria von Weber* by the New York Philharmonic under Artur Rodzinski, and in Chicago on 15 February 1944 for the premiere of *Ludus tonalis* by Willard MacGregor at the University of Chicago and also to give a lecture there the day before.

Paul Hindemith had been living in this country for only four years by 1944 but had already compiled a remarkable record of success, far more impressive than any of the other notable composers who had come here in the 1930s had been able to achieve. World premieres of important compositions written since his arrival had been given by the Boston Symphony, New York Philharmonic, Philadelphia Orchestra, and the Minneapolis Symphony, and many other orchestras were featuring performances of his music, with all of these events receiving ample attention from the U.S. news media. He had become firmly established at a major U.S. university as one of its most distinguished teachers, and his work as a scholar had been given public recognition by the leading musicologists of New York. These achievements hardly endeared him to the displaced composers who had preceded him here and some among them, not a little envious, were heard to grumble that Hindemith was more interested in commercial than artistic success. The composer, much amused by these inane charges, continued as before to achieve both.

With the war careening to its climax, the 1944–45 school year was one of marking time for most institutions and organizations in this country. Hindemith made only one public appearance outside the university, playing one of the two solo viola d'amore parts in a performance of J. S. Bach's *Passion According to St. John* by the Cantata Singers in All Souls Church in New York City on 25 April 1945. He was invited to do so by the conductor of the ensemble, Arthur Mendel, his good friend and collaborator from AMP, and was pleased to accept on one condition: he insisted that no special attention be paid to his presence as one of the instrumentalists. Hindemith greatly admired this masterpiece by his favorite composer and thoroughly enjoyed the experience, rare for him, to take part in its performance simply as one of the players.

Musical activities resumed their normal pace in the first postwar academic year of 1945–46 and Hindemith accepted eight outside engagements during its course. The first was as a conductor at a memorable "Festival of Three Concerts of Music by Paul Hindemith Celebrating the Composer's Fiftieth Birthday" held at the Juilliard School of Music in New York on 23–24 November 1945, presented by the school in collaboration with AMP. When Hindemith first learned from his friend Karl Bauer at AMP that such an event was being planned, he replied:

I find there is hardly anything meritorious in sliding slowly over the 50th birthday into gray old age. Many have already done it before and it is entirely lacking in originality. Furthermore, such celebrations are always held as a pitiful reminder to youth and as an occasion for the elderly to make satisfactory amends—"Just wait, old friend, soon you will be as rickety as me."

Would it not be more sensible and in keeping with the basic principle of "the less said the better" to take care of the whole thing with a private lunch and in general proceed as though nothing is happening, which is the truth.

It is very touching that you all want to go to all this effort and expense. I still remember the Town Hall concert we gave six years ago: the performances were very good and the moderate-sized audience was moderately pleased. All that was forgotten the next day when AMP and Schott had to put out $2,000 to cover the deficit. . . . If you and the others are going to persist in spite of my thoughts about it, then I must insist you make the whole thing as short and painless as possible. . . . I think that four concerts are too many. New York has only 8,000,000 inhabitants, and the number of concertgoers to fill the hall four times could only be distilled from a territory the size of Texas with a population density equal to the entire eastern United States."[5]

The composer's insistence on having only three concerts was heeded and he cooperated fully in planning the programs. There was no need for him to fret about covering the costs or filling the hall, for the festival was fully subsidized by Juilliard and AMP and the capacity audiences were comprised of invited guests.

The first concert, given on Friday evening, 23 November, included the *Sonata for Two Pianos,* played by Bruce and Rosalind Simonds, *Die junge Magd,* sung by Enid Szantho, *Sonata in C for Violin and Piano,* performed by Isaac Stern and Abraham Zakin, and the *Fifth String Quartet,* played by the Budapest String Quartet. The second concert, given the following afternoon, featured the *Ludus tonalis,* played by Bruce Simonds. It was preceded by the *Sonata for Trombone and Piano,* performed by Davis Shuman and Vivian Rivkind. The final concert, given that evening, offered choral and instrumental music, all conducted by the composer: *Herodiäde* (its first performance as a concert piece), *Five Songs on Old Texts,* and *The Four Temperaments,* with Jane Carlson as the solo pianist.

The birthday celebration continued in Detroit, where on 8 December Hindemith conducted the Detroit Symphony in a performance of his *Symphony: Mathis der Maler,* and in Chicago on 15 December, where an all-Hindemith concert was given in Orchestra Hall, with the composer conducting. An ad hoc ensemble of leading professional musicians from the city performed *Herodiäde, The Four Temperaments, Die junge Magd,* and the *Nobilissima Visione Suite. Time* magazine took note of this special event with an article describing the music as "shockingly pleasant" and not as "atonal" as was feared it might be. The article also included this report of a press conference with the composer:

> Today, at 50, he is a solid citizen of New Haven, Connecticut. "It's close to New York, if you need New York. I don't need New York." He teaches composition and theory at Yale University 16 hours a week. The rest of the time he works on composing. "Real composers get their ideas from heaven, but they never come to me that way," he said. When someone suggested he become a conductor, he laughed. "All my life I've tried to be an honest musician, and now you want me to become a conductor. Anybody can conduct—well, almost anybody."[6]

Hindemith disdained press interviews and could not resist making flip and often facetious replies to what he considered to be stupid questions asked by reporters. They would occasionally backfire, but he was not in the least concerned.

The composer's fiftieth birthday fell on 16 November 1945 and he received hundreds of letters and cards from all over the world wishing him well. To express his appreciation he wrote a brief four-voice canon on a quatrain from the *Rubáiyát* and had it printed on a card that was sent to everyone who had written him. This was the text:

> Oh, threats of Hell and hopes of Paradise!
> One thing at least is certain—this life flies;
> One thing is certain and the rest is lies—
> The flower that once has blown forever dies.

It was not intended for publication, but Music Press of New York requested and received permission to include it in a small volume called *Modern Canons* under the title *Oh, Threats of Hell,* published in 1947.

Hindemith's first and only public appearances in Canada were made in 1946, when he conducted the Canadian Broadcasting Corporation Orchestra in his *Symphony: Mathis der Maler* on 23 January in Toronto, gave a lecture on music theory at the Royal Conservatory of Music in Toronto the following day, and a similar talk at the Conservatoire Français in Montreal on 25 January. Hindemith was held in high regard by Canadian musicians and shortly after his death the Canadian Broadcasting Corporation broadcast nationally a series of five interviews with prominent musical figures in the country who had known the composer personally, called "The Legacy of Paul Hindemith."

The spring term of 1946 was heavily occupied with teaching, composing (the *Lilacs Requiem*), and preparing and conducting the first major Collegium Musicum concert. Hindemith had time for only two brief public appearances in New York: playing the viola d'amore in a performance of Bach's *St. John Passion* by the Cantata Singers under Arthur Mendel, and attending the world premiere of his *Lilacs Requiem* on 14 May.

That summer, at the invitation of Carlos Chavez, conductor of the National Symphony Orchestra of Mexico, Hindemith traveled to Mexico City to conduct the orchestra in two performances of an all-Hindemith program on 14 and 16 June. He had not forgotten his unhappy collaboration with Chavez at the 1937 Coolidge Festival in Washington, D.C., but this time he was in sole command. The two men got along splendidly and the concerts were a huge success, according to a letter sent to Willy Strecker. The Mexican audience heard performances of the *Symphony: Mathis der Maler*, *Cupid and Psyche*, *Nobilissima Visione Suite*, and the *Symphonic Metamorphosis*.

Hindemith's teaching obligations were heavier than ever in the 1946–47 school year, precluding the acceptance of any outside engagements except two. He agreed to attend the world premiere of his *Concerto for Piano and Orchestra* in Cleveland on 27 February 1947 and a repeat performance two days later. It was played by Jesús Maria Sanroma and the Cleveland Symphony under George Szell. Hindemith remained in the city until 3 March to give two lectures at the Cleveland Institute of Music.

All of Hindemith's professional activities during the summer of 1947 were carried on in Europe, where he had returned for the first time since emigrating in 1940. There were important conducting engagements in a dozen major cities of Italy, Austria, Switzerland, Belgium, and Holland. From this point on, conducting would become an increasingly important part of his professional life.

Resuming his university duties in the fall of 1947 Hindemith again found his work schedule much too heavy to accept any professional engagements until January. Since it entailed no travel, he agreed to conduct a subscription concert of the New Haven Symphony Orchestra on 12 January 1948, an event described in chapter 9. There were four appearances in New York during the spring of 1948. He attended the New York premiere of his *Symphonia Serena* by the New York Philharmonic under Bruno Walther at 2:00 p.m. in Carnegie Hall on 15 February and conducted the New Friends of Music Orchestra in his *Herodiäde* at 5:00 p.m., the same day in Town Hall. On 5 April he played one of the two solo viola d'amore parts (Howard Boatwright did the other) in a performance of Bach's *Passion according to St. John* in Carnegie Hall by the Juilliard Chorus under Robert Shaw. And he brought his Yale Collegium Musicum vocalists and instrumentalists to New York on 27 May for a repeat performance at the Metropolitan Museum of Art of the concert of early sixteenth-century music that had been given in New Haven on 20 and 21 May.

Hindemith's next public appearance in this country was not until a year later, when he attended the world premiere of his *Concerto for Woodwinds, Harp, and Orchestra* at Columbia University on 15 May 1949. Meanwhile, he had been on sabbatical leave from Yale, spending eight months in Europe, where he followed a heavy schedule of conducting and lecture engagements and completed two important new compositions.

In July 1949, the Hindemiths drove to Colorado Springs, Colorado, where he spent the first week in August at Colorado College holding special classes and seminars in music theory and preparing and conducting a concert to be performed by students and faculty on the final day. It took place on 5 August and included *Trauermusik*, *Six Chansons*, *The Four Temperaments*, and *Frau Musica*, all conducted by the composer, and the *Fifth String Quartet*, played by a faculty ensemble.

The most important of Hindemith's professional engagements outside Yale while living in the United States was his appointment as the Charles Eliot Norton Lecturer at Harvard University for the academic year 1949–50. The Norton lecturer was expected not only to deliver a series of public addresses designed for subsequent publication in book form (as described in chapter 10), but also to be at the university for at least six weeks each term carrying out an optional program of activities related to his specialty. Hindemith chose to give a credit course in theory and composition in the fall term, in addition to delivering the six Norton lectures. In the spring term he prepared and conducted two concerts by student ensembles and gave three additional lectures, not related to the Norton series. The first concert was given on 16 and 17 March, when he conducted a program of his own music including *Apparebit repentina dies, Demon of the Gibbet, Frau Musica,* and a special canon to be sung by the audience written in honor of the eightieth birthday of Mrs. Elizabeth Sprague Coolidge, who was present. The second was a concert of early music, "Perotin to Dufay," given on 31 March.

The three additional lectures in the spring were given before special groups: the American Academy of Arts and Sciences in Boston on 8 February, the students and fellows of Kirkland House at Harvard on 17 February, and a meeting of leading U.S. music critics attending a "Symposium on Music Criticism" at Harvard on 6 March. The lectures for the academy and the symposium dealt with music theory, but at Kirkland House he spoke on "The Duties and Rights of Music Consumers."

During this time, the Hindemiths continued to live in New Haven, but rented a small furnished apartment in Boston's Hotel Fensgate that could be used as needed. The composer's pocket diaries record that he spent a total of about forty days each term at Harvard, making twelve round trips between New Haven and Boston, nine of them by automobile (with Gertrude doing most of the driving) and three by train. He thoroughly enjoyed this Harvard interlude and could be pleased, for it was an enormous success on all counts. The university, too, was pleased. President James B. Conant gave a gala dinner in his honor and Hindemith was offered an honorary doctor of music degree to be awarded in June 1950. Unfortunately, he was obliged to decline the honor, since his concert commitments in Europe would interfere. Harvard, like Yale and many other universities, does not give honorary degrees in absentia.

Hindemith made two other public appearances during that academic year. One was on 4 November 1949, when he attended the world premiere in New Haven of his *Concerto for Trumpet and Bassoon with String Orchestra.* The other was in Louisville, Kentucky, on 1 March 1950, where he conducted the Louisville Symphony Orchestra in the world premiere of his *Sinfonietta in E,* a work that had been commissioned by the orchestra.

Hindemith was back in Europe for his third postwar visit during the summer of 1950 and completed a heavy round of conducting engagements. Returning to Yale late in September, he refused to accept any outside engagements during the first term, since all of his free time was needed to prepare the Norton lectures for publication.

The pressure had eased sufficiently as the second term began in 1951, so that Hindemith could fulfill three engagements in the Midwest. He gave a lecture at Oberlin College on 24 February entitled "Beyond Technique and Entertainment," and at Indiana University on 6 March, speaking on "The Emotional Approach." Both of these were based on materials from his Harvard lectures. Between these two appearances he spent a week at the University of Illinois, holding classes in theory, giving lectures, and rehearsing student instrumental and choral groups for a public concert of his own music that he conducted on 4 March. The program included the *Philharmonic Concerto, Six Chansons, The Four Temperaments,* and *Frau Musica.*

The "Fifth Annual Symposium of the International Federation of Music Students" was held at Yale during 12–17 March 1951 and Hindemith was asked by the local committee of Yale School of Music students to give the opening address. He flatly refused at first, since he wanted no part of an event intended primarily as a public showcase for compositions written by students from Juilliard, Eastman, New England Conservatory, Curtis Institute, the Royal Conservatory of Toronto, and Yale, an idea he heartily deplored. He was finally pressured into doing it by being told that such notable musical figures as Dimitri Mitropoulos, Paul Henry Lang, Otto Kinkeldey, and Susanne Langer had already agreed to appear at the symposium. Hindemith's talk on "Musical Inspiration" (actually chapter 4 of *A Composer's World,* not yet published) was heard by a capacity audience in Sprague Hall that responded with loud and sustained applause when he had finished. True to his convictions, he did not appear at any of the lectures and concerts given over the next five days. Gertrude explained what was happening in a letter to Willy Strecker: "There is a symposium now going on at which Paul gave a lecture on 'Musical Inspiration.' He did not paint a very happy picture for these would-be composers, but they applauded him loudly. One of his students told him that after this lecture they should logically have called off the symposium. But it is going on vigorously and teeming with would-be Stravinskys who are all playing their music for each other."[7] The International Federation of Music Students, begun at Juilliard in 1947, died a natural death in 1953 from fiscal anemia.

Hindemith gave two more public appearances before the spring term ended. He conducted the world premiere of his *Symphony in B♭ for Concert Band* by the U.S. Army Band in Washington, D.C., on 5 April, and a concert of sixteenth-century music by the Yale Collegium Musicum (a repeat performance of the program given at Yale on 21 May) on 4 June in New York in the Cloisters, an adjunct of the Metropolitan Museum of Art.

The Hindemiths were in Europe from August 1951 until late September 1952, where the composer taught at the University of Zürich for two terms and filled many conducting engagements in several countries. He was also the recipient of two high honors in Germany: the Bach Prize from the city of Hamburg on 2 March "for distinguished service to German music"; and the country's highest civilian decoration, the Order of Merit, from the president of the Federal Republic of Germany at ceremonies in Bonn on 31 May. His fatherland was clearly trying to make amends for having treated him so shabbily in the past, but it was too late. He had renounced his German citizenship on becoming a U.S. citizen in 1946 and was fully resolved never to return permanently.

Hindemith's first U.S. engagement after returning from Europe was in New York's Town Hall on 7 December 1952, when he conducted the New Friends of Music chamber orchestra in a concert of his own music that included the *Septet for Wind Instruments* (1948), *Kammermusik No. 3* (1925), *Concert Music for Piano, Brass, and Two Harps* (1930), and the once notorious but still exciting *Kammermusik No. 1* (1921). It is noteworthy that he was now willing to select three of the four pieces on the program from his earlier works, for ever since beginning his concert activities in the United States in 1937 he had insisted on featuring compositions written after 1935. Music critics had complained about this, but he had paid no attention. He was not heard to say why he decided to feature early pieces on the Town Hall concert, and one can only surmise that he was now willing to concede that some of them, at least, were still musically viable.

The concert was a success and the critics were pleased. In fact, the New York Music Critics Circle named the 1948 *Septet for Wind*

Instruments the best new piece of chamber music performed in the city in all of 1952. Ironically, this was the one and only piece on the program written after 1935. Gertrude Hindemith commented wryly about the award in a letter to Willy Strecker: "The nice little wind septet has suddenly become famous because the New York critics voted it the best chamber music piece of the year. We have no idea what the award really means, but congratulations are raining down on all sides and 'The Septet' lies suddenly on the lips of all grocers and fish dealers, who have now admitted us into the ranks of their most important customers."[8] A few weeks later, on 15 February 1953, Hindemith again decided to include an early work he had not done previously in this country when he conducted the student ensembles of the Peabody Conservatory of Music in Baltimore in a concert of his own music. Besides *Kammermusik No. 2*, written in 1924, the program included *Die junge Magd, Septet for Wind Instruments, Six Chansons,* and *Frau Musica.*

Hindemith's final appearance as an orchestral conductor while residing in the United States was with the Minneapolis Symphony on 13 March 1953, when he conducted an entire concert in a program that included the U.S. premiere of his *Symphony: Die Harmonie der Welt,* Weber's *Der Freischütz Overture,* and Mendelssohn's *Scottish Symphony.* It was the first time he had been invited by a major U.S. orchestra to do an entire program that included works by other composers, an invitation he had been waiting impatiently to receive ever since coming to this country. Since resuming his concertizing activities in Europe after the war he had rapidly gained recognition there as a conductor of first rank, but this fact had been completely ignored by orchestras here. Thus the Minneapolis engagement, although belated, gave him particular pleasure, for Dimitri Mitropoulos, at least, was now willing to acknowledge him as a professional peer. The concert was a great success.

Hindemith's final U.S. appearance before leaving for Switzerland was at the Metropolitan Museum of Art in New York on 18 May 1953, when he conducted the Yale Collegium Musicum in a repeat performance of the "From Perotin to Bach" concert they had given at the University on 14 May. The *Herald-Tribune* critic lavished praise on the concert and also expressed profound regret that Hindemith was leaving the United States. There was indeed cause for regret, for his decision to move his base of operations to Switzerland permanently meant that henceforth his participation in the musical life of this country would be severely curtailed. Hindemith insisted he would be returning frequently for extended periods, but circumstances dictated otherwise and almost six years were to pass before he resumed his concertizing in the United States.

Chapter 12

Recognition, Honors, Citizenship

NEVER ONCE as a U.S. resident did Paul Hindemith read or hear an unkind word in the news media about himself or his work here. He was warmly and deferentially received wherever he went and invariably complimented on whatever he did. Even those critics who found reason to question some of his music did so politely. Never before in his professional career had he enjoyed such an extended period free of critical attacks and controversy and he was extremely grateful.

He had won the esteem and admiration of the many leading musicians he met during his three previous visits here and they were delighted he had decided to live in this country. They accepted him immediately as a compatriot, even though it would be five years before he could receive his final papers as a U.S. citizen. The exclusive Institute of Arts and Letters, whose membership is limited to 250 U.S. citizens "qualified by notable achievements in art, music, or literature," elected him as an "honorary foreign member" in 1943 and a regular member in 1947, shortly after he became a citizen.

Hindemith thought it was meaningless to put national labels on contemporary composers and thus saw nothing significant in being asked by Columbia University to write a work for its Festival of Contemporary American Music in 1949. Nevertheless, it was further evidence of his recognition by the U.S. musical community as a member in good standing. His Columbia University piece, *Concerto for Woodwinds, Harp, and Orchestra,* was played on a program that included works by such well-known U.S. composers as Daniel Gregory Mason, Bernard Rogers, and Randall Thompson, and it undoubtedly surprised some to find Hindemith placed in such company as a "fellow American." However, it was a fact, and Columbia University did not hesitate in acknowledging it.

Hindemith received more commissions during this period than

any other contemporary composer living in this country, whether native, foreign, or naturalized. There were fourteen commissions in all, and the organizations and individuals for whom they were written comprise an impressive list, as does the great variety of forms reflecting Hindemith's extraordinary versatility as a composer. He wrote symphonic works for the Dallas and Louisville orchestras and the U.S. Army Band, ballet scores for George Balanchine and Martha Graham, concertos for Columbia University, the Connecticut Academy of Arts and Sciences and Benny Goodman, a cantata for Harvard University, an oratorio for Robert Shaw and his Collegiate Chorale, a male chorus for the Yale Glee Club, a string quartet for the Budapest String Quartet, a violoncello sonata for Gregor Piatigorsky, and a two-piano sonata for Dougherty and Ruzicka. Several more had to be refused for lack of time.

His activities here as a teacher, lecturer, and conductor generated enormous interest in Hindemith's music and it was widely and frequently performed, far more so than that of any other contemporary composer. The music editor of *Time* magazine was so impressed in 1948 that he wrote:

> Few living composers have ever had so much of their music played in one week. Everyone seemed to burst out playing the knotty dissonant music of Paul Hindemith.
>
> Violinist Robert Brink had just put his fiddle away after playing Hindemith's *Sonata in E* in Manhattan's Town Hall when the Guilet Quartet moved in to play a Hindemith quartet. Next night, in Carnegie Hall, the Boston Symphony marched through his *Symphony in E♭*, three blocks away the Ballet Society danced *The Four Temperaments* — music by Hindemith. Next night, in Carnegie Hall, George Szell put the Cleveland Symphony through Hindemith's *Symphonic Metamorphosis of Themes by Carl Maria von Weber*. The critics, who sometimes find Hindemith's music a bit dry, found the *Metamorphosis* gay and charming. In Boston the same night, the Boston Symphony was playing his *Symphonia Serena*.
>
> Two days later, Bruno Walther and the New York Philharmonic gave *Symphonia Serena* its New York premiere. At week's end, composer Hindemith, a short and shy man who now heads the music department at Yale [*sic*] capped it all by conducting his own *Herodiäde* at a New Friends of Music concert in Manhattan's Town Hall.[1]

The first of several special honors Hindemith received while living in the States was the Howland Memorial Prize Medal, Yale University's highest award, presented to him by President Charles Seymour in a public ceremony on 20 November 1940. The citation read in part: "The Howland Prize is awarded to the citizen of any country in recognition of achievements of marked distinction in the fields of literature, the arts, or the science of government. An important factor in the selection is the idealistic element in the recipient's work. . . . Tonight we confer it on one of the most distinguished composers of music now living. His music, although grounded in the great tradition of the past is, nevertheless, an eloquent expression of his own time."[2]

Hindemith received an honorary doctor of music degree from the Philadelphia Academy of Music in Philadelphia on 4 June 1945. American composer Roger Sessions gave a brief address, expressing his high admiration for Hindemith's achievements in music and concluding: "As a fugitive from tyranny, as were our forefathers from the earliest days of our country, he has come to our shores, and by his very presence has contributed inestimable riches to our musical life. It is therefore especially fitting that on this occasion he be greeted as one of our honored colleagues, not only because he is one of the first among musicians, but because we may shortly regard him, in the true American tradition, as one of our most distinguished compatriots."[3]

Columbia University also awarded Hindemith an honorary doctor of music degree, in June 1948. He remembered this occasion with special pleasure, for the president of the university, who conferred the honor on him, was none other than Dwight D. Eisenhower, who had become as much of a hero to the composer as to everyone else in the United States. Hindemith took diabolic delight in the fact that the hated Nazis had been destroyed by Allied military forces under the command of a U.S. general of German descent. President Eisenhower gave a dinner in honor of the degree recipients the evening before and Hindemith was pleased to report to friends that he had an opportunity for a long private conversation with Eisenhower on topics ranging from music to politics that he thoroughly enjoyed.

The last public honor Hindemith received while living in the United States was the New York Music Critics Circle award for having written the "most outstanding" new chamber music composition premiered in the city during 1952. As previously noted, this was for his 1948 *Septet for Wind Instruments,* performed in Town Hall on 7 December 1952. The award was of only local significance, yet he derived a certain satisfaction from it, since the critics, who had been insisting all along that his more recent pieces were less interesting than his earlier ones, were now citing one of his 1948 compositions as the best of its kind that they had heard that year.

Of greater importance to Hindemith than any other recognition or honor he received while here was his being made a citizen of the United States. He wrote to Gertrude one month after arriving as an immigrant: "I am constantly being urged to take out my 'first papers,' something one is not obliged to do at all. I believe one must wait until he sees how things are developing, for it can always be done later."[4] But with Gertrude safely in New Haven and his work at the university having begun auspiciously he no longer doubted the feasibility of staying and applied for citizenship in October 1940. He sent this revealing note to Hugo Strecker in London a few days later: "I have applied for my first citizenship papers. Your father will be shocked when he hears I intend to renounce my German citizenship, but I cannot help it. I must finally know where I belong."[5]

After the mandatory waiting period had elapsed, Hindemith appeared before an immigration officer in New Haven on 15 July 1945 for his final hearing, accompanied by Professors Richard Donovan and Robert D. French (master of Jonathan Edwards College, where Hindemith was an associate fellow) as his sponsors. He had spent a considerable amount of his time prior to this day studying U.S. history, the Constitution, the governmental system, and much more, in preparation for what he assumed would be a rigorous examination. After giving the correct answers to a few simple questions any schoolchild would have known, he was passed. The composer was furious when he left the office, saying to his friends that he felt he had been swindled.

Hindemith was finally sworn in as a U.S. citizen on 11 January 1946 at the Federal Court in Hartford, Connecticut, by Federal Judge Carroll Hincks. The oath is generally administered to large groups at the same time but Judge Hincks thought that Hindemith was too distinguished a person to be simply one in a crowd and invited him into his chambers, where he took the oath in a private ceremony. The judge was from New Haven and an excellent amateur musician who was well aware of Hindemith's eminence and wished to treat him accordingly. The composer appreciated this, but told some of his friends later he would have much preferred not receiving such special attention. However, he knew the judge meant well, and later sent him a manuscript copy of his song for solo voice and piano, *Sing on, There in the Swamp,* inscribed with a note of appreciation. The Judge was grateful but also concerned, for he feared such a gift might be considered by some to be a bribe of sorts. He quickly gave the manuscript to his friend Professor Ellsworth Grumman of the Yale School of Music, who later donated it to the university.

Gertrude applied for citizenship shortly after her husband and passed her final hearing on 9 January 1946. The happy occasion was celebrated at a merry dinner party at one of New Haven's best Italian restaurants, along with the Donovans and the Nosses. She was sworn in a few weeks later and could then join Paul in claiming U.S. citizenship, a distinction of which they were both very proud and one they never relinquished.

Chapter 13

Mr. and Mrs. Paul Hindemith of New Haven, Connecticut

GERTRUDE HINDEMITH finally made her way to New York by early September 1940, where she was met by her husband, and they came to New Haven on Sunday 15 September 1940. They engaged a room at the Taft Hotel and notified only Professor and Mrs. Richard Donovan that they were in town. The search for a furnished house to rent began the next morning and was completed satisfactorily by the end of the week. The Donovans informed them that the most attractive residential areas were in the northern and western sections of the city, adding that Yale faculty members preferred the northern. On hearing this, the Hindemiths immediately eliminated the northern area from consideration, for they knew Paul's time for composing would be limited because of his teaching duties and would have to be protected from interruptions by uninvited callers. Consequently they thought it advisable not to have very many professional colleagues as neighbors. They restricted their search to the western section and were fortunate in finding a small but trim and nicely furnished house at 134 West Elm Street in the Westville district, where they would live for the next five years.

Westville was a distinctly middle-class neighborhood but unusually attractive because of the wide streets, boulevards, and handsome trees. A large and beautiful city park comprised mostly of woodlands was nearby, ideal for walks. Hindemith described their situation in a letter to Willy Strecker: "We found a small furnished house in the western part of the city. Everything is again the way we like it. The location is convenient and beautiful as well. We can walk to the woods in five minutes—the most beautiful oak trees—and can see for great distances through the countryside. Next time you come you must join us on our hikes. Meanwhile, we will train for it."[1] They were located about three miles from the university but there was convenient bus service, and in April 1941 they purchased a secondhand Packard coupe in which he could be driven to and from the school by Gertrude. (Paul got his driver's license in 1949, but he seldom drove.)

The owner of the West Elm Street house found it necessary for personal reasons to move back in 1945, but he offered to sell the Hindemiths another house he owned in the same area. It was a much larger and quite handsome frame house, located at 147 Alden Avenue, and more satisfactory in every way. They bought it in October 1945 and lived there until leaving the United States in 1953.

The spacious house on Alden Avenue had to be completely furnished by the Hindemiths and they did so in a modest yet attractive fashion. Gertrude explained to her friends that since they were certain the beautiful belongings they had stored in Berlin had been destroyed during the final days of the war, they saw no reason for buying comparable furnishings only to lose them as well for one reason or another. It can be assumed that money was also a factor in their decision, for purchasing a house had obviously placed a considerable strain on their still rather limited resources.

Adapting to residential life in the United States was not difficult, since Paul was very familiar with this country and its ways and there had been ample opportunity to brief Gertrude on what to expect. Furthermore, both of them understood and spoke English very well. Thus they were able to move into the Westville district without attracting any special attention, much to their relief and delight, and were accepted by their neighbors as friendly and likable folks who caused no trouble and took good care of their property. It was precisely the kind of situation the Hindemiths had hoped to find and they were quite content to remain in the Westville area throughout all of their thirteen years in New Haven.

Their decision to live in a private residence rather than in an apartment was undoubtedly influenced by their recent happy experience as householders in Bluche, Switzerland, just before emigrating. That had been the first time they had ever done so and they had loved it. Gertrude wrote to friends that she was delighted with her new role as a full-time "Hausfrau" and that Paul had discovered particular pleasure and relaxation in gardening, a hobby he would pursue avidly the rest of his life. They engaged no domestic help in New Haven except the part-time services of a cleaning woman after moving into the large Alden Avenue house in 1945.

Gertrude did all of the cooking and Paul tended to the yard and garden. The author's wife, Osea Noss, was frequently invited to the Hindemiths' while he was away on military service and she recalls a highly amusing incident on one of her visits. She was in the kitchen chatting with Gertrude when Paul, who had been outside mowing the lawn, came in to announce gleefully that he had just been offered a job. A man passing by had been so impressed by the efficient and energetic way the composer was going about it (dressed in denim jeans and a T-shirt) that he stopped to ask if he could hire Hindemith to do his lawn. Paul said he explained to the gentleman politely that he regretted not being able to do so, for he already had all the jobs he could handle.

The Hindemiths were well satisfied with their living situation and were never heard to complain. They were comfortable, enjoyed privacy, and furthermore were not troubled with serious health or financial problems. The composer noted in his pocket diary that he had to take to his bed about ten times in the thirteen years because of influenza or gout (on four occasions with both at once) but for only a few days, and he was never hospitalized. Gertrude was also spared any long illness. Their financial situation stabilized within a year after their arrival in New Haven and improved steadily thereafter. Not only was Hindemith's salary from Yale sufficient to provide a comfortable living, but this was substantially augmented by royalties, commissions, and fees for conducting and lecturing.

Their house also served as Hindemith's studio and office. He had none at the school, by choice, preferring to keep his professional activities as a composer and performing artist completely separate from his teaching. He did all of his writing and met all of his business appointments at home, never divulging what he might be composing or what distinguished musical figure had been there to see him. Visitors who had appointments with him would go directly to his home and never appear at the School of Music. It was a completely private part of his life about which his faculty colleagues knew little if anything, and there are no documents that provide any information of consequence.

Gertrude Hindemith served very efficiently as her husband's executive secretary, managing his business affairs, tending to his correspondence, screening his appointments, controlling the social calendar, and doing whatever had to be done to assure him maximum time for composing. Her refusals to grant appointments or accept social invitations would ruffle feathers on occasion, and she is sometimes unfairly pictured in biographical accounts as a difficult person. Celebrity chasers of whatever social level did indeed find her "difficult," but her friends enjoyed her gracious company and greatly admired her for all she did to help her husband. The pressures of school and professional work were not unduly heavy during the war years and Gertrude took time to study at the Yale Graduate School for her master of arts degree in French philology under Henri M. Peyre, receiving it in June 1945. She also did volunteer work in one of the city hospitals between 1942 and 1945.

Gertrude was a devout Roman Catholic, having been converted to the faith shortly before coming to the United States. She attended Mass regularly on Sundays and frequently on weekdays at St. Thomas More Chapel, seat of the Roman Catholic Chaplaincy at Yale University, preferring that to her parish church of St. Aedan's in Westville because of its superior liturgical music. She was not aware of a local diocesan ruling then in effect (long since abrogated) that required Catholics to attend and support their parish church, and eventually the St. Aedan's priest called on her to remind her of this obligation. Gertrude reported to her friends that she had been greatly annoyed by this and bluntly told the startled priest that she thought the ruling was ridiculous and that she would continue attending St. Thomas More. However, she agreed to make a modest annual contribution to St. Aedan's.

Hindemith never accompanied his wife to Mass nor did he attend any other church, regarding himself as a "neutral" in these matters. Nevertheless, he was keenly interested in Catholic liturgical music, particularly the Gregorian chant, using it regularly in his teaching as a model of melodic construction. All of his degree students at Yale were required to learn the art of singing it in the Solesmes tradition from neumatic notation.[2]

The Hindemiths routinely refused all invitations to receptions and cocktail parties, not only disliking them per se but also considering them a waste of precious time. However, they enjoyed a relaxed evening with a small group of close friends when their heavy schedule permitted. Friends took their cue from Gertrude, who would let them know when Paul was ready for a break and the evening would be planned accordingly. Such evenings happened infrequently but were invariably good fun, featuring sophisticated parlor games that severely tested one's literary and musical wits, with Paul often devising highly ingenious ones himself. The composer's major students also enjoyed social evenings at the Hindemiths' home on occasion, and all were invited to a cookout at the end of the term each spring.

The largest evening party hosted by the Hindemiths was given in their home on 2 May 1953 as a farewell salute to their friends. It was an occasion never to be forgotten by the guests. Colorful invitations made by Paul were sent to about seventy-five people, who on arriving were astounded to find the walls of the entry hall, dining room, and kitchen covered with paper on which Hindemith had painted fantastic murals depicting spacious halls, marble staircases, crypts, and cemeteries, a project that had obviously required many hours to complete.

Hindemith also planned an elaborate program of entertainment, inviting a dozen of his faculty colleagues (including the author) and one of their wives to participate. A string quartet performed his famous *Minimax* parody and his spoof of the overture to *The Flying Dutchman*. A male quartet in bizarre dress sang humorous German partsongs. The attractive soprano Helen Boatwright, who had been the featured soloist in three of the Collegium concerts, sang sexy torch songs, and a baritone sang a group of Negro spirituals translated into outlandish German.[3]

The final act was a hilarious panel discussion involving four scholars attempting to identify a recent archeological find, all of it conceived, directed, and staged by Hindemith. To represent the find he had constructed a grotesque stuffed figure, featuring two arms and two legs, faces painted on both the front and back of the head, and painted undershorts. The four panelists were Yale professors of German, French, music history, and international relations, all in academic garb, and they argued heatedly in a babel of tongues. Eventually a scroll was brought in (actually a roller window shade) on which Hindemith had written a long message in a mysterious script. The panelists were finally able to decipher the message, which identified the figure as someone who had been interested in sports and entertainment, big in the middle, and small in the head, therefore it had to be a prehistoric "Yalie." A lavish supper followed the program and everyone stayed late, reluctant to bring to an end an occasion the like of which they knew they would never experience again.

Hindemith needed more opportunities to relax than afforded by the relatively infrequent social evenings with friends, and the resourceful composer found them without difficulty. He worked in the garden, took long walks with Gertrude in the nearby city park, created Christmas cards, painted Easter eggs, and made "house music" with his wife. He never attended concerts or recitals unless there was a compelling reason for doing so.[4] They enjoyed going to New Haven's famed Shubert Theater if the play and cast were of special distinction. When Paul occasionally encountered a block in his thinking while composing they would drop everything and walk to their neighborhood movie theater to see whatever was showing. Gertrude reported that Hindemith found grade-B Westerns particularly therapeutic.

During their first five summers here the Hindemiths enjoyed holidays in various areas of New England. In 1941, they remained in their rented country home near Lenox, Massachusetts, for a month after the Tanglewood session ended. They were on Cape Cod for three weeks in 1942 and in the White Mountains of New Hampshire in 1943, staying in resort hotels. In 1944 they decided to camp out on their own and rented a small cabin in a secluded coastal area near Boothbay Harbor, Maine, staying about three months and loving it. Gertrude wrote to Osea Noss:

> We have found an ideal place. We are hidden in the woods, have a huge property of our own and a sweet little enchanting house right on the ocean and with all the comforts of "civilization." After a period of continuous yawning and sleeping, Paul is now better than he was ten years ago.
>
> We are kept very busy. This highly desirable location is good for work but less so for getting food. We have to hike miles to get our daily bread, and if not, like yesterday, I have to *bake* my own! Don't laugh—it was VERY GOOD. The whole place is covered with berries and we could can enough for the entire winter if we had the equipment here. Now we are sawing wood for the fall. There are many fallen trees lying around and we do some of them every day. I am happy I now know how to handle a saw. Previously I always looked on them as strange animals. However, they are goodnatured, provided they stay in the wood and don't jump on your legs.
>
> You can see we have a full schedule—keeping house, gathering berries, sawing wood, and getting food—and the rest of the time is spent looking out into the open sea. When our eyes reach the horizon we know that it goes on and on to where the terrible destruction is taking place.[5]

The war in Europe was never far from their thoughts because of their deep concern for family and friends there. It is mentioned again in another letter Gertrude wrote to Mrs. Noss two weeks later: "Paul is feeling wonderful—his feet are youthfully active again. He is as busy as ever—writing, thinking, blazing trails, and picking berries for food. We have no radio and that is probably a blessing with all the news coming in every minute and being revoked the next day. A lot has happened since we left New Haven and it looks as if the world is pregnant with some big explosion."[6] Gertrude was right.

They returned to Maine the following summer of 1945, enjoying six weeks of isolated living and working in a camp on the seacoast near Bar Harbor. This time they rented two cabins, one of which Paul used as a studio. They also had an opportunity to make a little "house music," as Gertrude described in a letter to Osea Noss: "There is a tiny chapel nearby with a little reed organ that Paul repaired. We now play big organ pieces by Bach, Buxtehude, etc., on it. I play the pedal part and Paul the manual parts, all the time pumping with all his might. It is a strange combination of music and a bicycle race."[7]

In the summer of 1946, when Paul was engaged to conduct two concerts by the National Symphony Orchestra in Mexico City, the Hindemiths enjoyed a Mexican holiday. Since the restrictions on the use of gasoline had been lifted, they decided to drive all the way down from New Haven in their Packard, leaving 2 June and not returning until 24 August. Following the successful concerts in Mexico City they traveled widely throughout the country, making extended stops in Taxco and Agua Bianca. It was their first visit to this colorful land and they reported to friends that it had been a fascinating experience.

Paul and Gertrude's frequent visits to Europe, beginning in 1947, precluded their taking another summer holiday in the United States until 1949, and this proved to be their last. Hindemith's engagement to spend the first week in August as a guest teacher and conductor at Colorado College in Colorado Springs provided the incentive for a 5,000-mile excursion by car, this time in a new Pontiac and with an additional driver, for Paul had just acquired his driver's license. They left on 20 July, going out by a northern route, spent the week at Colorado College, relaxed for two weeks in Taos, New Mexico, and drove leisurely back to New Haven over a southern route, arriving home on 12 September.

Two brief auto trips by the Hindemiths, made in 1948 and 1953, merit special attention. They found time between 23 and 28 July 1948 to explore the Pennsylvania Dutch countryside, their first visit to this charming and quaint area, and Paul was much impressed with what he heard and saw. He would later invoke memories of this experience in writing his *Pittsburgh Symphony.*

Unfortunately, very little information is available about an extraordinary excursion they made during the spring vacation period in April 1953, since they said nothing about it to their friends and there are no references to it in their correspondence. The composer noted in his pocket diary that he and Gertrude motored to the Trappist Abbey of Our Lady of Gethsemane in Kentucky to meet with the noted author and monk Thomas Merton, who was living there as the master of the novices. Hindemith obviously discussed with Father Merton the possibility of his writing a text that could be set to music and would involve audience participation, for the priest did so. In *The Collected Works of Thomas Merton,* published by New Directions Press of New York in 1971, there is a substantial three-part poem called "A Responsary" with alternate stanzas for "Chorus" and "All the People" that is inscribed "For Paul Hindemith—1953." The visit was undoubtedly related to the UNESCO commission on which the composer was then working, for it is known he had encountered difficulties in finding a suitable text. It is highly probable that Gertrude urged him to see whether Father Merton might have written one that could be used. It is clear that he had not, since Hindemith began writing the music for Claudel's *Canticle to Hope* the day after they returned to New Haven. There was no time to wait for Merton to write one. It is not known whether Hindemith ever saw "A Responsary," or if he did, what his reaction was. He never did set it to music.

Their private lives as ordinary citizens of New Haven would have to be described as prosaic, but that is exactly what Paul and Gertrude Hindemith hoped they would be. The notion held by many Europeans that they were unhappy here and impatiently bided their time until they could return is completely false, and they would have been the first to deny it. They lived comfortably in their own private home, enjoyed the company of devoted friends, were highly respected in the university community, and had ample opportunities for interesting holidays and excursions. Above all, they were extremely grateful to have found security after seven years of agonizing uncertainty and bedevilment brought on by the political debacle in Germany. They fully intended to return each year for extended stays, combining professional engagements with holidays and visits with personal friends, but it was not to be quite like that.

PART 3
Expatriate, 1953–63

Introduction

The story of Paul Hindemith's association with the United States as an expatriate during the last ten years of his life follows a perfect "before and after" scenario. Before there was a satisfactory opportunity to resume his concertizing here, he was forced to wait almost six years and his enthusiasm for his adopted country steadily declined; after the success of his first reappearance, his faith was immediately and completely restored and all of the rancor that had been accumulating disappeared without a trace. Hindemith's professional activities then were concentrated almost entirely on composing and conducting, both pursued with characteristic vigor until the end. Part 3 deals only with those activities that relate directly to the United States, of which there were considerably more than is generally known.

Principal sources for the data used in preparing this section were long and informative letters the composer wrote to Oscar Cox, his attorney in the United States, and equally illuminating letters Gertrude Hindemith wrote to Cox and to the author's wife, Osea Noss. Hindemith was most fortunate in having the services of Oscar Cox, one of the top lawyers in Washington, D.C., who had previously held high legal positions in the federal government and thus could be of invaluable help in solving the composer's problems with U.S. income taxes and other regulations affecting citizens living abroad. Cox was also a Yale graduate, highly cultured in the arts, wrote poetry, greatly admired Hindemith and his music, and became the composer's personal friend.[1] Hindemith wrote very little to his other friends in the United States, depending upon Gertrude to keep them informed of his thoughts and activities and she did so faithfully. She carried on an active correspondence with Osea Noss throughout this period, filling her letters with details of their doings and including any specific comments her husband might wish to make. All of these letters were written in English and are now in the Paul Hindemith Collection at Yale University. The author's personal journal was also a useful source of information.

Chapter 14

Estrangement, 1953–58

THE HINDEMITHS' hopes of returning early and often to the United States soon faded when the offers of suitable engagements they had confidently expected to receive failed to materialize. Their initial reaction of surprise soon became one of annoyance, then anger, and finally bitterness and resentment. Problems over income taxes and their status as U.S. citizens also arose that intensified their feeling of alienation. There is ample documentation of their increasing disenchantment in the letters written to Oscar Cox and Osea Noss, but it must be added that they tell only their own side of the story, implying that everyone over here was somehow to blame for their predicament. There were many aspects of the concert business in the United States the Hindemiths did not fully understand, particularly those relating to symphony orchestras, and the composer's stubborn insistence on having his own way or none at all only exacerbated the situation. After almost six years of fighting the system to no avail, he was finally willing to adjust to the facts of the matter and agreed to accept three engagements early in 1959, only one of which met the conditions he had been demanding.

In 1953 the Hindemiths sold their Alden Avenue home and most of its contents, retaining a few light housekeeping items, which they stored in the attic with the new owner's permission. Gertrude explained that these would be useful when they returned for their extended stays in the United States while Paul fulfilled his concert engagements. She told friends they were planning to be back for the 1954–55 concert season. In a long letter sent to Osea Noss a few months later from Blonay, Switzerland, where they had purchased a handsome villa overlooking Lake Geneva, she mentioned that they would be on an extended concert tour in South America during the fall of 1954 and when it was over in December "we will come home to New Haven."

The first indication that things were not going according to plan came in a brief note sent by Gertrude to Mrs. Noss in April 1954: "Our trip to the USA is doubtful. Lots of concerts in South America but in *our* USA there is not enough 'demand' to pay for the trip! We might return directly from Brazil."[2]

Mrs. Noss replied, expressing regret that a U.S. tour might not materialize and suggesting they engage a concert manager over here. Gertrude's reaction was revealing:

> Your question about an agent hits the heart of the matter. Of course, we did not think we needed one, I don't know why—perhaps because we never used one since all of the European requests for Paul came directly to him in New Haven. We engaged our Zürich agent more or less as a friend, asking him to take care of the business correspondence because I could not do it all any more and also I did not like the bargaining part of the business.
>
> Stupidly enough, we thought that after we left America everyone would be calling for us!!! No, really and truly it is a matter of money. The South Americans are paying for the trip from Zürich to Buenos Aires and back for us both. They would have paid for the return trip to New York but we would have to pay our own way from New York back to Zürich. There was the possibility of a $1500 engagement in Los Angeles but it would have meant endless travel with no money left. So next year there will be an agent in charge and we hope to come to the USA in the spring of 1956.
>
> I feel sort of sad, for I really hoped to get back to Yale to see you all and to work a while in the beautiful Sterling Library, which has no equal anywhere. But as much as we would like to see our friends we cannot (since we have a house to pay for) just travel for pleasure.[3]

The Zürich agent mentioned by Gertrude was Walter Schulthess, a personal friend and professional musician who also did work as a concert manager. Gertrude was relieved of a heavy load of correspondence, to be sure, but since Schulthess made no pretense of being a concert promoter, their difficulties in getting U.S. engagements would continue. Later in 1955 they briefly explored the possibility of using the formidable Arthur Judson management in New York but did not like what they found, as will be described later in this chapter. Schulthess was retained as their agent until the end.

The South American concert tour in the fall of 1954 was an artistic triumph and an enjoyable experience for the Hindemiths on the whole, but they were greatly puzzled, not to say irked, that their visit received so little attention from U.S. Embassy officials. Gertrude described their experience in Bogotá, Colombia, in a letter to Oscar Cox, enclosing photos of Hindemith being greeted by the German ambassador and news clippings heralding the arrival of "the great German composer Hindemith":

> At our arrival here the German Ambassador stood in the rain and mud at the airport to meet us and has not ceased to be of help to us. The American official (a Cultural Attache) did not make a move. We invited him to the concert and he did not even come backstage. Yesterday, another American Embassy official came around and chatted with us as though we were from China. . . . Forgive this silly complaint, but this means more to us than we can say. People here just shrug their shoulders and say that Americans are only commercially minded.[4]

Their Washington friend and attorney was equally upset by this and brought pressure on the Department of State to do something about it. Gertrude next wrote to Cox from Rio de Janeiro reporting that U.S. officials there had paid some attention to their presence and adding that "your secret channels have worked already."

By April 1955 the Hindemiths had been gone from the United States not quite two years and they were already unhappy enough over the lack of invitations to return and their treatment by U.S. officials abroad. Now came another jolt. Hindemith was informed by Cox that although he was now technically a "nonresident citizen," having been without a permanent U.S. address for over 512 days, he was still liable for income tax payments. He recommended that the composer consider establishing some sort of permanent U.S. address since that would put him in a more favorable tax situation. He even offered his summer home in Maine as a possibility. The composer's lengthy reply, sent from Blonay in April 1955, was a veritable litany of complaints about the United States. He rejected the idea of having a permanent U.S. address, saying he would have to stay in Europe since he had more than enough concert engagements there to guarantee a comfortable living and time to compose. This was impossible in the United States in his opinion. Symphony orchestra conductors in the United States, he grumbled, have a "brotherhood worse than the locomotive engineers and will not let any outsider enter their realm." Cox had been sending him announcements and reviews of performances of his music in the United States but the composer was not impressed, saying, "They show mostly performances of my smaller works, with never an opera and almost never a symphonic piece." Numerous examples of how his visits in foreign countries had been ignored by U.S. Embassy people were cited. He was clearly unhappy about the situation and his resentment was growing.

Cox was now becoming deeply concerned over Hindemith's difficulties in obtaining U.S. engagements and recommended their Swiss agent enlist the help of the illustrious Arthur M. Judson management in New York. Gertrude sent this feisty reply:

> If Mr. Judson should suddenly display any interest, Schulthess will automatically turn all U.S. negotiations over to him. Because I know you like "facts," here are some that might be news to you.
>
> Men like Judson are usually mostly interested in their fees. His is 20%, as far as I know. These "gangsters" really do not go to work for you. However, if there is a man who is likely to bring in a number of well-paid engagements, they put their mighty hand over the affair and bestow upon the artist the great privilege of their favor. For Paul, of course it is a joke, but he cannot afford to have Judson AGAINST him, and that is why Schulthess thinks it is better to have him WITH us.[5]

Schulthess did write to Judson in January 1956, inquiring about a possible appearance with the Chicago Symphony and received the following reply (a copy of which Gertrude enclosed in her letter to Cox): "I am afraid there will be no chance for Hindemith in Chicago since Reiner does not seem to be interested in him. However, Pittsburgh is interested in having him in the first part of January 1957 for a fee of $1,000. Would Mr. Hindemith be willing to come for that one date? Please let me know immediately so as not to hold up Pittsburgh in its plans."[6] Gertrude was indignant, as is evident in her comments to Cox:

> Perhaps we are getting overly sensitive but we feel this letter is a document of impoliteness and almost insulting hostility. As there is still a year between now and the proposed date it is at least a lack of courtesy not to have added "I will do my best to get more dates," or something like that.
>
> We will leave it to Schulthess whether he wishes to continue with Judson. We feel it is hopeless and that there is a trend to keep Paul out of the US. You will probably understand that Paul's desire to return does not increase very much with these experiences.[7]

Needless to say, there were no further negotiations with Judson.

Hindemith now thought that Cox was becoming overly concerned about the difficulty of securing engagements and sought to put him at ease with these comments:

I am profoundly moved, if not rather embarrassed, by your efforts to make my music and/or person more palatable to American orchestras, trustees, and the like. I do not wish to discourage you, but I think that after a while you will find out that nothing can be done. In case we see you when you come to Europe we can talk about these problems. It is of no value to write about them since they are not that important. After all, it does not matter whether there are a few concerts in the States or not. Anyway, after next season I intend to curb my conducting in favor of composing. Nevertheless, it seems that through our agent Schulthess some American engagements are taking shape.[8]

Hindemith's claim that "it does not matter whether there are a few concerts in the States or not" was purely gratuitous and obviously added to allay his friend's concerns. There is overwhelming evidence in the Hindemith correspondence to refute this statement.

While the United States continued to ignore Hindemith, his prowess as a conductor gained ever-increasing recognition in Europe, and in April 1956 he led the Vienna Philharmonic Orchestra in fifteen concerts on a tour of Japan. As during the 1954 South American tour, U.S. Embassy officials paid little notice to their visit and Gertrude was again upset. She complained to Cox in a letter sent from Blonay after their return:

I am sorry to report we were not noticed at all by the American Embassy. We left our cards there soon after we arrived, but they were not returned. Since that is the second time this has happened I wonder if it is an American custom not to return visitors' calls, as is done in Europe. Of course, the traffic in the American Embassy is enormous, and the Ambassador is mostly involved with business—he was attending a trade fair in Osaka part of the time we were there. . . . However, the Tokyo Embassy has a large staff of cultural relations people, yet not a single one of them attended any of our concerts. . . . We attended a garden party at the American Embassy three days before our departure. We left early and were told afterward that the Ambassador was looking for us. How very nice of him!!![9]

In the same letter Gertrude reported that their return visit to the United States had been "indefinitely postponed." Several offers of engagements had been received but none was of sufficient importance either artistically or financially to warrant coming over and they had been declined.

With the prospects of obtaining suitable appearances in this country remaining so bleak, the Hindemiths were now beginning to worry about the regulation requiring U.S. citizens living abroad to reenter the country at least once every five years to retain their passports. They again appealed to Oscar Cox for help, who in turn appealed to his friend John Foster Dulles, then the secretary of state. Cox wrote to Dulles recommending that the Hindemiths be admitted into the special category of citizenship reserved for individuals who can be considered "national assets" because of the international recognition accorded their achievements in the arts or sciences. These so-called honorary citizens enjoy all of the rights and privileges of regular citizenship but are not subject to any restrictions on the length of their stay out of the country. Secretary Dulles accepted the recommendation without hesitation and Cox was happy to cable Hindemith in September 1956 that they were now exempt from the five-year regulation and need not fret any longer. Paul immediately sent this note, along with a postcard depicting a mountain range in the Alps: "The rock that dropped from our chest can only be compared to the stone pictured on this card. We don't know how to thank you."[10]

All would have been well at this point if some minor functionary in the Passport Division had not sent Hindemith a letter telling him he was now expected to promote American music abroad. The composer was furious, and he sounded off in a long letter written to Cox on 16 December 1956. The letter was essentially a year-end summary of details relating to his U.S. taxes and investments, but he included a final section under the heading "Citizenship," wherein he vented his spleen not only on the Passport Division but also on the U.S. musical scene in general. He deplored this country's treatment of the composer, "who is forced to live in medieval slavery, being the servant of all kinds of managers, union bosses, conductors, and professional societies, against whom no individual can do anything unless he has millions to spend." He resented the fact that "nobody ever bothered to call me an American musician, even though I wrote the piece that in due time . . . may become one of the

nation's few musical treasures (When lilacs last . . .)." He was insulted
that the passport people had put him in the same company with "the
little singers or their likes, who play and sing in all the America
Houses and drink all the cocktails offered." In sum, he was so
incensed he was beginning to think "it might be preferable to travel
on a stateless passport, as do some other artists."

This was a unique outburst, the first and last of its kind.
Hindemith had a temper that he rarely unleashed, but now the
combination of frustration over the lack of U.S. engagements, the
heavy pressure he was under to complete the score of his new and
very large opera *Die Harmonie der Welt,* and anger provoked by the
Passport Division's arrogance in telling him what to do was more
than enough to trigger it. Having gotten it all off his chest, however,
he concluded with this apologetic note, "Let's forget all this stupidity."

The first U.S. engagement Hindemith was willing to accept was
offered to him in 1957 when he was asked to conduct a series of three
concerts by the Chicago Symphony Orchestra at Ravinia Park in the
summer of that year. Ironically, he could not accept because his new
opera was to be premiered on 11 August in Münich. Gertrude
reported this in a letter to Osea Noss, along with these interesting
comments about Paul and the United States:

> I laughed about your hoping for a "magic carpet" to bring Paul
> back to the U.S. The truth is that in the U.S. not many know Paul
> as a performing musician. He is a "College Man," or better, the
> "Yale Professor," and probably most of the people think he is still
> there. The proof is that we still get letters addressed to Yale — even
> the Ravinia man wrote to Yale. He had no idea that over here Paul
> has quite a reputation as a conductor and has always been known
> as a orchestra man. Here in Europe it took them time to understand
> he was also a "Professor." In America they have fixed him forever
> as an interesting "conférencier."[11]

Hindemith also received another U.S. offer in 1957. In January
of that year, the Yale University Corporation had authorized the
School of Music to discontinue its undergraduate division and
offer only professional studies at the graduate level after September
1958. The author was then dean of the school and immediately
recommended that Hindemith be invited to return as a member of
the faculty. This was approved by President A. Whitney Griswold
and the composer was offered a very high salary and complete

freedom in arranging his own teaching program. The author knew Hindemith would never have agreed to return to the school he left in 1953, but there was a possibility he might be interested now that it would be open to graduate students only. He was not, as Gertrude explained in a letter to the dean:

> Paul was moved by your frank and spontaneous invitation, and if he were ten years younger he would not have hesitated to make any arrangement to follow the call. But Paul does not want to assume any more extended obligations in the field of teaching. He feels he has given well half of his life to it and he took it all very seriously, as you know. The results have not been too abundant, and for the remaining years of his life he feels he should concentrate on creative work. . . . He has so much to say in music and words that it seems to him there will never be sufficient time for it all.[12]

She went on to explain how their situation in Switzerland was "ideal" for Paul's professional work, since their proximity to all of the major European cities enabled him to fulfill his concert engagements with minimal difficulty. She complained again about his lack of recognition in the United States as a conductor: "America will always see in Paul the 'Yale Professor'—well, that's not so bad, and he is really very proud of that."[13] Gertrude ended her letter by writing: "Many thanks, Luther, for your good thoughts and efforts on behalf of calling Paul back. I do hope I have cleared up the situation and given you a picture of the complicated factors involved. Paul would love to come back to Yale for a short visit, if possible on some festive occasion. He would not be able to do any teaching, but could probably give a lecture or two." It was clear that there was no possibility of getting Hindemith back to Yale as a teacher and that it could only be done through a concert engagement.

The first definite step on what had proven to be a very long road back to the United States was taken in the fall of 1957 when Hindemith began negotiating with the Pittsburgh Symphony Orchestra over a commission to write a piece for the city's bicentennial celebration. The idea was proposed by William Steinberg, then conductor of the orchestra, and this led to problems, as Gertrude reported in a letter to Oscar Cox:

> William Steinberg wanted a piece written for his orchestra in connection with an anniversary. However, we turned the offer around and said Paul would come to conduct a concert and in that

case bring a new piece (he wanted to write one anyway). They agreed to $5,000 for the deal, but we met with Mr. Steinberg one night in Frankfurt and he was so business-minded and wanted so much publicity over the fact that "Hindemith Writes a Piece for the Pittsburgh Symphony" that Paul got mad, and when he came up to our hotel room later he had quite a fit, just like Maria Callas. I had to telephone Steinberg and tell him the deal was off. But now they have met again, and Paul agreed to conduct the concert provided there was no advance publicity about the new piece. I am afraid they will never agree to this and will cancel the whole thing and we'll be glad. Paul can't stand this type of mercenary musician and he is not about to spend several months writing a new piece just for the glory of Mr. Steinberg.[14]

The "deal" did not have to be canceled, for Pittsburgh accepted Hindemith's terms and the two concerts (one a repeat) were set for early in 1959. Gertrude was delighted to report this to Cox, adding, "We hope that *at last* the U.S. horizon is in sight!" She also asked Cox to spread the news to "all men of good will" that they would like to have a concert in New York or Washington while they were there. She wrote to the Nosses strongly recommending that if Yale was interested in having a Hindemith concert a time should be reserved as soon as possible "for other projects are about to join." Their friend Professor Beekman Cannon, then president of the New Haven Symphony Board, was sent a similar letter. Gertrude ended her letter to the Nosses by writing, "I can't tell you how much I am looking forward to this trip, and I only hope we will live long enough to get there."

Neither the author nor Beekman Cannon was able to arrange a New Haven concert because of insoluble calendar conflicts, and Cox could only get Leonard Bernstein to offer Hindemith a guest appearance with the New York Philharmonic simply to conduct one of his own pieces. This was rejected out of hand. One of Hindemith's former Yale students, Peter Ré, then on the music faculty at Colby College in Waterville, Maine, offered him $1,000 to conduct a concert by the college orchestra and chorus and this was accepted. A third and final event, to be given in New York's Town Hall, was arranged and sponsored by Associated Music Publishers. (Details of these three appearances are described in the following chapter.)

The Hindemiths were very unhappy that no Yale–New Haven appearance had been arranged, much more so, in fact, than their friends realized at the time, and the author and his wife were to find themselves direct targets of their resentment in July 1958. The Nosses had happily accepted Gertrude's invitation to stop briefly in Blonay while on their summer holiday in Europe, but when they arrived at their hotel in Geneva there was a note from her (along with a box of Swiss chocolates) saying they were "too busy" to receive any visitors. The travelers were not only dismayed by what was obviously a snub, but also mystified as to the real reason for it. This was not clarified until the Hindemith-Cox correspondence came to Yale ten years later. This included a letter from Gertrude to Oscar Cox written in July 1958 in which she expressed their "serious disappointment over our good old Yale School of Music" and how Dean Noss and the faculty had let them down. She went on to say: "The Nosses are now touring Switzerland but we found reasons not to see them. A discussion might have become unpleasant and we did not feel the urge to sit with a whiskey-soda and just chat. These people do not know how disappointing they are. After 13 years of Paul doing all he could for the School, it seems strange to realize what little effect it made."[15]

Osea Noss wrote to Gertrude later in the fall, sending local news of mutual interest, saying she was sorry the planned visit did not take place, and wishing the Hindemiths well on their forthcoming trip to the United States. Gertrude responded with a cordial letter just before Christmas, expressing their disappointment over not having a Yale engagement but saying she could understand how there might have been difficulties in arranging one. Her letter continued:

> Paul was always interested in participating in some School event when he returned and was willing to do anything, perhaps organize a School concert that could be repeated in New York. I can even say he decided to take the Pittsburgh engagement because it offered the possibility of his appearing at Yale. The fact that we will return without Yale on our program might lead to a mistaken impression. I have already heard it said that Paul "did not want to come back," and that he "was not interested in seeing his old school again." This is all very silly and embarrassing. You would do us a great favor if you told the truth: Paul was willing but nothing could be arranged.
>
> Forgive me for speaking out so frankly, but I felt it right to bring the subject up to avoid misunderstanding. We will be passing

through New Haven for a few hours, I guess. We might meet if you are not too busy. But Paul will decline any social affairs, for you know how he hates them. Happy New Year and best wishes as ever. Paul and Gertrude.[16]

The Hindemiths sailed for New York from Genoa on 10 January 1959, reentering the United States on 21 January, five years and eight months after moving to Switzerland. The Nosses were not "too busy" to see them in New Haven and cordial relations were instantly resumed. The long period of waiting and frustration was finally ended and the Hindemiths would never again have cause to question their status as U.S. citizens or the loyalty of their friends at "our good old Yale School of Music."

Chapter 15

Reconciliation, 1959–63

Six weeks before sailing to the United States for his first concert tour there since leaving in 1953, Hindemith sent this note to Oscar Cox: "It will be marvelous to see you again, but you will do us a great favor if you refrain from any mobilization of local authorities, press people, and so on."[1] Hindemith reminded him again a few weeks later: "Please do not send any ladies of honor or other dignitaries to the boat. Traditionally, Karl Bauer will be there with his old Chevvy, and the more anonymously we can arrive and stay in New York the happier we will be."[2] Karl Bauer also received a note from the composer: "Please do not let anyone know our New York address, not even my relatives, otherwise too many people will know about it."[3]

With only three unexceptional engagements on his schedule, Hindemith was obviously anxious to avoid any special attention being paid to his return. There is also reason to assume that the many doubts and questions about their current standing here raised by their difficulties in organizing a tour had made the Hindemiths a bit apprehensive and they thought it better to maintain a low profile until they saw what would happen.

There was no ceremonial welcome at the dock when they arrived in New York on 21 January, with only their close friend Karl Bauer and his "old Chevvy" there to take them to the Plaza Hotel, where they stayed until going to Pittsburgh three days later. Hindemith conducted a pair of subscription concerts by the Pittsburgh Symphony Orchestra on 30 January and 1 February, given in the Syria Mosque Auditorium. The program included Schumann's *Manfred Overture*, the composer's *Pittsburgh Symphony*, commissioned by the city for its bicentennial celebration, and Reger's *Variations on a Theme by Hiller*. The reviews were rather bland, giving credit for workman-like conducting and accepting the commissioned work as a rather interesting piece of "occasional music."

Hindemith's well-intentioned effort to give his twenty-three-minute symphony an appropriate parochial flavor by making thematic use of a Pennsylvania Dutch folksong and a quasi-folk pop tune extolling the city of Pittsburgh seems to have misfired. The Pittsburgh audience wondered what a Pennsylvania Dutch tune had to do with their city, and most of them had never heard the pop tune, written in 1941 by Woody Guthrie with the help of Pete Seeger for use in their own concerts. Andres Briner, who attended the premiere performance, has written in his biography of the composer that he overheard some members of the audience say they thought Hindemith was playing some kind of a joke on them and were not particularly pleased. Non-Pittsburghians are, of course, not disturbed by these elements and can fully enjoy one of the composer's most ingenious and brilliant orchestral scores. Hindemith himself seemed to have been pleased with it, for he included it on twenty-one concerts he conducted later.

Hindemith enjoyed the engagement at Colby College, where on 8 February he conducted the school orchestra and chorus in a program that included Mendelssohn's *Hebrides Overture,* his own *Five Songs on Old Texts,* Handel's *Water Music,* and Bruckner's *Mass in E Minor.* The demand for tickets was so great that the scheduled morning dress rehearsal was changed into an extra concert, open to the public for a fee.

Hindemith and his advisers had considered a New York appearance essential on his first visit back, but none of the possibilities offered had been deemed suitable. Consequently, Associated Music Publishers assumed the responsibility of organizing a concert and it proved to be very successful. A professional concert manager was engaged, who secured the composer's consent to hold a press conference at the Plaza Hotel a few days prior to the event, attended by the city's leading music editors. Hindemith had not wished to meet with U.S. "press people" on his arrival three weeks before, but meanwhile not only had his appearances at Pittsburgh and Colby College been successful, but he had also been offered and had accepted an engagement as one of the guest conductors of the New York Philharmonic Orchestra during the 1959–60 season, and he was now quite willing to meet the press. He was treated with utmost respect, and his sharp and frank answers to a variety of questions about contemporary music were given extensive coverage.

It is clear that the composer wanted to take advantage of the opportunity afforded by this visit to introduce some of his most recent music to U.S. audiences. Pittsburgh had heard his latest symphony, written late in 1958, and two works completed earlier that year were on the Town Hall program in New York: the *Octet* for winds and strings, and six of his *Twelve Madrigals.* Bruckner's *Mass in E Minor* was the final work on the program. Participating in the performance were instrumentalists from the National Arts Chamber Orchestra and singers from the Collegiate Chorale.

Hindemith could not have hoped for a warmer reception, being greeted by a standing ovation when he first appeared on stage and again at the end. All of the major music critics attended and were full of praise for what they saw and heard. The *Musical Courier* reviewer predicted that "Hindemith's command of conducting will soon carry him into the ranks of the masters in the baton field," and "music lovers may joyously anticipate next season's return of Paul Hindemith as a guest conductor of the Philharmonic." Howard Taubman wrote in the *Times* that "Mr. Hindemith will be conducting the New York Philharmonic next year and he will be appreciated with increasing ardor." Paul Henry Lang ended his *Herald-Tribune* review by saying, "I for one left the concert profoundly thankful to have had the opportunity to see this exceptional musical mind in action." The *Madrigals,* in fact, found such favor that they were later voted by the New York Music Critics Circle as being the best new contemporary choral music premiered in the city during 1959.

Several of the Hindemiths' Yale friends, including the Nosses, went backstage afterward, wondering not a little how Paul and Gertrude would react on seeing some of the people in whom they had been so "disappointed." The friends were greeted as warmly as ever before, and the Hindemiths immediately accepted an invitation from the Nosses for an overnight visit with them in New Haven, on the condition that no one was to know they would be there except a few friends they would specify. They came on 18 February and were given the use of the private guest suite in Silliman College, where the author was then serving as master. There was a small cocktail party to which the special friends they wished to see had been invited, and Professor and Mrs. Richard Donovan remained for dinner. Paul and Gertrude went alone the next morning to their former home on Alden Avenue to check on the household goods they had left there, and the Nosses joined them for lunch at a nearby restaurant, where Paul and the author began making plans for a

Yale concert in 1960. The Hindemiths returned to New York that afternoon. It had been a heartwarming visit for all concerned, and it must be recorded that neither Paul nor Gertrude made any reference during their visit, direct or indirect, to the fact that there had been no Yale concert scheduled. They were obviously pleased with the warm welcome they had received from their Yale friends and especially so to know there would definitely be a Hindemith appearance at Yale in 1960.

Hindemith's first return visit to the United States had been long in coming and short on promises, but the success of the New York concert alone made it worthwhile. The composer had convinced the tough New York critics that he really could conduct, and he would strengthen their conviction on subsequent visits. He could also enjoy the satisfaction of knowing that the 1960 tour was already taking shape, with firm offers to conduct the New York Philharmonic and a concert at Yale University. They sailed for Europe on 21 February and were home in Blonay by 2 March.

Plans for Hindemith's concert at Yale moved ahead without delay. Negotiations with Schulthess were completed by April and the date set for 19 February 1960. Hindemith immediately began working on program details, and it was clear from the many letters exchanged with the author that he was taking his "homecoming" concert at Yale very seriously indeed. Various possibilities were discussed over the next two months before a final plan evolved that pleased him and for which adequate instrumental and choral forces at the school were available. The program would begin with a Buxtehude cantata on the chorale *Herzlich Lieb hab' ich dich, O Herr,* for chorus and orchestra, sung in German. Gertrude wrote that Paul wanted to do "something special" at Yale and for this he selected three pieces from Giovanni Gabrieli's *Symphoniae Sacrae* as the second number on the program, none of which had ever been published in modern performance editions, and Hindemith made them to order for this occasion, based on the available instrumentation. The selections were: *Magnificat,* for three choirs and instruments, sung in Latin; *Canzoni septiemi et octavi,* arranged for an ensemble of recorders, krummhorns, oboes, bassoons, viols, and lute; and *Omnes gentes plaudite,* for four choirs and instruments, sung in Latin. The school requested that he include one of his own compositions and he agreed to open the second half with six of his *Twelve Madrigals,* of which four had been sung in the Town Hall concert but two would be U.S. premieres. He chose Stravinsky's *Symphony of Psalms* as the final number, saying that all "intelligent students" should learn this "inspiring" piece.

Organizing the 1960 U.S. tour was done without delay or difficulty. The New York and Yale appearances had been set as early as April 1959, and Oscar Cox was able to complete arrangements for a performance of the *Lilacs Requiem* in the Washington Cathedral, to be conducted by Hindemith on 6 March 1960. Earlier, Cox wrote that he would try to have the *Requiem* performed at the Capitol before a joint session of Congress on Lincoln's birthday with the composer conducting, but Gertrude quickly squelched that idea. She wrote to Cox on 30 April, "Dear Oscar, do not press the plan of a Congress performance, for so many Americans have written similar things (American Creed, Gettysburg Address, etc.) that the jealousy would be terrible."[4]

They arrived in New York on 8 February 1960, having sailed from Le Havre on the S.S. *United States,* and stayed at the Hotel Pierre until going to New Haven on 12 February. Hindemith had arranged his schedule to allow for a full week of daily rehearsals and began work within a few hours after his arrival. After hearing all of the various choral and instrumental groups perform their numbers over the next three days, he told the author that everything was so well in hand the concert could be given "tomorrow." They had been so carefully prepared by Professors Keith Wilson and Fenno Heath he found little more that needed to be done. Hindemith was delighted and very proud of his old school. The remaining rehearsals could now be used for added polishing, and the final performances were flawless. The capacity Sprague Hall audience rose to its feet and cheered at the end.

The Hindemiths greatly enjoyed their week back at Yale. They stayed at the Taft Hotel (by choice) but also had the use of the academic guest suite at Silliman College. There were opportunities to see all of the old friends they wished to see and a gala reception was given in their honor at the Silliman College Master's House after the concert. Gertrude sent the Nosses this note after returning to New York: "It was a glorious week in every respect—humanly, musically, spiritually, and emotionally—and it was good to be back. I never would have thought that the grim old Taft Hotel could be a magic place of delight, and our academic suite was a sweet and charming refuge. I hope now you can recover from the Hindemith ordeal."[5]

They returned to New York on 21 February and Hindemith's rehearsals with the Philharmonic began the following day. He conducted the first of four concerts on consecutive days in Carnegie Hall on 25 February in a program that included Cherubini's *Overture to "Medea,"* his own 1940 *Concerto for Violoncello and Orchestra,* and Bruckner's *Symphony No. 7.* The soloist in the concerto was Aldo Parisot, a brilliant young Brazilian-American cellist recently appointed to the Yale School of Music faculty. Hindemith had known him when Parisot was a student at Yale in the late 1940s.

All of the critics were impressed by Hindemith's conducting, notably his ability to project the musical essence of the work without resorting to virtuoso mannerisms. These were some typical comments: "When Mr. Hindemith leads the orchestra you know that a great musical mind is at work" (Paul Henry Lang in the *Herald-Tribune*); "He makes no pretense of being a heaven-storming wielder of the baton ... his ideas of the works he undertakes are conveyed with energy but without fuss" (Howard Taubman in the *Times*); and "He was a study in compact energy and concentrated gravity, an object lesson for all conductors" (Louis Biancolli in the *World-Telegraph and Star*).

For reasons known only to itself, the New York Philharmonic had waited an uncommonly long time before inviting Hindemith to conduct, being virtually the last of the major U.S. and European orchestras to do so. When it did, however, he was given a royal reception, and during the intermission at the third concert he was ceremoniously inducted into the Philharmonic Society as an honorary member, joining a highly exclusive company that included the likes of Liszt, Wagner, and Stravinsky. Wide publicity was given his appearance in the city and he was honored at two large receptions, one given by the society and the other by AMP. The author and his wife were with the Hindemiths after the final concert and found them elated over the success of this important engagement. Adding to their pleasure was the fact that Paul had received a standing invitation to return as a guest conductor whenever his schedule permitted and also a commission to write a work for the orchestra to be performed during its 1962–63 inaugural season in the new Philharmonic Hall in Lincoln Center.

Hindemith's third and final appearance on the 1960 U.S. tour was at the Washington Cathedral in the nation's capital, where on 6 March he conducted a performance of Bruckner's *Mass in E Minor* and his own *Lilacs Requiem*. Critic Paul Hume of the *Washington Post* was moved to write: "I doubt if we shall ever mourn Abraham Lincoln's untimely death more eloquently than in the words of Walt Whitman set to the music of Paul Hindemith; it is a work of genius and the presence of the genius presiding over its performance brought us splendor and profound and moving glory." The chorus and orchestra had been prepared by Paul Callaway, organist and choirmaster of the cathedral, with the composer doing the final rehearsals on the two days preceding the concert. The idea of doing the *Requiem* in the cathedral had originated with Oscar Cox, who also carried out all details of its organization.

The Hindemiths returned to New York and remained there until sailing for Le Havre on 12 March aboard the S.S. *United States.* On the day before leaving, Hindemith agreed to an interview over lunch at his hotel with Howard Taubman of the *Times,* who delayed publishing his story until 20 March, eight days after the composer had left the country and was safely out of firing range. Taubman reported that Gertrude was present and had cautioned her husband to watch his words, but he was obviously in an expansive mood and undoubtedly a bit chesty over the manifest success of his recently completed tour, and gave very frank answers to the interviewer's probing questions. He named Stravinsky and Bartok as the only twentieth-century composers whose music would endure, expressing serious doubts about Schönberg and his circle. He could not think of anyone in the United States who merited being called a genuine "composer" and complained that this country "pampered" its young writers by giving them too many grants, fellowships, and awards. His unwillingness to consider any U.S. composer as worthy of high ranking provoked an irate response from many readers, and even Taubman himself took issue, ending his article by writing, "Hindemith has earned the right to the proud title of composer, but we would only add that a few more names of the last 50 years might be added to his list." However, the publication of his critical opinion of U.S. composers did Hindemith no lasting harm and he was received here as cordially as ever when he returned again in 1961.

Back in their Blonay home by 18 March, the composer shortly began work on his unique one-act opera *The Long Christmas Dinner.* The story of this collaborative project between Hindemith and his New Haven friend and author Thornton Wilder offers further evidence of his deep and virtually lifelong interest in U.S. history and literature. He had been intrigued by the story after reading it in a 1931 volume of Wilder's one-act plays and thought it could be used as an opera libretto, provided certain revisions were made. He wrote to Wilder asking if he would be willing to make such revisions according to a plan the composer would outline. Wilder agreed and on 14 May received Hindemith's suggestions. He immediately began the revision, sending each scene to Blonay as soon as it was completed, where Hindemith spent most of June writing the score.

Work on the opera had to be interrupted long enough to write a commissioned four-minute *March* to be played during the academic procession at the ceremonial opening of the week-long celebration of the 500th anniversary of the University of Basel, held on 1 July. The author was there as the official representative of Yale University, and he and his wife enjoyed several private meetings over food and wine with the Hindemiths, who had driven over from Blonay for a few days of relaxation as special guests of the University of Basel. They were still savoring the pleasures and successes of their recent U.S. tour and were eager to hear all the latest news from Yale and New Haven. They also invited the Nosses to visit them in Blonay, a totally unexpected pleasure, for it was well known how zealously they guarded the privacy of their Alpine retreat, never divulging its exact location and rarely receiving visitors there.

The visit took place on 29 and 30 July and it was gratifying for anyone who had known Paul and Gertrude only in the relatively modest settings of their New Haven homes to see them now in their imposing villa above Lake Geneva, surrounded by the beautiful furnishings that had miraculously escaped destruction while stored in a warehouse near Berlin during the war. The guests were lavishly entertained and again there was much talk about Yale and the United States. Paul complained that he had been waiting impatiently for three weeks to receive the final scene of the opera from Wilder and asked the Nosses, who knew Thornton personally, to find out what was happening when they returned to New Haven in a few days. They did, and learned from Wilder's sister Isabel, who served as her brother's secretary, that the final scene was now on its way to Blonay. She explained that Thornton had always found it difficult to consider a manuscript "finished," feeling that there were improvements that could and should still be made.

Plans for the 1961 tour had begun early in 1960, when Hindemith

agreed to conduct the Santa Fe Opera in August, in three performances of his comic opera *News of the Day,* to be sung in English.
Knowing he had a standing invitation to conduct the Chicago
Symphony during its summer concert series in Ravinia Park on the
North Shore, he had his manager notify the orchestra he would be
available in July 1961 and he was promptly engaged for three separate concerts. Offers to conduct in the Hollywood Bowl and in
Vancouver were also received but declined, since Hindemith wanted
to have some time to relax while here. Gertrude told the author later
that Paul's arduous winter and spring concert activities had brought
on a minor heart problem and his doctor had cautioned him not to
take on too much work during the summer. Consequently, the 1961
tour was limited to only six appearances in six and a half weeks, but
all were of major importance and the fees were sufficient to make it
financially feasible.

They docked in New York on 18 July 1961 and two days later left
for Chicago by train, but arranged for a day's stop in Detroit, where
Hindemith took advantage of the opportunity to learn more about
this country's past by visiting "Greenfield Village and the Ford
Museum," as he noted in his pocket diary. They were in Chicago by
23 July.

The Ravinia Park concerts by the Chicago Symphony given on
25, 27, and 29 July were very successful. Chicago's leading music
critics were ecstatic in their praise of Hindemith's conducting, writing reviews that appeared under two-, three-, and even four-column
heads such as "Hindemith, 66, Thrills Ravinia," "A Rewarding
Ravinia Night by Hindemith," "Hindemith Scores Again," "Hindemith
Leads a Superior Schubert," "Hindemith's Performance Memorable,"
and "Hindemith's Triumph Worth Shouting About." It was a remarkable achievement for the orchestra as well, for three entirely different programs were played over a period of only six days, each one
including a demanding work by Hindemith that most of the players
had never done before.

The 25 July program offered Cherubini's *Overture to "Les
Abéncerages,"* Hindemith's *Concert Music for Strings and Brass,
Opus 50,* and Bruckner's *Symphony No. 7.* Hindemith's reading of
the Bruckner was described as one of "extraordinary and spellbind-
ing insight" that drew a standing ovation. This prompted another
critic to write, "Anyone who can win this sort of reception with an
unfamiliar score of more than an hour's duration deserves a place

among the most persuasive masters of the baton." Two nights later Hindemith conducted Mendelssohn's *Hebrides Overture,* his own *Pittsburgh Symphony,* and Schubert's *Symphony No. 9.* One reviewer wrote that the Schubert was done with "a stylistic authority that carried overwhelming conviction and established the most vital kind of communication between performer and listener." The third and final concert, given 29 July, included his *Concerto for Orchestra* from 1925, Beethoven's *Third Piano Concerto,* with Gary Grafmann as soloist, and Schumann's *Symphony No. 4.* The capacity audience arose and cheered at the end, joined by members of the orchestra, who broke out into a thunderous orchestral fanfare. The *Sun-Times* reviewer wrote, "The impressive thing was that for all his reputation as a composer, Hindemith got this reception the honest and hard and musically significant way by giving the audience a concert so fine that it made you want to shout."

Hindemith's spectacular success at Ravinia prompted Chicago Symphony officials to offer him an engagement during the 1961–62 subscription season in Orchestra Hall, but he could not accept because his concert schedule was already filled. However, he agreed to come in the spring of 1963, when he would conduct seven concerts by the orchestra in three different programs.

The invitation to conduct in Santa Fe was extended to Hindemith by the founder (in 1957) and general director of the Santa Fe Opera, John Crosby, a recent Yale College graduate who knew the composer at the university. Crosby proposed that *News of the Day* be sung in English and Hindemith agreed. He asked his Yale friends to help find a translator and Don Moreland, a graduate of the Yale School of Drama and a professional stage director, was recommended. When Hindemith was at Yale in February 1960 the author arranged for the two men to meet and an agreement was reached to have Moreland not only do the translation but also be the stage director for the production.

The Hindemiths went by train to Albuquerque, New Mexico, rented a car there and drove to Santa Fe, where they settled into the historic and colorful La Fonda Inn on 3 August. The world premiere of *News of the Day* in English on 12 August had a successful beginning but a disastrous finish. At the time, the Santa Fe Opera gave its performances in an outdoor theater located in the desert a few miles north of the city, a delightful setting provided the weather cooperated. That night it did not, as Gertrude reported in a letter to

Oscar Cox: "The opening night went beautifully until a cloudburst of super violence put an end to it in the middle, drenching the audience, conductor, singers, and the stage in an ocean of furious waters. The heroic people stood under hoods and umbrellas, shouting 'Bravo, bravo, more, more!' Now we are keeping our fingers crossed for the second performance this Wednesday night."[6]

The author and his wife attended the second performance and again there was a weather problem. However, the rains came with only five minutes remaining, and the conductor, orchestra, and cast braved it to the finish. The conductor and performers were given a rousing ovation. All of the critics lauded the music, conductor, orchestra, singers, and the production, but several thought the plot a bit silly, a reaction this comic opera has consistently drawn since it was first performed in 1929.

At lunch with Paul and Gertrude the following day, the Nosses were astonished when the composer suddenly asked if Yale University would be interested in receiving all of his music manuscripts as a bequest. He said the University of Zürich and the State Music Conservatory in Frankfurt had both made formal requests for them but he was not convinced either place was appropriate and was now thinking of Yale. This was incredible, coming as it did so soon after the Hindemiths' professed disenchantment with Yale, but apparently the great success of the February 1960 visit had obliterated any feeling of ill will they might have had. The author happily assured him that Yale would be honored to accept such a legacy, but first it would have to be determined whether the university could provide appropriate facilities for such a valuable collection. Preliminary planning for a new music center had recently been authorized and this offered an excellent possibility, but no definite answer could be given for two or three years. Hindemith said he was willing to wait. Unfortunately for Yale, it was not to be, for delays in the building plans and the composer's untimely death in 1963 put an end to any further negotiations.

The Hindemiths were home in Blonay by 8 September and would remain in Europe until returning for a fourth visit in 1963. A full schedule of nineteen major conducting engagements had been arranged without difficulty, ample evidence that Hindemith was now recognized in this country as a conductor of first rank. Several additional offers had been received but had to be declined. Meanwhile, there would be eighteen months of intense professional activity, including fifty major appearances as a conductor in Germany, Austria, Switzerland, Italy, and England, and the composition of two large works, the *Mainzer Umzug,* and the *Concerto for Organ and Orchestra.*

Hindemith continued to receive attention by the U.S. press while he was out of the country. The *New York Times* carried stories about the December 1961 world premiere of *The Long Christmas Dinner* in Mannheim, Hindemith's appointment as a guest conductor of the New York Philharmonic for the 1962–63 season, and his commission by the Philharmonic to write a work in celebration of its first season in Lincoln Center. *Time* magazine published an article on the premiere of the *Mainzer Umzug,* an oratorio written to commemorate the 2000th anniversary of the city of Mainz. He was also honored in 1962 by being elected to membership in the prestigious American Philosophical Society, a very "American" organization founded in Philadelphia in 1743 and whose earlier presidents included Benjamin Franklin and Thomas Jefferson. This was in recognition of his work as an author and theorist as well as composer, for membership in the society is restricted to outstanding scholars and scientists.

The Hindemiths arrived in New York to begin their fourth visit on 6 March 1963, having sailed from Le Havre on the S.S. *America.* Paul went to the Juilliard School of Music that same evening to take over rehearsals for *The Long Christmas Dinner,* which would be performed for the first time in its original English version on 13 March. It was given on four consecutive evenings, paired with his 1924 ballet *The Demon* on the first two nights and his 1944 ballet *Herodiäde* on the other two. Hindemith conducted only the first two performances, with Jorge Mester of the Juilliard faculty, who had done all of the preliminary rehearsals, taking over on the third and fourth. The critics were much impressed by this unusual Hindemith-Wilder music drama. Irving Kolodin of the *Saturday Review* wrote, "A unique blend of talent introduced a new composite of beauty in Paul Hindemith's setting of Thornton Wilder's *The Long Christmas Dinner*" and described the score as "filled with beautiful sonorities." Paul Henry Lang of the *Herald-Tribune* commented that "the work testifies to the exceptional rank Mr. Hindemith occupies among 20th-century composers by virtue of his wide knowledge, which is in the service of a persuasive style controlled by an extraordinarily musical sensitivity."

The Juilliard production was transported to Washington, D.C., where the opera and *The Demon* were performed in the Linser Auditorium on 17 and 18 March, conducted by Hindemith. This was sponsored by the Opera Society of Washington and organized by Oscar Cox, who was the treasurer of the society.

Hindemith was next in Chicago, where he faced the demanding task of conducting the Chicago Symphony Orchestra in six concerts of three different programs within a period of nine days. On 28 March he conducted a regular subscription concert in Orchestra Hall that included Brahms's *Academic Overture,* his own *Concert Music for Strings and Brass, Opus 50,* and Bruckner's *Symphony No. 7.* The concert was repeated the following afternoon, after which Hindemith was the guest of honor at a reception by the Bruckner Society, and again in the Pabst Theater in Milwaukee on 1 April. He did another pair of subscription concerts in Orchestra Hall on 4 and 5 April, offering Schumann's *Manfred Overture,* Reger's *Variations on a Theme by Beethoven,* Wagner's *Siegfried Idyll,* and his own *Sinfonietta in E.* His final program, the following day, began with the same Schumann and Reger pieces but ended with Beethoven's *Grosse Fuge* and Hindemith's *Nobilissima Visione Suite.* The reviews of these concerts were uniformly excellent.

Paul and Gertrude were not back in New York until 15 April, nine days after the final Chicago concert. The only record of their whereabouts and activities during this interval is found in the composer's pocket diary: evidently, Hindemith was having difficulties with his stomach and kidneys, and they went to Hot Springs, Virginia, to consult with doctors and presumably try the mineral waters. The diary contains no further mention of medical problems during the remainder of this visit, but friends who saw him in New York the following week sensed something was wrong, for he did not look well.

It had to be difficult under these circumstances to carry out his heavy two-week schedule of eight concerts and a four-hour recording session with the New York Philharmonic, but Hindemith rose above them and the critics detected no weakening of his many strengths as a conductor. For his first series of four concerts, given 18 through 21 April, he chose to do his *Lilacs Requiem* and Reger's *Psalm 150* for chorus and orchestra, a work Hindemith had recently rescored. The Schola Cantorum of New York, prepared by its regular conductor Hugh Ross, provided the choral forces and George London was the baritone soloist in the *Requiem*. Hindemith conducted the same performers in a recording of the *Lilacs Requiem* for Columbia Records on 23 April.

The featured work on the second series of four concerts Hindemith conducted on 26 through 29 April was his *Concerto for Organ and Orchestra* that had been commissioned by the New York Philharmonic. He had opted for this format when he learned there would be a new organ in Philharmonic Hall, but the results were not entirely satisfactory. Many of the musical subtleties of this powerful and complex work were lost because of the organ's tonal deficiencies. The excellent soloist was the distinguished Viennese organist Anton Heiller. Weber's *Euryanthe Overture* and Reger's *Variations on a Theme by Hiller* were the other works on the program. Many of the Hindemiths' Yale friends attended the first performance and went backstage after the concert to wish them bon voyage. Gertrude was her usual ebullient self, but Paul was uncharacteristically subdued and looked very fatigued. They both said they were looking forward to returning for another tour next year. It was the last time their friends would ever see them.

The Hindemiths left the United States on 2 May, and this time they would never return. Paul died on 28 December 1963, and Gertrude's expressed intentions of coming back to visit her friends were never realized before her own death in March 1967. The news of Paul Hindemith's untimely death at the age of sixty-eight was given prominent and extensive coverage in all of the leading U.S. newspapers, many of which included special articles by their music editors eulogizing his life and work. It was the kind of media attention accorded only to the passing of a national celebrity. Every major orchestra in the United States paid a musical tribute to his memory, including a national telecast by the New York Philharmonic conducted and narrated by Leonard Bernstein, called "The Legacy of Paul Hindemith."

Early in 1964, plans were begun to establish a Paul Hindemith Collection at Yale to preserve documents already at the university and to assemble more material relating to his life and work in the United States. It was formally inaugurated during a convocation commemorating the composer's thirteen years at Yale, held on 7 and 8 November 1964 and attended by over 200 of his friends and former students from all parts of the country. Gertrude Hindemith was invited but regretfully declined, saying the emotional strain would be too much for her to bear. To demonstrate her appreciation of the invitation and her lasting affection for Yale she gave to the university the original full score of the *Lilacs Requiem*, which arrived in time to be shown at the convocation along with many other items of Hindemith memorabilia in a large exhibit prepared by the Music Library. Convocation events included three concerts of his music, a reception and dinner for all the guests, and a memorial Mass in St. Thomas More Chapel with the Ordinary sung to the music of Hindemith's last composition, his *Mass* for a cappella chorus.

When he renounced his German citizenship and took an oath to defend the United States upon becoming a citizen in 1946, Hindemith could neither understand nor appreciate the fact that he continued to be referred to by the U.S. media as a German more often than not. He never considered himself to be an "American" composer nor did he expect to be known as one, but he was, after all, a U.S. citizen, and it irked him not to be considered as such, for it was a matter of great personal pride to him. The successes of his U.S. tours from 1959 on had begun to improve this situation, but most of the obituary stories left the impression that he was really a German who just happened to have a U.S. passport. Auspicious recognition as a compatriot was finally accorded him thirteen years after his death, when the National Music Council in the bicentennial year of 1976 included his name in the select list of "Americans who have made notable contributions to this nation's musical heritage during the first 200 years of its history." A bronze plaque now hangs in the foyer of Sprague Memorial Hall at Yale University, where Paul Hindemith did all of his teaching and conducting while on the faculty, that reads:

A LANDMARK OF AMERICAN MUSIC, PAUL HINDEMITH (1895–1963). COMPOSER, PERFORMER, TEACHER, AUTHOR, AND ONE OF THE MOST INFLUENTIAL MUSICIANS OF THE 20TH CENTURY, HINDEMITH EXCELLED IN EVERY FORM OF COMPOSITION FROM OPERA TO BALLET. HE WAS A SUPERB VIOLIST AND KNEW THE TECHNIQUES AND POTENTIALITIES OF EVERY INSTRUMENT OF THE ORCHESTRA. AS A THEORIST HE WROTE TEXTS THAT ARE MASTERPIECES OF EDUCATIONAL EXPERTISE. AT YALE UNIVERSITY (1940–53) HE EXERTED A LASTING INFLUENCE OVER COUNTLESS ASPIRING AMERICAN COMPOSERS. PRESENTED BY THE NATIONAL

MUSIC COUNCIL AND CONNECTICUT STATE FEDERATION OF MUSIC AND DANCE CLUBS. AMERICAN REVOLUTION BICENTENNIAL, 1776–1976.

Notes

Acknowledgments

1. Geoffrey Skelton's *Paul Hindemith: The Man behind the Music* is a notable exception. Refer to the Bibliography for further details.

Part 1: Early Associations, 1920–40

Chapter 1: Early Associations with the United States, 1920–37

1. Hindemith's chance discovery of these Walt Whitman poems sparked a keen and lasting interest in the work of the great poet. He immediately obtained a copy of *Leaves of Grass* and used it as a "reader" for the studies in English he had now begun to undertake seriously. This was the composer's introduction to Whitman's moving tribute to the memory of Abraham Lincoln that he would set to music twenty-six years later in his oratorio *When Lilacs Last in the Dooryard Bloom'd: A Requiem for Those We Love*, as detailed in chapter 10.

2. The *Concert Music for Strings and Brass, Opus 50* was the last composition to which Hindemith assigned an opus number. He discontinued the practice after 1930.

3. Letter: Hindemith to Mrs. Coolidge, 8 May 1930.

4. Letter: Hindemith to Mrs. Coolidge, 19 August 1930.

5. Letter: Mrs. Coolidge to Hindemith, 18 October 1930.

6. Letter: Willy Strecker to Hindemith, 8 March 1937.

7. Letter: Gertrude Hindemith to Willy Strecker, 11 March 1937.

8. Letter: Willy Strecker to Hindemith, 16 March 1937.

Chapter 2: The First U.S. Concert Tour, 1937

1. Letter: Oliver Strunk to Hindemith, 12 September 1936.

2. Otto Klemperer had fled Germany and was now conducting the Los Angeles Symphony Orchestra.

3. Hindemith's creative work while living in the United States was greatly facilitated by the close and willing cooperation of Associated Music Publishers in New York and he was grateful for it. However, when royalties owed to him by Schott-Mainz and Schott-London were finally released to him in

1951 by the office of the Alien Property Custodian in Washington, D.C., where they had been legally impounded ever since the United States had entered the war, he was greatly upset. He found reason to believe that faulty accounting practices by AMP had done him out of a fair amount of money he was due and threatened to cancel his contract with Schott unless the president of AMP was replaced immediately. Willy Strecker was alarmed and immediately hurried over to settle the dispute. He succeeded in having the president replaced and Hindemith withdrew his threat.

4. Letter: Oliver Strunk to Hindemith, 12 September 1936.

5. Letter: Hindemith to Oliver Strunk, 9 December 1936.

6. The four choral pieces were so well received at the festival that AMP urged Schott to publish them with English translations. Hindemith added a new piece in 1938 and the five were eventually published by AMP in 1943 as *Five Songs On Old Texts*. (Schott was unable to do so because of the war.)

7. Letter: Hindemith to Gertrude Hindemith, 2 April 1937.

8. Journal: 2 April 1937.

9. Letter: Ernest Voigt to Willy Strecker, 16 April 1937.

10. Ibid.

11. Journal: 2 April 1937.

12. The young Mexican composer-conductor Carlos Chavez was then in the United States doing a series of concerts with the Philadelphia Orchestra. Mrs. Coolidge was interested in promoting his career and had invited him to participate in the Washington Festival.

13. Journal: 9 April 1937.

14. Journal: 6 April 1937.

15. Journal: 8 April 1937.

16. Journal: 10 April 1937.

17. *New York Times*, 11 April 1937.

18. Letter: Ernest Voigt to Willy Strecker, 16 April 1937.

19. *New York Times*, 12 April 1937.

20. Hindemith came to have high regard for Fiedler's ability as a conductor and collaborated with him in making a Victor recording of *Der Schwanendreher* on his 1939 U.S. tour.

21. Journal: 13 April 1937.

22. Letter: Ernest Voigt to Willy Strecker, 16 April 1937.

23. Letter: Hindemith to Gertrude Hindemith, 14 April 1937.

24. Journal: 15 April 1937.

25. *New York Times*, 16 April 1937.

26. Journal: 17 April 1937.

27. Journal: 18 April 1937.

28. Hindemith was in Chicago two days later and happened to stay in a hotel where Paul Whiteman and his famous "Symphonic Jazz" orchestra was playing for dinner dancing. He stopped in to listen a while and later (20 April) wrote in his journal: "It was nothing special—I am accustomed to something different from the Cotton Club experience."

29. Journal: 21 April 1937.

30. Franco Autori was the regular conductor of the Buffalo Philharmonic

Orchestra. He was an Italian-American with considerable ability, then thirty-four years old, who had been appointed only a few months before.

31. Journal: 23 April 1937.
32. Journal: 26 April 1937.
33. Ibid.
34. Letter: Hindemith to Ernest Voigt, 30 April 1937.
35. Letter: Hindemith to Mrs. Coolidge, 29 April 1937.
36. No plans for teaching at Northwestern University ever materialized.
37. Letter: Hindemith to Willy Strecker, 3 May 1937.

Chapter 3: The Second U.S. Concert Tour, 1938

1. Journal: 23 February 1938.
2. Journal: 24 February 1938.
3. The noted composer Walter Piston was then chairman of the Department of Music at Harvard University.
4. Journal: 25 February 1938.
5. Journal: 26 February 1938.
6. Details of Klaus Liepmann's involvement with Hindemith's concert at Yale on 27 February 1938 are found in a letter Liepmann wrote to Prof. Beekman Cannon on 29 March 1972, now in the Hindemith Collection at Yale.
7. Journal: 27 February 1938.
8. Letter: Hindemith to Gertrude Hindemith, 28 February 1938.
9. Journal: 1 March 1938.
10. Journal: 3 March 1938.
11. Journal: 6 March 1938.
12. Journal: 7 March 1938.
13. Journal: 8 March 1938.
14. Journal: 19 March 1938.
15. Journal: 25 March 1938.

Chapter 4: The Third U.S. Concert Tour, 1939

1. The German edition of *Unterweisung im Tonsatz, Part I*, published by Schott in 1937, had attracted international attention among musicians and had sold very well. The publisher and Hindemith had agreed that an English translation of the exercise book should be made available as soon as possible. Otto Ortmann, then director of the Peabody Conservatory of Music in Baltimore, was selected as the translator; it was published by AMP in 1941.
2. Letter: Hindemith to Gertrude Hindemith, 21 February 1939.
3. Ibid.
4. Letter: Hindemith to Gertrude Hindemith, 26 February 1939.
5. Letter: Hindemith to Gertrude Hindemith, 2 March 1939.
6. Ibid.
7. Letter: Hindemith to Gertrude Hindemith, 18 March 1939.
8. Ibid.
9. Letter: Hindemith to Gertrude Hindemith, 27 March 1939.

10. Letter: Hindemith to Gertrude Hindemith, 26 April 1939.
11. Ibid.
12. Ibid.
13. *New York Times,* 24 April 1939.

PART 2: RESIDENT, 1940–53

Chapter 5: Emigration, 1940

1. Letter: Hindemith to Willy Strecker, 20 November 1939.
2. Letter: Ernest Voigt to Nicholas Nabokov, 7 September 1939.
3. Letter: Ernest Voigt to Nicholas Nabokov, c. 10 December 1939.
4. Letter: Hindemith to Gertrude Hindemith, 12 February 1940.

Chapter 6: The First Seven Months

1. Letter: Hindemith to Gertrude Hindemith, 1 March 1940.
2. Ibid.
3. Letter: Hindemith to Gertrude Hindemith, 20 March 1940.
4. *A Song of Music* was published by AMP in 1941 with the English text. Hindemith later made a German translation under the title *Lied von der Musik* and the piece was published by Schott in 1958 with both the German and English texts.
5. The plan had to be modified to accommodate the different spring vacation breaks at both schools. Four of the appearances could be synchronized, but it was necessary for Hindemith to make two separate visits to each school to complete the series of six lectures.
6. Letter: Dean David Stanley Smith to President Charles Seymour, 11 January 1940.
7. Letter: Hindemith to Gertrude Hindemith, 31 March 1940.
8. Letter: Hindemith to Gertrude Hindemith, 7 April 1940.
9. Letter: Hindemith to Gertrude Hindemith, 12 April 1940.
10. Letter: Hindemith to Gertrude Hindemith, 27 April 1940.
11. Letter: Hindemith to Gertrude Hindemith, 15 March 1940.
12. Letter: Hindemith to Gertrude Hindemith, 21 March 1940.
13. Letter: Hindemith to Gertrude Hindemith, 15 July 1940.
14. Letter: Hindemith to Gertrude Hindemith, 5 August 1940.
15. Letter: Hindemith to Gertrude Hindemith, c. 20 August 1940.
16. Letter: Hindemith to Gertrude Hindemith, 15 March 1940.
17. Ibid.
18. Letter: Hindemith to Gertrude Hindemith, 12 April 1940.
19. Letter: Hindemith to Gertrude Hindemith, 27 April 1940.
20. Letter: Hindemith to Gertrude Hindemith, 14 July 1940.
21. Letter: Hindemith to Gertrude Hindemith, 6 August 1940.
22. Letter: Hindemith to Gertrude Hindemith, 3 March 1940.
23. Letter: Hindemith to Gertrude Hindemith, 7 March 1940.

Chapter 7: Professor at Yale

1. Letter: Hindemith to Willy Strecker, 27 October 1940.
2. Letter: President Charles Seymour to Hindemith, 22 January 1941.
3. Letter: Charles Seymour to Hindemith, 11 February 1941.
4. Letter: Hindemith to Willy Strecker, 30 May 1941.
5. Letter: Hindemith to Dean Bruce Simonds, 11 November 1948.
6. Hindemith suggested Arnold Schönberg, then teaching at the University of California in Los Angeles, as his temporary replacement. The invitation was spurned in a curt note saying that he was not interested in being a substitute for Hindemith or anyone else and that the salary being offered was so low it was ridiculous.
7. Letter: Gertrude Hindemith to Willy Strecker, 12 January 1953.
8. Letter: Provost Edgar Furniss to Hindemith, 15 December 1952.

Chapter 8: Teacher at Yale

1. The written qualifying test in harmony and counterpoint prepared by Hindemith was so difficult that a mark of 50 out of a possible 100 was considered to be excellent (and the highest ever achieved). The composer once told an applicant who had complained about the severity of the test that if he could pass all of it there would be no need for him to do further study with anyone.
2. The other composition teachers during Hindemith's tenure were Richard Donovan, Hope Leroy Baumgartner, David Stanley Smith (until 1946), and Quincy Porter (after 1946).
3. Letter: Hindemith to Ernest Voigt, 8 June 1942.
4. Letter: Hindemith to Willy Strecker, 27 October 1940.
5. The forty-seven students who earned their degrees in theory or composition under Hindemith are named below. The single asterisk denotes those who received degrees in composition, the double asterisk those who received degrees in both composition and theory; the others received their degrees in theory.

Barbieri, Anthony	Hwang, Philip
* Berkowitz, Leonard	Iadone, Joseph
Blackwood, Easley	King, Alvin
Blumenfeld, Harold	**Kraehenbuehl, David
**Boatwright, Howard	Lam, George
Boykan, Martin	* Lewin, Frank
Brotman, Michael	Loach, Donald
Carlucci, Joseph	Miller, Carl S.
Collins, Walter S.	Moran, Jean Todd
* Cowell, John	Morris, Franklin
Crawford, John C.	Quashen, Ben
Darling, James	Ré, Peter
de Almeida, Antonio	Rice, William
Di Bonaventura, Sam	Richter, Eckhart
**Dunlap, Joseph	Rudas, Hans
Durkee, Charlotte	* Sarason, Leonard

England, Nicholas
* Etler, Alvin
Goodman, Thomas
Gottlieb, Robert
Hickok, Robert
Howard, Lee
Hunter, George

* Schönthal, Ruth
* Shackford, Charles
Smith, Frank
Strauss, John
**Thorarinsson, Jon
* Weigel, Eugene
Widdis, Frank
Wyner, Yehudi

The following list gives the names of other degree candidates in the school who did a substantial amount of their work in theory with Hindemith, enrolling in all or most of his courses. They included majors in performance, music history, or in theory or composition under other teachers. Several were talented composers who were accepted into Hindemith's "composition minor" class.

Archer, Violet
Bagger, Louis
Barnard, Parke
Bixler, Martha
Chessid, Herman
Cumberworth, Sterling
Diemer, Emma Lou
Einstein, Ralph
Fraker, Charles
Frost, Thomas
George, Graham
Gratch, Olga
Herrmann, Virginia Hitchcock
Jacobson, George
Keats, Donald

Lester, Eugene
McClellan, Mildred Nolte
Main, Alexander
Martens, Mason
Mason, Neale
Maynard, Paul
Miller, Timothy
Moehlenkamp, Jack
Pollak, Louis
Powell, Mel
Ruff, Willie
Samuel, Gerhard
Sinclair, George
Skelton, William
Withrow, Miriam

Hindemith admitted into his major composition class the following students who were not candidates for degrees at the School of Music. This was done only during the war years. The single asterisk denotes Yale College undergraduates; the double asterisk denotes School of Music graduates.

* Brown, David W.
* Buttolph, David
Dello Joio, Norman
Foss, Lukas
Harrison, Francis Llewellyn
* Hemingway, Louis Jr.
Kay, Ulysses
Klenz, William

**Levine, Maurice
Osborne, Wilson
Paulson, Herbert
Tam, Shau-Kwong
* Thorne, Francis
**Vinitsky, Ruth
**Woldt, John

Chapter 9: Performer at Yale

1. Letter: Hindemith to Gertrude Hindemith, 7 March 1940.
2. The original is in the Yale Hindemith Collection.

3. Yale University News Bureau release, 10 May 1946.

4. One of the three was Gertrude Hindemith, an accomplished soprano, who sang in each of the Collegium concerts.

5. Hindemith returned to Yale in February 1960 and conducted student groups in a memorable concert of choral music, fully described in chapter 15.

6. *New York Herald-Tribune,* 22 May 1953.

7. The Collegium concerts of 1951 and 1953 were recorded and Hindemith approved the release of two albums containing selections from each program. They were issued by Overtone Records in 1954 and are no longer available, but they exist in many private collections and school libraries.

Chapter 10: Creative Work

1. Letter: Hindemith to Ernest Voigt, early October 1940.

2. Letter: Hindemith to Ernest Voigt, 25 April 1941.

3. Letter: Hindemith to Willy Strecker, 30 May 1941.

4. Delighted with the success of the *Four Temperaments,* Balanchine urged the composer to write another and larger ballet that would fill an entire evening. Hindemith was interested, but circumstances prevented his ever doing so. Nevertheless, the choreographer's interest in his music remained lively and in 1952 Balanchine designed a ballet to the music of *Symphonic Metamorphosis of Themes by Carl Maria von Weber,* with the composer's approval. Hindemith attended the performance in New York's City Center and liked it, writing to Willy Strecker that it was "very gay and beautifully done." Many years later, in 1978, Balanchine choreographed another Hindemith score, *Kammermusik No. 2,* the piano concerto written in 1924, and it was highly praised by the New York dance critics. Ironically, he had asked the composer for permission to do this some forty years before, but Hindemith had refused.

5. Letter: Hindemith to Ernest Voigt, 16 February 1941. Howard Boatwright learned later from Hindemith that at the reception following the premiere of his cello concerto in Boston on 7 February 1941 Koussevitzky told the composer, "I think we should wait a little longer before we do the symphony." The maestro was never entirely comfortable in doing contemporary music, had had problems with the cello concerto, and apparently did not savor the idea of tackling another at the moment.

6. Letter: Hindemith to Ernest Voigt, late November 1941.

7. Letter: Hindemith to Ernest Voigt, 1 September 1941.

8. Letter: Hindemith to Ernest Voigt, late October 1941.

9. Letter: Hindemith to Ernest Voigt, 8 September 1942.

10. Letter: Hindemith to Ernest Voigt, 24 October 1942.

11. Letter: Hindemith to Ernest Voigt, 24 November 1942.

12. *New York Times,* 21 January 1944.

13. Ibid.

14. Preparing and publishing the concert band arrangement of the *Symphonic Metamorphosis* that Hindemith had in mind from the start proved to be a protracted and extremely frustrating operation. The chief cause was the inability of Schott and AMP to agree on how the performing rights fees were to

be shared. A settlement seemed to have been reached by 1960 and Schott asked the composer to proceed with the arrangement. His heavy schedule would not permit this, but he strongly recommended "my former colleague at Yale," Professor Keith Wilson, chairman of the Wind Instrument Department and director of University Bands. Wilson was approached and accepted the assignment, completing a symphonic band arrangement by 1962. Further disagreements now erupted, dragging on over the next ten years before the score and parts were finally published. However, the situation remains complicated, for only the score and parts of the fourth movement can be purchased, the other three movements being available on rental only.

15. Gertrude's mother died during the war, her health impaired by the struggle to survive the Allied bombardments of Frankfurt. Hindemith's mother escaped injury in the Frankfurt raids, dying of natural causes in 1948. The composer saw her after the war.

16. Letter: Hindemith to Karl Bauer at AMP, 7 March 1955.

17. Letter: Hindemith to Willy Strecker, 20 January 1947.

18. Baritone George Burson would later achieve world fame under the name George London.

19. Letter: Gertrude Hindemith to Luther Noss, 6 October 1964.

20. Letter: Hindemith to Karl Bauer, early February 1947.

21. Letter: Hindemith to Hugo Strecker, 1 December 1947.

22. Letter: Gertrude Hindemith to Willy Strecker, 16 December 1950.

23. Letter: Gertrude Hindemith to Eugene Ormandy, 2 January 1953.

24. Letter: Eugene Ormandy's secretary to Gertrude Hindemith, 16 January 1953.

25. Letter: Hindemith to Willy Strecker, 19 March 1949.

26. Several of the details relating to the Columbia University commission were obtained directly from conversations with Professor Luening in 1974.

27. The CBS Symphony was the major orchestra used by the Columbia Broadcasting System for its national broadcasts. It had no connection with Columbia University.

28. Several of the details relating to the concerto written for the Connecticut Academy anniversary were obtained from the academy's historical papers on deposit in the Yale University Library. The original manuscripts of the sketches and full scores of all three movements of the concerto are now at Yale University, given by the composer just before he took permanent leave from New Haven in June 1953. He came to the school to pay farewell calls on his friends, including the music librarian, Brooks Shepard. After his brief visit, Hindemith suddenly produced the manuscripts and tossed them on Shepard's desk, saying, "Here's something to remember me by," and left immediately.

29. The Marshall Bartholomew diaries are in the archives of the Yale School of Music Library.

30. Letter: Gertrude Hindemith to Willy Strecker, 9 November 1950.

31. Letter: Gertrude Hindemith to Willy Strecker, 16 December 1950.

32. Letter: Hindemith to Oscar Cox, 14 December 1956.

33. See "The Genesis of a Masterpiece," an article by Richard E. Thurston published in the July 1981 issue of the *Instrumentalist.*

34. Letter: Hindemith to Willy Strecker, 28 November 1952.

Chapter 11: Professional Activities

1. Howard Boatwright has pointed out that one problem in getting engagements was that Hindemith did not belong to the musicians' union. Hindemith defended his refusal to join, saying, "I got away from one dictator and don't want to be under another [Caesar Petrillo]." However, he finally joined the New Haven Local 234 in February 1950.

2. Letter: Hindemith to Ernest Voigt, 10 February 1941.

3. Letter: Hindemith to Willy Strecker, 23 September 1941.

4. Dimitri Mitropoulos also conducted the New York Philharmonic in the New York premiere of the *Symphony in E♭* on 26 December 1941. Hindemith willingly accepted the maestro's invitation to attend the performance and take a bow.

5. Letter: Hindemith to Karl Bauer, 11 September 1945.

6. *Time* magazine, 24 December 1945.

7. Letter: Gertrude Hindemith to Willy Strecker, 14 March 1951.

8. Letter: Gertrude Hindemith to Willy Strecker, 17 January 1953.

Chapter 12: Recognition, Honors, Citizenship

1. *Time* magazine, 23 February 1948.

2. From the President Charles Seymour Papers, Yale University Archives.

3. A complete copy of Roger Sessions's remarks is in the Paul Hindemith Collection at Yale University.

4. Letter: Hindemith to Gertrude Hindemith, 21 March 1940.

5. Letter: Hindemith to Hugo Strecker, 9 November 1940.

Chapter 13: Mr. and Mrs. Paul Hindemith of New Haven, Connecticut

1. Letter: Hindemith to Willy Strecker, 27 October 1940.

2. The Collegium Musicum concert of 21 May 1951 included a composite Mass of music by various sixteenth-century composers. Hindemith brought his chorus to St. Thomas More Chapel the morning before, Whitsunday, where they sang the Mass at the service. The Propers were also sung, done in Gregorian chant.

3. Members of the string quartet were Joseph Fuchs, first violin; Howard Boatwright, second violin; Paul Hindemith, viola; and Luigi Silva, violoncello. The baritone soloist was Carl Lohmann, secretary of Yale University.

4. He did attend the few student recitals at which he was asked by the dean to serve as one of the faculty judges.

5. Letter: Gertrude Hindemith to Osea Noss, 10 August 1944.

6. Letter: Gertrude Hindemith to Osea Noss, 27 August 1944.

7. Letter: Gertrude Hindemith to Osea Noss, 6 September 1945.

PART 3: EXPATRIATE, 1953–63

Chapter 14: Estrangement, 1953–58

1. Hindemith set two poems by Oscar Cox for solo voice and piano that were published by Schott in 1955 as *Two Songs: Image* and *Beauty, Touch Me.* The attorney refused to accept any payment for his services, but Hindemith insisted on showing his appreciation by giving to Cox the original scores of his *Concerto for Clarinet and Orchestra* and the *Concerto for Horn and Orchestra.* Both manuscripts were donated to Yale University by Mrs. Cox after her husband's death.

2. Letter: Gertrude Hindemith to Osea Noss, 12 April 1954.
3. Letter: Gertrude Hindemith to Osea Noss, 28 June 1954.
4. Letter: Gertrude Hindemith to Oscar Cox, 19 October 1954.
5. Letter: Gertrude Hindemith to Oscar Cox, 4 January 1956.
6. Letter: Arthur Judson to Walter Schulthess, early January 1956.
7. Letter: Gertrude Hindemith to Oscar Cox, 23 January 1956.
8. Letter: Hindemith to Oscar Cox, 26 February 1956.
9. Letter: Gertrude Hindemith to Oscar Cox, 12 June 1956.
10. Letter: Hindemith to Oscar Cox, September 1956.
11. Letter: Gertrude Hindemith to Osea Noss, 28 January 1957.
12: Letter: Gertrude Hindemith to Luther Noss, 6 June 1957.

13. Hindemith told the author personally two years later that he had been genuinely pleased to be invited to rejoin the Yale faculty and how much he regretted not being able to accept. He expressed continuing interest in the School of Music and his willingness to help advance its progress in any way he could. This was actually the second time since 1953 that Hindemith had been invited back to Yale. The Corporation voted to award him an honorary doctor of music degree in 1955 but Hindemith was obliged to refuse, since his previous concert commitments in Europe prevented his meeting the requirement of being present at the June commencement exercises to receive it.

14. Letter: Gertrude Hindemith to Oscar Cox, 3 February 1958.
15. Letter: Gertrude Hindemith to Oscar Cox, 22 July 1958.
16. Letter: Gertrude Hindemith to Osea Noss, 23 December 1958.

Chapter 15: Reconciliation, 1959–63

1. Letter: Hindemith to Oscar Cox, 25 November 1958.
2. Letter: Hindemith to Oscar Cox, 1 January 1959.
3. Letter: Hindemith to Karl Bauer, 29 December 1958.
4. Letter: Gertrude Hindemith to Oscar Cox, 30 April 1959.
5. Letter: Gertrude Hindemith to Osea and Luther Noss, 22 February 1960.
6. Letter: Gertrude Hindemith to Oscar Cox, 14 August 1961.

Bibliography

Published materials relating to Paul Hindemith's life and work in the United States are exceedingly few in number. Of these, the following were useful in preparing this volume:

Boatwright, Howard L. "Paul Hindemith as a Teacher." *Musical Quarterly*, vol. 50, no. 3 (1964).

— — —. "Hindemith's Performances of Old Music." *Hindemith-Jahrbuch* 3 (1973).

Noss, Luther. *A History of the Yale School of Music*. New Haven: Yale School of Music, 1984.

Richter, Eckhart. "A Glimpse into the Workshop of Paul Hindemith." *Hindemith-Jahrbuch* 6 (1977).

— — —. "Hindemith as Director of the Yale Collegium Musicum." *Hindemith-Jahrbuch* 7 (1978).

Thoburn, Crawford R. "Hindemith at Wells College." A two-part article in *Wells Express*, the school's alumnae magazine, 1966 December and 1967 January.

A selected list of general biographies:

Briner, Andres. *Paul Hindemith*. Zürich: Atlantis-Verlag, 1971. Available only in German.

Kemp, Ian. *Paul Hindemith*. Monograph. No. 6 in Oxford Studies of Composers. London: Oxford University Press, 1970.

Schubert, Giselher. *Paul Hindemith*. Monograph. Hamburg: Rowohlt Taschenbuch Verlag, 1981. Available only in German.

Skelton, Geoffrey. *Paul Hindemith: The Man behind the Music*. London: Victor Gollancz, 1975. Contains an excellent but necessarily limited account of the composer's U.S. experience.

Hindemith did not want anyone to write his biography and refused to cooperate with authors who wished to do so. However, he permitted B. Schott's Söhne of Mainz to issue an annotated pictorial biography in 1961, and his widow allowed a sequel to be published in 1965. These are:

Paul Hindemith: Zeugnis in Bildern. Mainz: B. Schott's Söhne, 1955. Also published in English.

Paul Hindemith: Die letzen Jahre. Mainz: B. Schott's Söhne, 1965.

Index of Names and Places

Amar, Lico, 6
Amar-Hindemith String Quartet, 6–7
American Academy of Arts and
    Sciences, Boston, 149
American Ballet Company, 29, 49
American Musicological Society,
    New York Chapter, 143
American Philosophical Society,
    Philadelphia, 193
Archer, Violet, 203 ch. 8, n. 5
Associated Music Publishers (AMP),
    1, 13–14, 17, 24, 29, 31, 40–42,
    52–53, 75, 98, 100, 104, 110–11,
    114, 116–18, 120–21, 140–41,
    144–45, 179, 183, 187, 199 ch. 2,
    n. 3
Autori, Franco, 27, 200 n. 3

Bach Prize, Hamburg, Germany, 151
Baden-Baden, Germany, 7, 130
Bagger, Louis, 203 ch. 8, n. 5
Baird, Cameron, 27–28, 61, 64, 66–67
Balanchine, George, 29, 44–46, 49, 79,
    110–12, 205 ch. 10, n. 4
Barbieri, Anthony, 203 ch. 8, n. 5
Barnard, Parke, 203 ch. 8, n. 5
Barrere, Georges, 18, 20
Bartholomew, Marshall, 104, 132
Bartok, Bela, 188
Basel Chamber Orchestra, 137
Basel, University of, 189
Bauer, Karl, 28, 43, 54–55, 58,
    144, 182
Baumgartner, Hope Leroy, 85, 203 ch.
    8, n. 2
Beethoven Association, 28
Berlin Staatliche Hochschule für
    Musik, 6, 65, 85, 99, 103
Bennington College, 39
Berkowitz, Leonard, 203 ch. 8, n. 5

Berkshire Music Center (see
    Tanglewood)
Berkshire String Quartet, 9
Bernstein, Leonard, 179, 195
Biancolli, Louis, 187
Biggs, E. Power, 75
Billboard Publications, xii
Bixler, Martha, 203 ch. 8, n. 5
Blackwood, Easley, 203 ch. 8, n. 5
Blonay, Switzerland, 171, 185, 188–89,
    192
Bluche sur Sierre, Valois, Switzerland,
    43, 59, 160
Blumenfeld, Harold, 203 ch. 8, n. 5
Boatwright, Helen, 102, 108, 163
Boatwright, Howard, xii, 20, 103, 148,
    203 ch. 8, n. 5, 205 ch. 10, n. 5, 207
    ch. 11, n. 1, 207 ch. 13, n. 3
Boepple, Paul, 18, 53
Boston, Mass., 22, 34, 149
Boston Symphony Orchestra, 8, 23,
    31, 33, 35, 61, 72–73, 75, 78,
    112
Boulanger, Nadia, 20, 24
Boult, Sir Adrian, 61
Boykan, Martin, 203 ch. 8, n. 5
Brain, Dennis, 130
Breitkopf and Haertel, 5
Briner, Andres, 183
Brotman, Michael, 203 ch. 8, n. 5
Brown, David W., 203 ch. 8, n. 5
Bryn Mawr College, 32
Budapest String Quartet, 118, 123, 131,
    140, 145
Buffalo, N.Y., 27, 39, 64
Buffalo Philharmonic Orchestra, 27
Buffalo, University of, 61, 63–67,
    102
Burson, George (see London, George)
Buttolph, David, 203 ch. 8, n. 5

211

Callaway, Paul, 188
Canadian Broadcasting Corporation, 146–47
Cannon, Beekman, 179, 201 ch. 3, n. 6
Cantata Singers, 144, 147
Carlson, Jane, 145
Carlucci, Joseph, 203 ch. 8, n. 5
Carnegie Hall, 24, 52–53, 148, 187
Caspar, Walter, 6
Chavez, Carlos, 18, 21–22, 147, 200 n. 12
Chessid, Herman, 203 ch. 8, n. 5
Chicago, Ill., 10, 146
Chicago Symphony Orchestra, 9, 25, 31, 36–37, 174, 177, 190–91, 194
Chicago, University of, 44, 118, 142
Claudel, Paul, 138
Cleveland Institute of Music, 147
Cleveland, Ohio, 43
Cleveland Symphony Orchestra, 123, 147
Cloisters, The, New York City, 108
Club, The (Yale University), 92–93
Colby College, 179, 183
Collegiate Chorale, 124–25, 184
Collegium Musicum Concerts, Yale, 9, 103–9
Collins, Walter, 203 ch. 8, n. 5
Colorado College, 133, 148
Columbia Broadcasting System Symphony, 130, 206 n. 27
Columbia Records, 25, 195
Columbia University, 130–31, 154, 156
Conant, James B., 149
Connecticut Academy of Arts and Sciences, 131, 206 n. 28
Conservatoire Français, Montreal, Quebec, 147
Coolidge, Elizabeth Sprague, 1–3, 6–8, 9–10, 13, 16, 20, 23, 29–30, 62, 122, 149, 200 n. 12
Copland, Aaron, 72–74
Cornell University, 61, 64, 68–69
Cotton Club (New York City), 25–26
Cowell, John, 203 ch. 8, n. 5
Cox, Oscar, 135, 169, 171, 173–76, 178–80, 182, 186, 188, 192, 194, 208 ch. 14, n. 1
Crawford, John, 203 ch. 8, n. 5
Crosby, John, 191
Cumberworth, Sterling, 203 ch. 8, n. 5

Curry, Capt. Hugh B., 136
Curtis Institute of Music, 23–24

Dali, Salvador, 49–50, 76–78
Dallas Symphony Orchestra, 124
Darling, James, 203 ch. 8, n. 5
Dartmouth College, 48
de Almeida, Antonio, 203 ch. 8, n. 5
Dello Joio, Norman, 203 ch. 8, n. 5
Denham, Serge, 45–46, 49
Denver, Colo., 50
Dessoff Madrigal Singers, 18
Detroit, Mich., 39
Detroit Symphony Orchestra, 145
DiBonaventura, Sam, 203 ch. 8, n. 5
Diemer, Emma Lou, 203 ch. 8, n. 5
Disney, Walt, 39, 46–48, 52
Donovan, Richard, 68–71, 84–85, 104, 157, 159, 184, 203 ch. 8, n. 2
Dorati, Antal, 125
Dougherty, Celius, 115–16
Downes, Olin, 21–22, 24, 33, 40, 73, 120
Driscoll, The Reverend Mr., 74
Dulles, John Foster, 176
Dunlap, Joseph, 203 ch. 8, n. 5
Durkee, Charlotte, 203 ch. 8, n. 5

Einstein, Ralph, 203 ch. 8, n. 5
Eisenhower, Dwight D., 156
Ellington, Duke, 25–26
England, Nicholas, 203 ch. 8, n. 5
Erskine, John, 28
Etler, Alvin, 203 ch. 8, n. 5

Fiedler, Arthur, 22–23, 52–53, 200 n. 20
Foss, Lukas, 74, 103, 111, 203 ch. 8, n. 5
Fox Studios, Hollywood, 46
Fraker, Charles, 203 ch. 8, n. 5
Frankfurt am Main, Germany, 3–4
Frankfurt State Opera Orchestra, 4, 7
French, Robert D., 157
Fromm, Herbert, 79
Frost, Thomas, 203 ch. 8, n. 5
Fuchs, Joseph, 207 ch. 3, n. 3
Furniss, Edgar, 84, 93
Furtwängler, Wilhelm, 11, 61

Garris, John, 108
Geiringer, Karl, 115
George, Graham, 203 ch. 8, n. 5
Gephart, William, 104
Goebbels, Paul, 11

Goodman, Benny, 126–28
Goodman, Thomas, 203 ch. 8, n. 5
Gottlieb, Robert, 203 ch. 8, n. 5
Graham, Martha, 122
Gratch, Olga, 203 ch. 8, n. 5
Greenwich House Music School, New York City, 28
Griswold, A. Whitney, 177
Grumman, S. Ellsworth, 158

Hanau, Germany, 3
Hannover, Germany, 129
Harlem, New York City, 25
Harris, Jean F., 123
Harrison, Francis Llewellyn, 203 ch. 8, n. 5
Harrison, Jay, 109
Hartt School of Music, Hartford, Conn., 143
Harvard University, 34, 53, 89, 125, 134, 149
Harvard University Press, 89
Havemann, Gustav, 6
Heath, Fenno, 186
Hegner, Anna, 4
Heiller, Anton, 195
Hemingway, Louis, 203 ch. 8, n. 5
Herrmann, Virginia Hitchcock, 203 ch. 8, n. 5
Hickok, Robert, 203 ch. 8, n. 5
Hincks, Carroll, 157
Hindemith, Gertrude, 1–2, 7, 10, 12, 61, 76, 79–82, 87, 91, 113, 115, 123–24, 127, 131, 133–35, 140–41, 150, 152, 157–67, 169–80, 181–86, 188, 190, 192, 195–96, 205 ch. 9, n. 4
Hindemith, Gustave, 17–18, 36
Hindemith, Paul, selected comments of special interest: Manhattan skyline, 16; Broadway, 18; Empire State Building, 19; U.S. food and drinks, 19–20; Duke Ellington, 25; Twentieth-Century Limited, 36; *Snow White,* 39; Walt Disney, 46–47; Hollywood, 51; Salvador Dali, 77; fiftieth birthday, 145; U.S. citizenship, 176
Hindemith, Robert Rudolf, 3–4
Hindemith, Rudolf, 4, 6
Hindemith, Rudolph, 17–18, 43
Hindemith, Toni, 4

Hindemith Collection, Yale, xi, xii, 1, 101, 170, 193
Hindemith Commemoration, Yale, 195
Hindemith Foundation, xi
Hindemith Institute, Frankfurt am Main, Germany, xi, xii, 1, 126
Hitler, Adolf, 11
Hoch Conservatory of Music, Frankfurt am Main, 4
Hoffmann-Behrendt, Lydia, 32–33, 39, 43, 48, 50, 52
Howard, Lee, 203 ch. 8, n. 5
Howland Memorial Prize, Yale, 7, 134, 156
Hull, Cordell, 81–82
Hume, Paul, 188
Hunter, George, 203 ch. 8, n. 5
Hurok, Sol, 46, 78
Hutcheson, Ernest, 28
Hwang, Philip, 203 ch. 8, n. 5

Iadone, Joseph, 203 ch. 8, n. 5
Illinois, University of, 150
Indiana University, 150
Institute of Arts and Letters, 154
International Federation of Music Students, 150–51

Jacobson, George, 203 ch. 8, n. 5
Jaegel, Frederick, 18, 20
Johnson, Thor, 131
Jonathan Edwards College, Yale, 35, 92
Judson, Arthur M., 172, 174–75
Juilliard Chorus, 148
Juilliard School of Music, 23, 28, 144–45, 193

Kahn, Eric Itor, 129
Kay, Ulysses, 203 ch. 8, n. 5
Keats, Donald, 203 ch. 8, n. 5
King, Alvin, 203 ch. 8, n. 5
Kinkeldey, Otto, 150
Kirkland House, Harvard, 149
Kirkpatrick, Ralph, 103
Kirshbaum, Morris, 103
Klemperer, Otto, 13, 51, 199 ch. 2, n. 2
Klenz, William, 203 ch. 8, n. 5
Kolodin, Irving, 193
Kortschak, Hugo, 9–10, 35
Koussevitsky, Serge, 8, 10, 13, 23, 33–34, 36, 53–54, 72–76, 80, 112–13, 140–42, 200 ch. 10, n. 5

Kraehenbuehl, David, 203 ch. 8, n. 5
Kupper, Annaliese, 129

Lam, George, 103, 203 ch. 8, n. 5
Landsberger, Max, 66
Lang, Paul Henry, 150, 184, 187, 193
Lange, Hans, 26, 37
Langer, Susanne, 150
Lenox, Mass., 64, 72, 74, 76, 80
Lester, Eugene, 203 ch. 8, n. 5
Levine, Maurice, 203 ch. 8, n. 5
Lewin, Frank, 203 ch. 8, n. 5
Library of Congress, 8, 20, 30
Liegl, Ernst, 118
Liepmann, Klaus, 35, 201 ch. 3, n. 6
Loach, Donald, 203 ch. 8, n. 5
Lohmann, Carl, 92, 207 ch. 13, n. 3
London, George, 124, 194, 206 n. 18
Los Angeles, Calif., 46, 51
Los Angeles Symphony Orchestra, 51
Louisville, Ky., 136, 149
Louisville Symphony Orchestra, 133,
   135–36, 149
Lübbecke-Job, Emma, 8–10
Luening, Otto, 130–31, 206 n. 26

McClellan, Mildred Nolte, 203 ch. 8,
   n. 5
McCulloh, Judith, xii
MacGregor, Willard, 118
Main, Alexander, 203 ch. 8, n. 5
Martens, Mason, 203 ch. 8, n. 5
Mason, Neale, 203 ch. 8, n. 5
Massine, Leonide, 42, 44–46, 48–50, 55,
   59, 76–79, 110, 120
Mendel, Arthur, 99–100, 134, 144, 147
Mendelssohn, Arnold, 4
Merton, Father Thomas, 166
Mester, Jorge, 193
Metropolitan Museum of Art, New
   York City, 104, 106, 108–9, 148
Metropolitan Opera Company, New
   York City, 38–39
Mexico City, Mexico, 124, 147
Meyer, Mrs. Eugene, 20–21
Miller, Carl S., xii, 203 ch. 8, n. 5
Miller, Deborah, xii
Miller, Timothy, 203 ch. 8, n. 5
Minneapolis Symphony Orchestra, 112,
   137, 142, 152
Mitropoulos, Dimitri, 112, 142, 150,
   152, 207 ch. 11, n. 4

Moehlenkamp, Jack, 203 ch. 8, n. 5
Monte Carlo Ballet Company, 42–43, 45
Montesi, Robert, 132
Monteux, Pierre, 44–45
Montreal, Quebec, 147
Moran, Jean Todd, 203 ch. 8, n. 5
Moreland, Don, 191
Morgenthau, Henry, 21
Morris, Franklin, 203 ch. 8, n. 5
Mühlheim, Germany, 4
Music Press, New York City, 146
Musical Courier, 184
Musical Quarterly, The, 143

Nabokov, Nicholas, 48, 54, 60–63, 67–68
National Music Council, 196
National Symphony Orchestra of
   Mexico, 124, 147
Nauheim, Germany, 3
New Friends of Music Chamber
   Orchestra, New York City, 148, 151
New Haven, Conn., 57, 64, 71, 181
New Haven Symphony Orchestra, 103,
   141, 148
New York Herald-Tribune, 109, 119,
   152, 184, 187, 193
New York League of Composers, 25
New York Music Critics Circle, 151,
   156, 184
New York Philharmonic Orchestra, 22,
   24, 120, 148, 179, 183–85, 187, 193–95
New York Philharmonic Society, 187
New York Times, 7, 11, 16–17, 21–22,
   24, 54, 89, 120, 184, 187–88, 193
New York World-Telegram and Star,
   187
Noehren, Robert, 79
Northwestern University, 30, 201 n. 36
Norton, Charles Eliot, Lectureship,
   Harvard, 89, 134, 136, 148
Noss, Luther, 85, 92, 100, 104, 134,
   142, 163, 177–81, 184–87, 189–92,
   208 n. 13
Noss, Osea, xii, 161, 164–65, 169–72,
   177, 180–81, 184, 187, 189, 192

Oberlin College, 150
Order of Merit, Germany, 151
Ormandy, Eugene, 118–19, 126–27, 143
Ortmann, Otto, 201 ch. 4, n. 1
Osborne, William, 203 ch. 8, n. 5
Overtone Records, 205 ch. 9, n. 7

Paramount Studios, Hollywood, 36, 46
Parisot, Aldo, 187
Paulee, Mona, 124
Paulson, Herbert, 203 ch. 8, n. 5
Peabody Conservatory of Music,
  Baltimore, 152, 201 ch. 4, n. 1
Peyre, Henri M., 162
Philadelphia Academy of Music, 156
Philadelphia Orchestra, 52–53, 118–19,
  126, 143, 200 n. 12
Philharmonic Hall, Lincoln Center,
  New York City, 187, 195
Piatigorsky, Gregor, 80, 114, 128, 140
Piston, Walter, 34, 201 ch. 3, n. 3
Pittsburgh Symphony Orchestra, 174,
  178, 182
Pittsfield, Mass., 3
Pollak, Louis, 203 ch. 8, n. 5
Porter, Quincy, 203 ch. 8, n. 2
Powell, Mel, 203 ch. 8, n. 5
Princeton University, 26

Quashen, Ben, 203 ch. 8, n. 5

Raisin, Blanche, 132
Ravinia Park, Chicago, 190–91
Ré, Peter, 179, 203 ch. 8, n. 5
Rebner, Adolf, 4
Rebner String Quartet, 4, 7
Reiner, Fritz, 174
Rexroth, Dieter, xii
Rice, William, 203 ch. 8, n. 5
Richter, Eckhart, xii, 203 ch. 8, n. 5
Rivkind, Vivian, 145
Rodzinski, Artur, 24, 120
Rosenfeld, Jay C., 2
Ross, Hugh, 40, 194
Rottenberg, Ludwig, 7
Royal Conservatory of Music, Toronto,
  147
Rudas, Hans, 203 ch. 8, n. 5
Ruff, Willie, 203 ch. 8, n. 5
Ruzicka, Vincenz, 115–16

Sacher, Paul, 137
St. Thomas More Chapel, Yale, 162,
  196, 207 ch. 13, n. 3
Samuel, Gerhard, 203 ch. 8, n. 5
Samuel, Harold E., xii
San Francisco Symphony Orchestra, 44
Sanroma, Jesús Maria, 18, 20, 32,
  34–35, 39, 53, 55, 102, 122, 147

Santa Fe Opera, 190–92
Sarason, Leonard, 203 ch. 8, n. 5
Saturday Review, The, 193
Schiff, Judith, xii
Schnabel, Arthur, 118
Schola Cantorum, New York City, 194
Schönberg, Arnold, 188, 203 n. 6
Schönthal, Ruth, 203 ch. 8, n. 5
Schott, B., and Sons, London, 126, 133,
  199 ch. 2, n. 3
Schott, B., and Sons, Mainz, 5, 13, 24,
  113–16, 121, 128–29, 132–33, 138,
  199 ch. 2, n. 3, 205 n. 14
Schrade, Leo, 103
Schubert, Giselher, xii
Schulthess, Walter, 172, 174–75, 185
Schünemann, Georg, 103
Seefried, Irmgard, 113
Seeger, Charles, 89
Seemann, Carl, 129
Sekles, Bernhard, 4
Sessions, Roger, 156
Seymour, Charles, 69, 83, 86, 156
Shackford, Charles, 203 ch. 8, n. 5
Shaw, Robert, 124–25, 148
Shepard, Brooks, 206 n. 28
Shuman, Davis, 145
Silliman College, Yale, 184, 186
Silva, Luigi, 207 ch. 13, n. 3
Silver Burdett Company, Chicago, 40
Simon, Eric, 126
Simonds, Bruce, 85, 88–91, 145
Simonds, Rosalind, 145
Sinclair, George, 203 ch. 8, n. 5
Skelton, William, 132, 203 ch. 8, n. 5
Skidmore College, 48
Smith, David Stanley, 35, 69–70, 85,
  87, 203 ch. 8, n. 2
Smith, Frank, 203 ch. 8, n. 5
Smith College, 39–40
South Egremont, Mass., 121
South Mountain Festival, 3
Southwest Radio Orchestra, Germany,
  130
Stein, Fritz, 12
Steinberg, William, 178–79
Stern, Isaac, 145
Stock, Frederick, 50
Stokowski, Leopold, 13, 47
Strauss, John, 203 ch. 8, n. 5
Stravinsky, Igor, 24, 29, 35, 72, 135,
  187–88

Strecker, Hugo, 126, 157
Strecker, Ludwig, 5
Strecker, Willy, 1–2, 5, 10, 12–14, 16–17, 21, 23, 30, 32, 58–60, 75, 83, 86, 89, 91, 99, 111, 123, 127–30, 133–35, 138, 141, 152, 159, 199 ch. 2, n. 3
Strunk, Oliver, 1, 13–15, 25–26, 29
Strunk, Mrs. Oliver, 20, 25–26, 29
Szantho, Enid, 145
Szell, George, 122, 147

Tam, Shau-Kwong, 203 ch. 8, n. 5
Tanglewood (Berkshire Music Center), 10, 35, 53–55, 64, 67, 72–76, 100, 104, 112–14, 128, 142
Taos, N.M., 133
Taubman, Howard, 184, 187–88
Thoburn, Crawford R., 60
Thomson, Virgil, 119
Thorarinsson, Jon, 203 ch. 8, n. 5
Thorne, Francis, 203 ch. 8, n. 5
Toch, Ernst, 51
Tompkins, Merritt, 17, 26
Toronto, Ontario, 147
Tourel, Jennie, 129
Town Hall, New York City, 52–54, 116, 129, 148, 151, 179, 184
Turkish Government Project, 11, 30
Tyler, George, 68

UNESCO, 138
U.S. Army Band, 136–37, 151

Vassar College, 48
Victor Recording Company, 22, 25, 44, 53, 55
Vienna Philharmonic Orchestra, 175
Vinitsky, Ruth, 203 ch. 8, n. 5

Voigt, Ernest, 1, 14–15, 17–18, 20, 21, 23, 25, 28–29, 31–32, 35, 38, 52, 55, 60–63, 80–82, 98, 110–12, 114–17, 120, 140

Walther, Bruno, 147
Washington, D.C., 151, 194
Washington Cathedral, 187
Washington Post, 188
Weaver, Paul J., 68
Weigel, Eugene, 203 ch. 8, n. 5
Weissman, Adolf, 7
Wellesley College, 140
Wells College, xii, 48, 54–55, 60–61, 64–65, 67–68, 100
Whiteman, Paul, 200 n. 28
Whitman, Walt, 199 ch. 1, n. 1
Widdis, Francis, 203 ch. 8, n. 5
Wilder, Isabel, 189
Wilder, Thornton, 188–89
Wilson, Keith, xii, 127, 131–32, 137, 186, 205 n. 14
Woldt, John, 203 ch. 8, n. 5
Wyner, Yehudi, 203 ch. 8, n. 5

Yale Collection of Musical Instruments, 106
Yale College, 106, 121
Yale Glee Club, 132–33
Yale Graduate School, 162
Yale News Bureau, 90
Yale School of Music, 35–36, 83, 113, 177, 180
Yale University, 36, 57, 64, 66–67, 69–72, 81, 127, 185, 192, 208 n. 13
Yale University Press, 136

Zakin, Abraham, 145
Zürich, University of, 89–90, 108, 137, 151

Index of Works Cited

A Frog He Went A-Courtin' (see
  *Variations for Violoncello
  and Piano*)
Apparebit repentina dies, 125, 149

Bach, Johann Sebastian: Heritage and
  Obligation, 136
Brueghel Ballet, 49–50, 59, 76–79, 110

Canticle to Hope, 138–39, 166
Cardillac, 6, 137–38
Childrens Crusade (ballet), 45, 49
Clarinet Quartet, 42, 53–54
*Composer's World, A: Horizons and
  Limitations*, 134–36
*Concert Music for Piano, Brass, and
  Two Harps, Opus 49*, 10, 151
*Concert Music for Strings and Brass,
  Opus 50*, 8, 33, 44, 75, 190, 194, 199
  ch. 1, n. 2
*Concert Music for Wind Orchestra,
  Opus 41*, 136–37
Concerto for Clarinet and Orchestra,
  126–27, 208 ch. 14, no. 1
Concerto for Horn and Orchestra, 130,
  208 ch. 14, n. 1
Concerto for Orchestra, Opus 38, 6,
  191
Concerto for Organ and Orchestra
  (1962), 193, 195
Concerto for Piano and Orchestra
  (1945), 122–24
*Concerto for Trumpet, Bassoon, and
  String Orchestra*, 131–32, 149, 206
  n. 28
*Concerto for Violoncello and
  Orchestra, Opus 3*, 5
*Concerto for Violoncello and
  Orchestra* (1940), 80, 140, 187,
  205 ch. 10, n. 5

Concerto for Violin and Orchestra, 59,
  72, 78
*Concerto for Woodwinds, Harp, and
  Orchestra*, 130–31, 148, 154
Craft of Musical Composition, The
  (see *Unterweisung im Tonsatz*)
Cupid and Psyche (*Farnesina*), 118–19,
  147

Demon, The, 193–94
Demon of the Gibbet, The, 132–33, 149
Die junge Magd, Opus 23.2, 27,
  145–46, 152
Duets for Bassoon and Violoncello, 115

Elementary Training for Musicians, 99

*Five Pieces for String Orchestra, Opus
  44-IV*, 27–28, 35, 140
Five Songs on Old Texts, 20, 53, 145,
  183, 200 n. 6
Frau Musica (revision), 120, 148–50,
  152

Harmonie der Welt, Die (opera), 59–60,
  123, 137, 177
*Harp That Once Thro' Tara's Halls,
  The*, 75
Herodiäde, 122, 145–46, 148, 193
Hin und zurück, 75, 143

In einer Nacht, Opus 15, 6
Ite, angeli veloces, 138–39

Jaeger aus Kurpfalz, Opus 45-III,
  27–28

Kammermusik No. 1, 15, 37
Kammermusik No. 2, 152, 205 ch. 10,
  n. 1

217

Kammermusik No. 3, 151
Kammermusik No. 5, 8, 33, 35
Kammermusik No. 7, 7

Little Sonata for Violoncello and Piano, 115
Long Christmas Dinner, The, 188–89, 193
L'Orfeo, 121
Ludus tonalis, 115–18, 145

Madrigals, Twelve, 184–86
Mainzer Umzug, 193
March (Basel), 189
Marienleben, Das, 6, 59, 113, 128–29
Mass, 196
Mathis der Maler (opera), 11, 38–39, 42
Mörder, Hoffnung der Fraunen, Opus 12, 5–6
Motets, Thirteen, 113
Minimax, 163

News of the Day, 7, 25, 190–92
Nine Songs for an American School Songbook, 40
Nobilissima Visione (ballet), 31, 42, 45–46
Nobilissima Visione Suite, 42, 51–52, 103, 141, 146–47, 194

Octet, 184
Oh, Threats of Hell, 146

Philharmonic Concerto, 150
Piano Quintet, Opus 7, 5
Pittsburgh Symphony, 166, 178–79, 182–83, 191
Plöner, Musiktag, 28

Quintet for Woodwinds, Opus 24.2, 23, 52

Schwanendreher, Der, 13, 18, 21–24, 26–27, 37, 44, 51, 53, 200 n. 20
Sechs Lieder nach alten Texten, Opus 33, 15
Septet for Wind Instruments, 129, 151–52, 157
Serenaden, Die, Opus 35, 14, 16
Sinfonia Serena, 124–25, 147
Sinfonietta in E, 133, 135–36, 194

Six Chansons, 59, 148, 150, 152
Sonata for Althorn and Piano, 121
Sonata for Bassoon and Piano, 42
Sonata for Clarinet and Piano, 59
Sonata for Double Bass and Piano, 133
Sonata for English Horn and Piano, 114
Sonata for Flute and Piano, 15, 25, 118
Sonata for Harp, 59
Sonata for Horn and Piano, 59
Sonata for Oboe and Piano, 42
Sonata for Organ, No. 3, 75, 79
Sonata in A for Piano, No. 1, 33, 35, 43
Sonata in B♭ for Piano, No. 3, 15, 20, 43
Sonata for Piano, Four Hands, 42, 53, 55, 118, 138
Sonata for Two Pianos, 115–16, 145
Sonata for Trombone and Piano, 114, 145
Sonata for Trumpet and Piano, 59, 79
Sonata in E♭ for Violin and Piano, Opus 11.1, 5
Sonata in D for Violin and Piano, Opus 11.2, 5
Sonata in E for Violin and Piano, 27
Sonata in C for Violin and Piano, 59, 145
Sonata for Solo Viola, Opus 11.5, 5
Sonata for Solo Viola, Opus 25.1, 14–15, 20, 23, 25–27, 33–35, 43
Sonata for Solo Viola (1937), 25–27
Sonata for Viola and Piano, Opus 11.4, 5, 33, 35, 43
Sonata in F for Viola and Piano (1939), 42, 48, 53, 55, 102
Sonata for Viola d'Amore and Piano, Opus 25.2, 33, 43
Sonata for Violoncello and Piano, Opus 11.3, 5
Sonata for Violoncello and Piano (1948), 128
Song of Music, A, 68, 200 ch. 6, n. 4
Songs, Solo, with Piano:
  Two Ballads, 116
  Nine English Songs, 116
  The Frog, 92
  Two Songs on Oscar Cox Texts, 208 ch. 14, n. 1
  Four Songs on Hölderlin Texts, 15, 20, 21

Spielmusik, Opus 43.1, 7
String Quartet, Opus 2, 5
String Quartet in F Minor, Opus 10, 5, 7
String Quartet in C Major, Opus 16, 3, 6
String Quartet, Opus 22, 14, 26
String Quartet in E♭ (1943), 118, 142, 145, 148
String Quartet (1945), 123
Suite of French Dances, 128
Symphonic Dances, 31, 37, 44–46, 49, 53
Symphonic Metamorphosis of Themes by Carl Maria von Weber, 77–79, 119–20, 147, 205 ch. 10, nn. 4, 14
Symphony: Die Harmonie der Welt, 137, 152
Symphony: Mathis der Maler, 27, 73, 75, 118, 143, 146–47
Symphony in B♭ for Concert Band, 136–37, 151
Symphony in E♭, 80, 112–13, 147, 149, 207 ch. 11, n. 4

Theme with Four Variations: The Four Temperaments, 79, 103, 110–12, 145–46, 148, 150

Three Easy Pieces for Violoncello and Piano, 42
Three Hymns by Walt Whitman, Opus 14, 6
Three Pieces for Violoncello and Piano, Opus 8, 5
Three Songs for Soprano and Large Orchestra, Opus 9, 5
Traditional Harmony, A Concentrated Course in, 98
Traditional Harmony, Part II, 100
Trauermusik, 27, 35, 75, 102, 148
Traumwald, Opus 13, 5
Trio for Heckelphone, Viola, and Piano, Opus 47, 14

Unaufhörliche, Das, 76
Unterweisung im Tonsatz, 11, 15–16, 19, 43–44, 48, 55, 80, 94, 99, 103, 113, 117, 128, 133, 201 ch. 4, n. 1

Variations for Violoncello and Piano on an Old English Children's Song, A Frog He Went A–Courtin', 114

When Lilacs Last in the Dooryard Bloom'd: A Requiem for Those We Love, 123–24, 177, 186, 188, 194–95, 199 ch. 1, n. 2

A Note on the Author

Luther Noss is professor emeritus of music and curator of the Hindemith Collection at Yale University. He was a member of the School of Music faculty from 1939 to 1976 and served as dean of the School of Music from 1954 to 1970. He is the author of *A History of the Yale School of Music, 1854–1970* (1984) and editor of *Paul Hindemith Sämtliche Werke,* vol. 3, no. 8 (1977), among other works.

Books in the Series Music in American Life

Only a Miner: Studies in Recorded Coal-Mining Songs
Archie Green

Great Day Coming: Folk Music and the American Left
R. Serge Denisoff

John Philip Sousa: A Descriptive Catalog of His Works
Paul E. Bierley

The Hell-Bound Train: A Cowboy Songbook
Glenn Ohrlin

Oh, Didn't He Ramble: The Life Story of Lee Collins
as Told to Mary Collins
Frank J. Gillis and John W. Miner, Editors

American Labor Songs of the Nineteenth Century
Philip S. Foner

Stars of Country Music: Uncle Dave Macon to Johnny Rodriguez
Bill C. Malone and Judith McCulloh, Editors

Git Along, Little Dogies: Songs and Songmakers of the American West
John I. White

A Texas-Mexican *Cancionero*: Folksongs of the Lower Border
Américo Paredes

San Antonio Rose: The Life and Music of Bob Wills
Charles R. Townsend

Early Downhome Blues: A Musical and Cultural Analysis
Jeff Todd Titon

An Ives Celebration: Papers and Panels of the Charles Ives
Centennial Festival-Conference
H. Wiley Hitchcock and Vivian Perlis, Editors

Sinful Tunes and Spirituals: Black Folk Music to the Civil War
Dena J. Epstein

Joe Scott, the Woodsman-Songmaker
Edward D. Ives

Jimmie Rodgers: The Life and Times of America's Blue Yodeler
Nolan Porterfield

Early American Music Engraving and Printing: A History
of Music Publishing in America from 1787 to 1825
with Commentary on Earlier and Later Practices
Richard J. Wolfe

Sing a Sad Song: The Life of Hank Williams
Roger M. Williams

Long Steel Rail: The Railroad in American Folksong
Norm Cohen

Resources of American Music History: A Directory of Source Materials
from Colonial Times to World War II
D. W. Krummel, Jean Geil, Doris J. Dyen, and Deane L. Root

Tenement Songs: The Popular Music of the Jewish Immigrants
Mark Slobin

Ozark Folksongs
Vance Randolph; Edited and Abridged by Norm Cohen

Oscar Sonneck and American Music
Edited by William Lichtenwanger

Bluegrass Breakdown: The Making of the Old Southern Sound
Robert Cantwell

Bluegrass: A History
Neil V. Rosenberg

Music at the White House: A History of the American Spirit
Elise K. Kirk

Red River Blues: The Blues Tradition in the Southeast
Bruce Bastin

Good Friends and Bad Enemies: Robert Winslow Gordon
and the Study of American Folksong
Debora Kodish

Fiddlin' Georgia Crazy: Fiddlin' John Carson, His Real World,
and the World of His Songs
Gene Wiggins

America's Music: From the Pilgrims to the Present
Revised Third Edition
Gilbert Chase

Secular Music in Colonial Annapolis: The Tuesday Club, 1745-56
John Barry Talley

Bibliographical Handbook of American Music
D. W. Krummel

Goin' to Kansas City
Nathan W. Pearson, Jr.

"Susanna," "Jeanie," and "The Old Folks at Home": The Songs of
Stephen C. Foster from His Time to Ours
Second Edition
William W. Austin

Songprints: The Musical Experience of Five Shoshone Women
Judith Vander

"Happy in the Service of the Lord": Afro-American Gospel
Quartets in Memphis
Kip Lornell

Paul Hindemith in the United States
Luther Noss